'On
the
side
of
light'

Cathal by Rachel Giese Brown

# 'On
# the
# side
# of
# light'

*critical essays on the poetry*
*of Cathal Ó Searcaigh*

James Doan and Frank Sewell (editors)

ARLEN
HOUSE

first published in December 2002 by

Arlen House
PO Box 222
Galway

and

42 Grange Abbey Road
Baldoyle
Dublin 13
Ireland

ISBN 1-903631-30-0 paperback

www.arlenhouse.com
www.arlenacademic.com

Printed by ColourBooks, Baldoyle, Dublin 13
Typesetting: Arlen House

# CONTENTS

# LIST OF ILLUSTRATIONS

## Texts by Cathal Ó Searcaigh

| | |
|---|---|
| *MC* | *Miontraigéide Cathrach* (An Fálcarrach: Cló Uí Chuirreáin, 1975) |
| *SS* | *Súile Shuibhne* (Dublin: Coiscéim, 1983) |
| *S* | *Suibhne* (Dublin: Coiscéim, 1987) |
| *ABB* | *An Bealach 'na Bhaile/Homecoming* (Cló Iar-Chonnachta, 1993) |
| *NBB* | *Na Buachaillí Bána* (Indreabhán: Cló Iar-Chonnachta, 1996) |
| *OO* | *Out in the Open* (Indreabhán: Cló Iar-Chonnachta, 1997) |
| *ATLS* | *Ag Tnúth leis an tSolas* (Indreabhán: Cló Iar-Chonnachta, 2000) |

## DEDICATION

Do Chathal Ó Searcaigh an leabhar seo/
this book is dedicated to Cathal Ó Searcaigh

# ACKNOWLEDGEMENTS

The editors wish to express their 'seven thanks'/seacht mbuíochas to the following individuals: Prof. Robert Welch for suggesting this book project in the first place; to all of the contributors for offering their expertise and the fruits of their research; to Bobby Hanvey for his illuminating photography; to Mutsuo Takahashi for allowing us to publish a translation of his 'reply' to Ó Searcaigh's 'tobar'/well of poetry and tradition; to Andrew Tomlinson for his perspicacious proof-reading and closely-considered corrections; and to Arlen House, our publisher. Finally, and most importantly, we congratulate Cathal Ó Searcaigh on the forthcoming publications of his books on Donegal, and on Nepal, and in 2003, his next collection of poems. Typically, Cathal has assisted and advised all of our contributors, I believe, at one time or another, providing unique insights into his own work, and the Irish poetry and cultural scene in general. He also provided for this publication, an enlightening and entertaining interview which is invaluable to anyone interested in his writing and in the true, transgressive nature of 'tradition'. Bail, beannacht agus rathúnas ort go deo, a Chathail.

The publisher wishes to thank all the copyright holders of the photos reproduced in this volume, Cathal Ó Searcaigh and Cló Iar-Chonnachta for the use of the extracts, and Nollaig Mac Congáil, NUI, Galway for his excellent proof-reading.

Special thanks to Cathal for exploring and making accessible his personal collection of photos, for his energy and enthusiasm and for his dedication to this volume.

'On
the
side
of
light'

Cathal on a reading tour of Germany in 1998 sits underneath a statue of Schiller in Leipzig (photo: Cathal Ó Searcaigh)

## AN TOBAR

*(do Mháire Mhac an tSaoi)*

'Cuirfidh sé brí ionat agus beatha,'
arsa sean-Bhríd, faghairt ina súile
ag tabhairt babhla fíoruisce chugam
as an tobar is glaine i nGleann an Átha.
Tobar a coinníodh go slachtmhar
ó ghlúin go glúin, oidhreacht
luachmhar an teaghlaigh
cuachta istigh i gclúid foscaidh,
claí cosanta ina thimpeall
leac chumhdaigh ar a bhéal.

Agus mé ag teacht i méadaíocht
anseo i dtús na seascaidí
ní raibh teach sa chomharsanacht
gan a mhacasamhail de thobar,
óir cúis mhaíte ag achan duine
an t-am adaí a fholláine is a fhionnuaire
a choinníodh sé tobar a mhuintire:
ní ligfí sceo air ná smál
is dá mbeadh rian na ruamheirge
le feiceáil ann, le buicéad stáin
dhéanfaí é a thaoscadh ar an bhall
is gach ráithe lena choinneáil folláin
chumhraítí é le haol áithe.

Uisce beo bíogúil, fíoruisce glé
a d'fhoinsigh i dtobar ár dteaghlaigh.
I gcannaí agus i gcrúiscíní
thóg siad é lá i ndiaidh lae
agus nuair a bhíodh íota tarta orthu
i mbrothall an tsamhraidh
thugadh fliuchadh agus fuarú daofa
i bpáirceanna agus i bportaigh.
Deoch íce a bhí ann fosta

a chuir ag preabadaigh iad le haoibhneas
agus mar uisce ionnalta
d'fhreastail ar a gcás ó bhreith go bás.

Ach le fada tá uisce reatha
ag fiaradh chugainn isteach
ó chnoic i bhfad uainn
is i ngach cisteanach
ar dhá thaobh an ghleanna
scairdeann uisce as sconna
uisce lom gan loinnir
a bhfuil blas searbh súlaigh air
is i measc mo dhaoine
tá tobar an fhíoruisce ag dul i ndíchuimhne.

'Is doiligh tobar a aimsiú faoi láthair,'
arsa Bríd, ag líonadh an bhabhla athuair.
'Tá siad folaithe i bhfeagacha agus i bhféar,
tachtaithe ag caileannógach agus cuiscreach,
ach in ainneoin na neamhairde go léir
níor chaill siad a dhath den tseanmhianach.
Aimsigh do thobar féin, a chroí,
óir tá am an anáis romhainn amach:
Caithfear pilleadh arís ar na foinsí.'

(Cathal Ó Searcaigh, *ABB* pp. 42–4)


## THE WELL

*'It'll set you up for life',*
*said old Bríd, fire in her eyes,*
*handing me a bowl of well-water,*
*the cleanest in all Gleann an Átha*
*from a well kept by her people's*
*people, a family heirloom*
*tucked away in a secluded spot*
*with a ditch like a moat around it*
*and a flagstone for a lid.*

*When I was coming into my own*
*back in the early sixties here,*
*there wasn't a house around*
*without the same sort of well;*
*everyone was all chuffed then*

*about how clean and healthy*
*theirs was kept and wouldn't let*
*a speck of dust cloud its silver*
*lining; and if a hint of red-rust*
*was found, they bailed it out*
*right away using a tin bucket;*
*then to keep their well sweet,*
*freshened it regularly with kiln-lime.*

*From our family well sprang*
*bright springwater full of life.*
*With tins and crocks, they dipped into it*
*day after day and any time their throats*
*were parched by summer's heat,*
*it slaked and soothed them in fields*
*and bogs - a true pick-me-up*
*that set them hop, skip and jumping*
*for joy, refreshing them all their lives.*

*For a long time now, running water*
*snakes towards us from distant hills*
*and in every kitchen, both sides*
*of the glen, water spits from a tap,*
*drab lacklustre water that leaves*
*a bad taste in the mouth while*
*among my people the real thing*
*is forgotten about. Bríd once said,*
*'it's hard to find a well these days',*
*as she filled up another bowl.*
*'They're hidden in bulrushes and grass,*
*choked by weeds and green scum*
*but for all the neglect, they've lost*
*not a drop of their true essence.*
*Find your own well, my lad,*
*for the arid times to come.*
*They dry up who steer clear of sources.'*

(trans. F. Sewell, *OO* pp. 19–21)

# UNCOVERING A WELL

'Everyone,' he said, 'should have their own well.'
Those words of wisdom, fresh as sundried hay,
were brought home to us once we'd passed
hill after hill of bogland. Our guide's well
lay deep in a hollow, and as the wooden lid
was lifted, a shallow mass of bog-coloured water
shivered. I recalled the sealed-up, oil-stained well
in my own backyard far across the world.
I really should clean that well when I return.
Or no; first, I should find the well inside
myself and make it clean. Far worse than leaves
dropping dead and clogging my well back home,
I thought, is all the apathy holed up in me.
Here, the clear spring-water drawn from the well
and stored in the jug for passing round and drinking,
was sharp and crisp as the blue patch of sky
peeking through a break in the heavy clouds;
and it thrilled my tongue and throat with delight.

(Mutsuo Takahashi; trans. M. Ohno & F. Sewell)

Cathal with poet, Mutsuo Takahashi, Donegal 2002 (photo: Nobuaki Tochigi)

## LOOSENING THE TONGUE

Born in 1956 in the hamlet of Mín a' Leá near the town of Gortahork, Co. Donegal, situated at the foot of Mt. Errigal, the poet Cathal Ó Searcaigh writing in the Irish language has been considered a leading voice of his generation for the past twenty years or so. This is the first collection of critical essays dealing with his poetry, and gathered together here are eight essays by Irish, American and Japanese scholars, as well as an interview with Ó Searcaigh, addressing various issues explored in his poetry, including the roles of language and place; gender and sexuality; and also the influence of other poets — both Irish and foreign.

Celia de Fréine's contribution 'What's In a Label?', examines 'the overwhelming sense of place [...] how the language changes when the poet moves from his beloved Donegal to the urban landscape of Dublin or London, and further afield to America and Kathmandu'. Focusing on the poetry contained in his second bilingual edition, *Out in the Open*, she finds the collection 'wonderfully rich in language, themes and characters'. Unlike other Irish poets concerned with the buried past and its effects on the present, she states that 'he is not preoccupied with unearthing the past and, although some poems involve the earth and what it yields, the poet consistently moves on in search of other pastures, both here and abroad'.

James Doan's essay, 'Cathal Ó Searcaigh: Gay, Gaelach agus Galánta — Gay, Gaelic and Gorgeous', foregrounds the Irish-language and gay elements in the poet's first bilingual collection, *Homecoming/An Bealach 'na Bhaile*. Finding Cathal to have a strong sense of his place within the Irish literary tradition, Doan points out his links with the Old Irish tradition found in works such as *Táin Bó Cuailnge* ('The Cattle-Raid of

Cooley'), the Irish folksong tradition, and contemporary Irish poets such as Máire Mhac an tSaoi and Nuala Ní Dhomhnaill. Throughout, he alludes to Cathal's use of a gay perspective as a key element in the expression of his distinctive poetic voice.

Kieran Kennedy's '"Oirféas ag gach orifice": The Irish Language Question, Globalization and Homosexuality' takes its title from the poem, 'Do Jack Kerouac', referring to the myth of Orpheus who, after unsuccessfully seeking his wife in the underworld, turned to sexual pleasure with boys and girls to assuage his grief. Also dealing with the explicit sexuality in much of Cathal's verse, Kennedy states that 'Ó Searcaigh enters the silence surrounding gay male sexuality in the Irish language by interrogating English formations of sexual subjectivity. In other words, he draws on the language associated with the shameful destruction of Gaelic in order to fabricate queer subjectivity in Gaelic'. Kennedy finds a number of shifts in terms of the conventional order in Ó Searcaigh's poetry; shifts which 'challenge the epistemological privilege granted to the imperial metropolis over the rural periphery'. In Kennedy's view, Ó Searcaigh's work 'offers the rural as a locus of enunciation' while the metropolis, too, 'becomes a locus of the enunciated,' leading ultimately to a synchronic hybridization of the two.

Eoin Mac Cárthaigh's 'Placing Cathal Ó Searcaigh' examines three key aspects of his poetry: his homeland, his people and the Irish literary tradition. Mac Cárthaigh finds a strong spiritual dimension in the way Ó Searcaigh 'deifies the land' in poems such as 'Cuisle an Chaoráin'/Mountain Pulse, in which the poet taps into 'the pre-Christian view of land as goddess'. He also looks at the relations between Ó Searcaigh and Irish poets from the seventeenth to the twentieth century, including Eochaidh Ó hEódhasa (O'Hussey), Antaine Ó Reactabhra (Raifeirtí), Seán Ó Ríordáin and Máirtín Ó Direáin.

Niall McGrath's revealing interview with Ó Searcaigh also focuses on diverse elements in his poetry: home and the Donegal landscape; the influences, for example, of Robert Burns and the Beat poets; the triadic role of Christianity, Irish folk beliefs and Buddhism; the Irish language; translation; and sexuality. This wide-ranging and entertaining discussion provides a helpful introduction to, or useful reminder of, the world and world view of this eagle-eyed poet as he nestles in his 'family of mountains'.

Brian Ó Conchubhair's contribution examines several themes and key aspects in Ó Searcaigh's works, including language and tradition. Placing him within the context of other contemporary poets writing in Irish, Ó Conchubhair concludes that Ó Searcaigh 'writes poetry which is rooted in the urban cosmos of the late twentieth century. This poetry is informed by a long tradition [...] which the poet can call upon at will; it never threatens to engulf him and obscure the unique voice which sounds in these poems'.

Mitsuko Ohno questions issues of gender in Ó Searcaigh's work by focusing on the speakers, voices, personae or masks adopted and adapted by the poet. Using four short love poems — two each by Ó Searcaigh and Nuala Ní Dhomhnaill — she asked colleagues to identify the gender of the poet in each case. Based on their responses, she concludes that at times he adopts a 'female' mask, perhaps as a 'protective guise of gay writing'. In addition, she examines the further-complicating issues of translation; and provides an in-depth reading of Ó Searcaigh's epoch-marking poem 'Gort na gCnámh'/'Field of Bones' in comparison with work by other contemporary Irish poets writing in Irish or English.

Frank Sewell's essay examines various influences on the poet's early works, including Burns, Eliot, Ó Ríordáin and Ó Direáin, but it also reveals the important influence of the great Russian master, Yevgeny Yevtushenko. The latter influence is seen largely in the translations and adaptations which Ó Searcaigh undertook for his first collection, *Miontraigéide Cathrach/A Minor City-tragedy* (1975); and also in the increasingly public role which Ó Searcaigh has adopted not just to criticise sexual and other intolerance in Irish society but, in Yevtushenko's words, to take part in his people's 'heroic struggle for the future'.

Nobuaki Tochigi's contribution deals with Cathal's 'representation of the Irish native' both abroad in London and at home in Donegal. Tochigi views Ó Searcaigh as a writer attempting to 'rectify stereotypical images of the Irish language and its native speakers'. He concludes that Ó Searcaigh's resilient stance toward the language has helped him gain a new audience, and that his flexible imagination has allowed him 'to modify existing forms or themes — indigenous or not — for his poems'.

Towards the end of 1999, Ó Searcaigh was one of only ten leading poets invited to edit an anthology of twentieth century Irish poetry.[1] Each editor was allowed to select only ten poems to represent the poetry of a given decade. The two Irish language poets Cathal Ó Searcaigh and Nuala Ní Dhomhnaill were, significantly, asked to edit the sections featuring poetry of the two most recent decades, the 1980s and 1990s, respectively. Ó Searcaigh chose his particular ten poets and poems because, in his words, they:

> responded to life in the Ireland of the '80s with creative eagerness and exuberance... The ten poems I have selected represent man's spirit coming to terms with the anguish of being. They all aspire, either openly or covertly, to the redemptive and affirmative condition of boundlessness.[2]

Ó Searcaigh's own poetry in Irish has been 'responding to life', from Donegal to Nepal, since the 1970s with the eagerness of work such as 'An Lilí Bhándearg'/'The Pink Lily' (OO p. 236) and the exuberance of 'Searmanas'/'Ceremony' (ABB p. 156). Boundless and bountiful as the view from any, or all, of his beloved mountains — Errigal, Fujiyama, Kathmandu — Ó Searcaigh's empowering poetry has broken down boundaries with the jazzy hornblasts of poems such as 'Jericho' (OO p. 54), the seductive 'Serenade' of 'Laoi Chumainn' (OO p. 86) and the *contrappunto* of 'Cainteoir Dúchais'/'Native Speaker' (OO p. 134). To the shock-horror of some and the delight of most, Ó Searcaigh has loosened the Irish tongue and set it freer to challenge silences, taboos and injustices such as those brought 'out in the open' in 'Gort na gCnámh'/Field of Bones (OO p. 66), 'Rúnsearc'/'Secret Love' (OO p. 92) and

'Caoineadh'/'Lament' (*ABB* p. 208). Ultimately, he truly earns the title of *file*/poet (literally, *seer*) by focusing far into the whatness of what is before him in poems such as 'Cathaoir Uilline'/'Armchair' (*OO* p. 202); and by composing moving laments against destruction that are, in the same breath, rousing reveilles to, and for, life —

> ba mhaith liom a dhearbhú duitse, a fhile, a d'fhán go diongbháilte
> i mbun d'fhocail, a labhair le lomchnámh na fírinne ó ár an chatha —
> go bhfuil mise fosta ar thaobh an tSolais, fosta ar thaobh na Beatha.

> *I want to assure you, poet whose truth*
> *was bared to the bones in World War 1,*
> *I too am on the side of Light, and of Life.*

(*OO* p. 242)

This remarkably diverse collection of critical essays is a testament to the expansive vision and international appeal of Cathal Ó Searcaigh — one leading poet in Ireland's continuing, dual-language literary tradition. We, the editors, hope that this literary critical intervention will help introduce new readers to Ó Searcaigh's poetry, and also prompt new readings of, and fresh returns to, his work by those already familiar with it in Irish and/or in translation into other world languages. The Ó Searcaigh reader, wherever he/she hails from, tends to feel like Heraclitus — never stepping into the same river twice:

> the flow goes on, a ripple in the rockpools here, a cascading torrent there. Sometimes breaking its banks, extending its limits; at other times languishing in backwaters. But always an outward flow, out to the ocean, unbounded.[3]

These comments by Ó Searcaigh on Irish poetry in general are equally applicable to his own work, and account also for our current desire to chart some of the tracks and transgressions of his world-embracing, tradition-expanding imagination and craft.

Jim Doan and Frank Sewell,
*Fort Lauderdale and Portstewart*

## Notes

1    Dorgan, Theo and N. Duffy (eds.), *Watching the River Flow: A Century in Irish Poetry* (Dublin: Poetry Ireland, 1999).
2    *Ibid.*, p. 185.
3    *Ibid.*

Laurence Ferlinghetti, Beat poet, close friend of Ginsberg, Kerouac, Corso and Snyder signing a book for Cathal, New York, 1994 (photo: Rachel Giese Brown)

## (as) Anseo ag Stáisiún Ch'aiseal na gCorr

Anseo ag Stáisiún Chaiseal na gCorr
d'aimsigh mise m'oileán rúin
mo thearmann is mo shanctóir. [...]
Thíos agus thuas tím na gabháltais
a briseadh as béal an fhiántais.
Seo duanaire mo mhuintire;
an lámhscríbhinn a shaothraigh siad go teann
le dúch a gcuid allais.
Anseo tá achan chuibhreann mar bheadh rann ann
i mórdhán an mhíntíreachais.
Léim anois eipic seo na díograise
i gcanúint ghlas na ngabháltas
is tuigim nach bhfuilim ach ag comhlíonadh dualgais
is mé ag tabhairt dhúshlán an Fholúis
go díreach mar a thug mo dhaoine dúshlán an fhiántais
le dícheall agus le dúthracht
gur thuill siad an duais.
Anseo braithim go bhfuil éifeacht i bhfilíocht.

(*ABB* 94–6)

## (from) HERE AT CAISEAL NA GCORR STATION

Here at Caiseal na gCorr Station
I discovered my hidden island,
my refuge, my sanctuary. [...]
Above and below, I see the holdings
farmed from the mouth of wilderness.
This is the poem-book of my people,
the manuscript they toiled at
with the ink of their sweat.
Here every enclosed field is like a verse
in the great poem of land reclamation.
I now read this epic of diligence
in the green dialect of the holdings,
understand that I'm only fulfilling my duty
when I challenge the void
exactly as my people challenged the wilderness
with diligence and devotion
till they earned their prize.
Here I feel the worth of poetry.

(trans. by Gabriel Fitzmaurice)

Eoin Mac Cárthaigh[1]

## Placing Cathal Ó Searcaigh

I am concerned here with three aspects of where Cathal Ó Searcaigh is coming from in his poetry — his homeland, his people and the Irish literary tradition. I have taken his own advice as a starting point: 'Caithfear pilleadh arís ar na foinsí' (*S* p. 142; *'We must return again to the well-springs'*).

His home place 'thart faoi bhun an Eargail' (*S* p. 47; *'around the base of Errigal Mountain'*) is the primary 'foinse' (*'source'* as well as *'well-spring'*) of his inspiration. His muse is not a Maud Gonne or an 'Emer'. It is his home place, and he states this explicitly in 'Cuisle an chaoráin' (*NBB* p. 48):

> i dtobainne, agus é ag trasnú
> Abhainn Mhín a' Mhadaidh, mar a bheadh rud inteacht
> ag borradh i mbéal a chléibhe.
>
> Bhí sé i bhfianaise na Bé ...
>
> *suddenly, as he crossed*
> *Mín a' Mhadaidh river, as though something*
> *were swelling in the pit of his stomach.*
>
> *He was in the presence of the Muse ...*

This is his Parnassus:

> Anois nuair a labhrann sé amach
> i bhfilíocht, labhrann, mar nár labhair ariamh,
> go macnasach mórchroíoch ...
> as croí an tsléibhe ...
>
> *Now when he speaks out*
> *in poetry, he speaks, as never before,*
> *exuberantly, with all his heart ...*
> *from the heart of the mountain ...*

It is as though the place has answered his prayer in an earlier poem: 'deonaigh cor úr a chur i mo dhán' (Fitzmaurice's translation, *'add a fresh dimension to my poem'*, will suffice for now[2]). His poetic inspiration has a truly spiritual dimension. He deifies the land:

> Chrom sé agus phóg sé
> plobar úscach an tsléibhe —
> cíocha silteacha Bhríde, bandia na gcríoch, Bé:
> deoch a bhí lena mhian.[3]

> *He stooped and kissed*
> *the oozing slush of the mountain —*
> *the streaming breasts of Bríd, goddess of the land, Muse:*
> *a drink that satisfied him.*

It is, perhaps, no coincidence that the wise woman who offers him a drink in 'An tobar' (*S* p. 140) is also named Bríd, or that 'Meadhbh', the name of another pre-Christian goddess, means *'she who intoxicates'*.[4] By seeing the land in this way, Ó Searcaigh is returning to sources at an even deeper level.

He is saying much the same thing in 'Tearmann' (*S* p. 127), when he rejects the Christian God — 'Dia na nDeor ... na nDealg/... na Tíorántachta ... na Trócaire' (*'the God of Tears, of Thorns, of Tyranny, of Mercy'*) — in favour of the pre-Christian God of Nature. Many would see the story of early Irish Christianity as a process whereby new doctrines were grafted onto an older core of beliefs. In this poem, the opposite process is at work. Christianity is peeled back to reveal the older core. Ó Searcaigh's God is spoken of in terms of the God he replaces: a carpet of moss becomes the aisle; shrubs are pews; a gentle breeze shaking heather incense is the priest; this God, 'foinse gach fuinnimh' (*'the source of all energy'*), expresses himself through creation, not words; the poet breathes him in 'chomh friseáilte le harán, chomh fionnuar le fíon' (*'as fresh as bread, as cool as wine'*).

Cathal, Agnes, his mother and the lambs Laurel and Hardy
(photo: Rachel Giese Brown)

Visions of the home place as muse and deity are fused with one another in his masterpiece, 'Cor úr' (S p. 29). Here, once more, the land is a woman, but this time she is also depicted as a lover — a lover who welcomes him home by revealing herself to him in all her beauty. Her 'srutháin gheala' (*'bright streams'*) become 'géaga .../ag sní thart orm go lúcháireach' (*'limbs weaving around me joyously'*). The 'lochanna ... maorga' (*'majestic lakes'*) of her eyes gaze upon him. She divests herself of 'crios atá déanta as ceo bruithne' (*'a heat-haze belt'*) so that he sees the 'críocha ionúine' (*'beloved territories'*) of her body, every 'cuar agus cuas' (*'curve and hollow'*), every 'ball seirce' (*'love spot'*) that he had forgotten. He appeals to her to enfold him 'anseo ... idir chabhsaí geala do chos' (*'here ... between the bright paths of your legs'*). His highly effective use of place-names in this poem has been commented on elsewhere[5] but bears repetition here, as he gazes upon her 'ó Log Dhroim na Gréine go hAlt na hUillinne/ón Mhalaidh Rua go Mín na hUchta' (where 'droim' can be translated literally as *'back'*, 'alt' as *'joint'*, 'uillinn' as *'elbow'*, 'mala' as *'brow'* and 'ucht' as *'breast'*).

This love is not a one-way process. If she is a lover, so too is the poet. While Fitzmaurice's translation of 'cor úr' in the title and the closing line as *'a fresh dimension'* is not incorrect, it misses the ambiguity of the word 'cor' — which means not just *'a twist'* but also *'a contract'* — and thus fails to capture the mutuality of the poet's love affair with his home place. She welcomes and inspires him; he rejoices in her and, by the very act of composing this poem (his 'dán' to her, in the sense of *'poem'* or *'gift'*), invests her with new meaning. Just as, in a religious context, God's revelation of himself to humanity does not end with the initial revelation but continues with humanity's inspired interpretation of it, so too his home place's revelation of itself to Ó Searcaigh requires his poetic response to celebrate it and make it whole.

In this poem, he is mining a deep vein in Irish literature. We have already seen him tapping into the pre-Christian view of land as goddess. Here he is also tapping into a literary extension of this — the depiction (persisting into the Christian era) of the land as a woman who requires her rightful spouse so that she may flourish. This is seen in the *aisling* (vision) poetry of the eighteenth century, in which Ireland is portrayed as a wife who is wasting away because she has been parted from her rightful husband, the Stuart king. It is also found in a more local context — for instance, in the *caointe* (laments) which have survived from the eighteenth and nineteenth centuries, where it is often implied that because the land has lost her husband she is now barren. It is a recurring motif in *dán díreach* (the classical verse of the later middle ages): in elegies, the land is pictured as a widow who has been made barren by bereavement; conversely, in praise poems to living lords, she is flourishing because she has found her rightful husband. Above all, this notion was central to the ritual of royal inauguration, in which the contract between a king and his people was sealed by a marriage between king and land. A late example (from 1310 AD) will serve by way of illustration:

> Agus ar bhfeis d'Fheidhlimidh ... re cóigeadh Connacht, do-roinne a oide a fhriotháileamh an oidhche-sin do réir chuimhne na seandaoine agus na seinleabhar; agus is í sin banais ríghe is oireaghdha do-rónadh i gConnacht riamh gus an laithe-sin.[6]

In 'Cor úr', Ó Searcaigh adds a fresh twist to this established motif. His 'cor úr' is a marriage contract between poet and land. His poem is the epithalamium that both celebrates and consummates a new 'banais' — his union with his home place.

This union is obviously a fruitful one for Ó Searcaigh as a poet, in that, as we have seen, his home place is his muse, and it is from his muse's 'broinn mhéith' (*'fertile womb'*) that his 'clann bheag bhéarsaí' (*'little family of verses'*) are born (*NBB* p. 13). However, the place also provides him with an environment in which he feels that poetry has meaning, and reaffirms him as a person in his own life. We find these two ideas side by side in 'Anseo ag stáisiún Chaiseal na gCorr' (*S* p. 48):

> Anseo braithim go bhfuil éifeacht i bhfilíocht.
> Braithim go bhfuil brí agus tábhacht liom mar dhuine
>
> *Here I feel poetry has force.*
> *I feel I have meaning and importance as a person.*

Any distinctions between a poet's life and a poet's art become irrelevant here. Indeed, since 'dán' can mean *'destiny'* or *'lot in life'* as well as *'poem'*, Fitzmaurice might equally well have translated the closing line of 'Cor úr', 'deonaigh cor úr a chur i mo dhán', as *'add a fresh dimension to my life'*.

The place is life-giving. The road he travels on his return from the city to his home place is a road from death to life. In 'Aon séasúr den bhliain' (*S* p. 24; *'Any season of the year'*), the life-giving sun never calls in through the window of his city bed-sit; neither nature nor human love can flourish 'anseo i saol seargtha/an bhrocsholais' (*'in this withered half-lit world'*). In 'Triall' (*S* p. 23), he dreams of escaping 'ó fhuaraíocht thuamúil na sráide' (*'from the tomblike coldness of the street'*); he speaks of 'a bhfuil curtha anseo de m'óige' (*'all I have buried here of my youth'*) 'i reilig bhrocach na n-árasán' (*'in the filthy graveyard of flats'*). In 'Maigdiléana' (*S* p. 11), 'tachtann sealán aibhléise/aoibh shoilseach na spéire' (*'a noose of electricity chokes/the sky's bright smile'*); the young prostitute wanders 'sa mharbhsholas chnámhach' (*'in the bony dead-light'*); this Magdalene, 'ag cuartú a Calvaire go heaglach' (*'fearfully seeking her Calvary'*), will be crucified among 'scáilí na gcros teilifíse' (literally *'the shadows of the television crosses'*), but no resurrection awaits her 'i dtumba folamh an underground' (*'in the empty tomb of the Underground'*), and the posters there advertising the Christian God's love for his creatures are cold comfort.

In contrast, Ó Searcaigh is reborn in his home place. He emerges from darkness into light when he returns from the city:

> Ó bhaitheas go bonn, bogaim le teocht
> is altaím le méid mo bhuíochais
> an glaochsholas a leánn domhsa ...
> siocfhuacht an dorchadais.
>
> ('Maidin i Mín an Leagha', *ABB* p. 106)

> *From head to toe, I soften with warmth*
> *and I give thanks with all my heart*
> *to the calling light that melts for me ...*
> *the frosty cold of the darkness.*

Here, once more, he makes effective use of a place-name. It is not surprising to find the sun 'ag leá' ('*melting away*') the coldness of the city from him here in Mín an Leagha (pronounced — and, elsewhere in his poetry, spelt — 'Mín a' Leá'). Likewise, since Mín an Leagha might be translated as '*the physician's land*', it is fitting that he should describe it in 'Triall' (*S* p. 23) as 'áit a bhfaighidh mé goradh agus téarnamh ann' ('*a place where I will find warmth and recuperation*'), where there is a:

> teangaidh shólásach ina cógas leighis
> le léim a chur arís i mo shláinte
>
> *comforting language that, like medicine,*
> *will bring me back to full health.*

Even when he is away from home, the place sustains him. He carries it within him as a focus in his life, as a yardstick against which he will measure 'amhrán mo shiúlta' (*S* p. 9; '*the song of my wanderings*'). This is beautifully put in 'Cíoradh' (*S* p. 15), when even the most banal of everyday actions — combing his hair — reminds him of:

> siorradh gaoithe ó Mhám an tSeantí
> ag slíocadh fraoigh go síoraí in Altán
>
> *a blast of wind from Mám an tSeantí*
> *stroking heather forever in Altán.*

It can also be seen in 'Is glas na cnoic' (*ABB* p. 206), where he can only feel 'sa bhaile i gcéin' ('*at home abroad*') because he has projected his imagination's map of his homeland onto London:

> piocaim suas Mín a' Leá agus Mayfair
> ar an mhinicíocht
> mhire mhíorúilteach amháin i m'aigne
>
> *I pick up Mín a' Leá and Mayfair*
> *on the same mad miraculous*
> *frequency in my mind.*

The traffic is 'ag méileach' ('*bleating*') 'mar thréad caorach á gcur chun an tsléibhe' ('*like a flock of sheep being driven to the mountain*'[7]); the office buildings are

> á ngrianú agus á n-aoibhniú féin
> faoi sholas na Bealtaine
>
> *sunning and delighting themselves*
> *in the May [sun]light*
> *(or under the [sun]light on Bealtaine [mountain]).*

However, it finds its clearest expression in a poem composed on his return — specifically, in his careful choice of the phrase 'oileán rúin':

> Anseo ag stáisiún Chaiseal na gCorr
> d'aimsigh mise m'oileán rúin
> mo thearmann is mo shanctóir.
>
> (*S* p. 47)

> *Here at Caiseal na gCorr station*
> *I have found my 'oileán rúin'*
> *my place of refuge, my sanctuary.*

Hughes sees echoes here of Seán Ó Ríordáin's 'Oileán agus oileán eile',[8] but this is to miss the point. The phrase 'oileán rúin' is straight from the poetry of Máirtín Ó Direáin. And this is not an example of what Gabriel Rosenstock[9] characterises in another context as 'gadaíocht-i-ngan-fhios' ('*unintended pilfering*') — it is clearly intended to echo Ó Direáin's work. Ó Searcaigh does not say 'd'aimsigh mé m'oileán rúin' ('*I have found my "oileán rúin"*'), but rather 'd'aimsigh mise m'oileán rúin' ('*I* [with emphasis] *have found my "oileán rúin"*'), the point being that, whereas Ó Direáin's 'oileán rúin' is Árainn, our poet's is to be found 'anseo ag stáisiún Chaiseal na gCorr'. By using these words, Ó Searcaigh is recruiting the whole canon of Ó Direáin's poems of exile, as distilled into this one phrase, to his cause.

With this in mind, Fitzmaurice's translation of this phrase — 'hidden island' (*ABB* p. 95) — is unsatisfactory. Even if he had chosen the preferable 'secret island' this could hardly be otherwise, given that 'rúin' means both 'secret' and 'beloved'.

A clear line of development can be seen in Ó Direáin's compositions. This begins with earlier poems such as 'Faoiseamh a gheobhadsa' (1942), 'Cuireadh do Mhuire' (1943) and 'An t-earrach thiar' (1949), in which Árainn is Ó Direáin's 'beloved island', a pastoral haven from the madness of city life. It progresses to the likes of 'Cuimhne an Domhnaigh' (1957), in which Ó Direáin first acknowledges the hardship and heartbreak of island life, and to such poems as 'Bua na mara' and 'Deireadh ré' (also 1957), in which he accepts that his 'beloved island' is a thing of the past. It reaches its culmination in 'Strainséir' (1966), in which he realises that he no longer belongs in his home place, and most particularly in 'Berkeley' (1966), in which, accepting that his 'beloved island' is now dead and gone, he chooses instead the 'secret island' of his memories as an alternative guiding star. By using the phrase 'oileán rúin', Ó Searcaigh is telling us that his own home place is both *'beloved island'* and *'secret island'* — both beloved place of refuge and chosen spiritual home and point of reference.

The place that gives Ó Searcaigh life, the landscape he gazes upon, is largely (as noted emphatically by Ó Dúill[10]) a made landscape, the work of human hands:

> Seo duanaire mo mhuintire;
> an lámhscríbhinn a shaothraigh siad go teann
> le dúch a gcuid allais.
>
> ('Anseo ag stáisiún Chaiseal na gCorr', *S* p. 47.)

> *This is the poem-book of my people;*
> *the manuscript they wrought forcefully*
> *with the ink of their sweat.*

His people's struggle with the land is a heroic one: 'Léim anois eipic seo na díograise/i gcanúint ghlas na ngabháltas' ('*I now read this epic of fervour/in the green dialect of the landholdings*'). This is a people 'a thug ... dúshlán an fhiántais' ('*who challenged the wilderness*'), who fought for 'breis agus trí chéad bliain' ('*more than three hundred years*') to win 'na gabháltais/a briseadh as béal an fhiántais/.../i mórdhán an mhíntíreachais' ('*the landholdings/that were snatched from the mouth of the wilderness/.../in the great poem of making the desert bloom*'). He is humbled by 'Dúthracht seo an ghaiscígh/a dheonaigh do do shinsear fómhar i gcónaí' (S p. 46; *This heroic devotion/that granted your ancestors a harvest always*). Just as Heaney commits himself to following in the furrows dug and tended by his father and grandfather by digging with his pen,[11] Ó Searcaigh, 'ag feidhmiú mar chuisle de chroí mo chine' (*functioning as a pulse in my race's heart*), will continue his forebears' epic struggle by reshaping his homeland in poetry.

If Ó Searcaigh's relationship with his homeland in 'Cor úr' is a two way process, the same is true of his people's relationship with it. The place is a less forgiving lover for the old man in 'Cré na cuimhne' (*NBB* p. 79):

> ... An síol a scaip sé lá dá shaol
> chan ar ithir mhéith mná a thit sé
>
> Ach ar dhomasach dubh an tsléibhe a dhiúl
> sú na hóige as a chnámha gan a dhúil a shásamh ...
>
> ... *The seed he scattered long ago*
> *did not fall on a woman's fertile soil*
>
> *But rather on the black peat of the mountain that sucked*
> *the sap of youth from his bones without satisfying his desire.*

As he shapes the land, it shapes him, and just as the land is spoken of in personal terms in 'Cor úr', this old man is spoken of in terms of the land. His facial features are topographic features: 'lena gháire mór cineálta/A d'éirigh ar íor a shúl is a spréigh anuas go solasta/thar leargacha a leicne' (*with his big kindly laugh/That rose on the horizon of his eyes and spread down brightly/over the slopes of his cheeks*); names slip 'as altán a bhéil' (*from the ravine of his mouth*); his Sunday tie is 'comh righin le bata draighin' (*as stiff as a blackthorn stick*); in 'ceapóg a bheatha' (*the tillage plot of his life*), he draws stories from 'cruach na cuimhne' (*the [turf- etc.] stack of memory*). He is like the subject of 'Taispeánadh' (S p. 66), who is 'cosúil le carraig á creimeadh i dtuilidh sléibhe' (*like a rock being eroded in a mountain flood*). He is so shaped by his surroundings that it becomes hard to distinguish him from them or them from him.

Cathal with local soccer team (8th from left with headband) playing in Fána Bhuí, 1987 (photo: Rachel Giese Brown)

And so we see landscape and community blending into each other. Throughout Ó Searcaigh's poetry, people and place are inextricably linked. (Remember that, by drawing on the notion of a 'banais ríghe' with the land, he is also implying the union with its inhabitants that the 'banais ríghe' symbolised.) His people too are his 'foinse'. If his people shaped his homeland, they also shaped him — the words of the old woman in 'Bean an tsléibhe' (*S* p. 63) fall 'mar shíolta ... in úir mhéith m'aigne' ('*like seeds ... in the fertile soil of my mind*'). If he drinks from the well-spring of his homeland, he also drinks from the well-spring of his people — he comes to the subject of 'Uchtach' (*S* p. 55) 'ag tóraíocht meala, lón anama,/a thaiscím i gcoirceog mo dháin' ('*seeking honey, food for the soul,/that I hoard in the beehive of my poetry*', or '*... of my life*'). If he is inspired by his homeland, he is also inspired by his people — the words of the storyteller in 'Oícheanta geimhridh' (*S* p. 68) are 'drithleoga dearga .../ag lasadh na samhlaíocht' ionainn' ('*red sparks .../igniting our imagination*'). This people have given him much — not only the collective memory contained in their stories but also, more importantly, 'caint mhiotalach mo dhaoine' ('*the metallic speech of my people*'), the raw material in which he, a 'gabha focal' ('*word-smith*'), chooses to work (*S* p. 26).

And again, he does not receive without giving. Poems such as 'Uchtach', 'Bean an tsléibhe', 'Caoradóir' and 'Oícheanta geimhridh' in the 'Bunadh na gcnoc' ('*Hill-folk*') series in *Suibhne* are living monuments to the people whose hard lives are sympathetically explored in them. So too is 'Cré na cuimhne' (*NBB* p. 79), a poem whose preface captures an element of what Ó Searcaigh's duty of '*functioning as a pulse in my race's heart*' (see above) means:

> Agus ach gurb é gur chan mé thú i mo dhán, a dhuine,
> rachadh d'ainm i ndíchuimhne ...
>
> *And if it wasn't for me singing of you in my poem, man,*
> *your name would be forgotten ...*

A third 'foinse' of Ó Searcaigh's is the Irish literary tradition. We have already seen him drawing on the depiction — echoing down through Irish language literature almost from the start — of the land as woman or goddess. This is not the only occasion when a familiarity with earlier Irish literature will give further depth to the reader's appreciation of Ó Searcaigh's poetry. Hughes draws our attention to another — the fact that 'Súile Shuibhne' (*S* p. 115) draws on a ninth-century text, *Buile Shuibhne* ('*The madness of Suibhne*').[12] Like Ó Searcaigh in the poem, Suibhne is estranged from his homeland and its people and seems to feel threatened by them. Like Ó Searcaigh, he flees human company and spends cold nights on windswept mountains. Suibhne's madness is the result of him challenging the authority of the church. Has Ó Searcaigh too come into conflict with the arbiters of acceptable behaviour? Whatever the answer might be, the general sense of emotional crisis — and even instability — pervading his poem will obviously be heightened for those who have read the madman's tale. It will be heightened still further by the knowledge that our poet is not just being looked *at* by the 'súile Shuibhne' ('*eyes of Suibhne*') of the poem's title and last line, but also — by presenting himself as being comparable with Suibhne — looking *through* these eyes.

Likewise, the ambiguous nature of the 'geasa' Ó Searcaigh is placed under in the poem of that title (*NBB* p. 13) will gain in emphasis from a knowledge of the *fianna* cycle of tales and ballads from which this word can hardly be separated. In these tales, 'geasa' can have either a negative import (entailing the notion of taboo) or a positive import (entailing the notion of being honour-bound to do something); thus, whereas Goll is under 'geasa' not to do a woman's bidding, Gráinne places Diarmaid under 'geasa' to do just that. Understanding this helps to bring out the double-edged nature of Ó Searcaigh's 'geasa' — the dawning realisation of his sexual orientation is not only a negative thing 'mar mhiodóg/ag gabháil ionam go putóg' (*'like a dagger/stabbing into my guts'*) but also a positive thing from which springs the duty to compose. An image central to the poem 'Fios' (*S* p. 102; '*(Carnal) knowledge'*) is also from the *fianna* cycle. The 'bradán feasa' — '*salmon of knowledge'* — from which Fionn mac Cumhaill gained his prophetic wisdom becomes a '*salmon of carnal knowledge'* in Ó Searcaigh's poem.

Another example of our poet drawing on earlier Irish literature is the fact that (as noted by Hughes[13]) the title 'Ceist! Cé a tharrthálfadh dán?'(*S* p. 91; '*A question! Who would rescue a poem?'*) echoes the opening line of a *dán díreach* poem from the seventeenth century, 'Ceisd! Cia do cheinneóchadh dán?'[14] ('*A question! Who would buy a poem?'*). The concern of both poets is the relationship between poet and poem and audience — the question of what becomes of a poem after it is composed. The earlier poet has reached the conclusion that, since there is no longer a market for his poetry, he will give up composing altogether. However, Ó Searcaigh cares little for the market; his direct involvement with the poem he has composed ends with the act of composition. After 'an ghin/a toirchíodh i m'intinn' ('*the child/that was planted in* [the womb of] *my mind'*) is born, he leaves it to its fate. The recalling of the earlier poem serves to focus the reader's attention on Ó Searcaigh's theme. The contrast with the earlier poet's answer to this question serves to strengthen the impact of Ó Searcaigh's own answer.

While on the subject of *dán díreach*, it may be as well to address the suggestion made by Ó Dúill[15] and by the poet himself[16] that Ó Searcaigh's gay love poetry may have a precedent in Irish in the compositions of Eochaidh Ó hEódhasa, who died in 1612.

(To be fair, neither commits himself fully on this.) Much the same point is made by Ó Laoire, who says that the society that produced *dán díreach* was one in which 'physical affection between males was validated in a homosocial ordering of relations, within which the eroticisation of male relations was naturalised'.[17] However, I can only see these observations as constituting an attempt to find validation for modern values by projecting them back onto the people and literature of an earlier era.

It is true that Ó hEódhasa often speaks of his patrons in amorous terms. For instance, in the poem 'A-tám i gcás eidir dhá chomhairle'[18] he refers to his lord as a 'leannán' ('*lover*') whose bed he misses sharing, as his 'céile' ('*spouse*'), and as 'm'Aodh féine, mo ghrádh tar Ghaoidhealaibh' ('*my own Hugh, my darling in preference to all other Irishmen*'). In another (unpublished) poem, 'Fada óm intinn a hamharc' ('*The one I am thinking of is far away from me*') to Hugh's half-brother, he is even more explicit:

> Gibé leaba a luigh sinne
> a-tám, do thaoibh inntinne,
> ar chorp a chéile is ó Cuinn
> a-nocht, is Éire eadrainn.

> *No matter what bed we lie in, and though the length of Ireland separates us, Conn's descendant and I are on top of each other's bodies tonight in our minds.*

However, in all of this he is simply employing a motif that was part of the standard stock in trade of his profession — the poet presenting his relationship with his lord as that of a besotted woman with an attractive man who would (or already does) make a good husband, i.e. a good partner in a stable contractual poet-patron arrangement. Indeed, this representation of the ideal poet-patron relationship as a marriage should not seem strange to the reader in light of what we have seen of the symbolic representation in Gaelic Ireland of the contract between a king and his people as a marriage between king and land. While it may be the case that, as suggested by Carney,[19] Ó hEódhasa was fonder of such imagery than many of his contemporaries, this tells us nothing of his sexual orientation. It is better seen as a tribute to the ability of this highly talented poet to breathe new life and depth into one of the established conceits of *dán díreach* (literally 'straight verse'!).

Returning to more direct comparisons, we find that the opening lines of Ó Searcaigh's 'Mise Charlie an scibhí' (*ABB* p. 202) depend for much of their impact on their contrast with the beginning of a poem placed on the lips of Antaine Ó Reachtabhra (died 1835). Compare Ó Searcaigh's 'Mise Charlie an scibhí,/lán éadóchais agus crá' (*'I am Charlie the scivvy,/full of hopelessness and torment'*) with Ó Reachtabhra's 'Mise Raifteirí, an file, lán dóchais is grá'[20] (*'I am Raftery, the poet, full of hope and love'*) and Ó Searcaigh's loneliness in London is brought into sharper focus. Those who have missed the contrast between Ó Reachtabhra's optimism as he stands 'le m'aghaidh ar Bhalla/ag seinm cheoil do phócaí falamh'[21] (*'with my face towards Balla [in Co. Mayo]/playing music to empty pockets'*) and Ó Searcaigh's pessimism, 'is mo chúl le balla' (*'with my back to the wall [?]'*) in Trafalgar Square, are relieved of their illusions by our poet: 'is a Raiftearaí' (*'and, Raftery,'*), he says, *'fuck this for a lark'*!

The fact that our poet draws on the Irish song tradition in love poems such as 'Ceann dubh dílis' and 'Tá mé ag síorshiúl sléibhe' (*S* pp. 108–9) has been pointed out by several commentators[22] but is explored most fully by Ó Laoire,[23] who — himself a noted bearer of this tradition — is uniquely placed to do so. Since I could not hope to add anything to the latter's analysis, I will confine myself to drawing the reader's attention to his writings and to recording some of his key observations here for the sake of completeness. Ó Laoire shows how Ó Searcaigh adds to the emotional charge of his own poems by adopting (and adapting) the idiom — metrical, stylistic and linguistic — of the songs, and especially their lack of emotional restraint and their almost exclusive reliance on the first and second persons; how the song tradition, which often deals with unrequited or forbidden love, provides an ideal vehicle for our poet to express his own brand of forbidden love; and how gay love can be expressed within this tradition by exploiting the songs' ambiguity in regard to gender, where men might sing a song with a female narrator or vice versa.

Ó Searcaigh's exploration of the Irish literary tradition as a source of imagery and idiom and inspiration does not end here. The compositions of many twentieth-century Irish language poets have had a major impact on his work. This is particularly true of his earlier work, as found in collections such as *Miontraigéide cathrach* (1975) and *Tuirlingt* (1978) — published, in my view, before he had fully developed a distinctive poetic voice of his own. Many of the poems in them echo the poetry of some of his more contemporary forebears so closely that they could be considered derivative.

To take a few examples from his 1975 collection, it is not hard (as pointed out by Ó Dúill[24]) to see that the author of 'Adieu' (*MC* p. 64) was very familiar with Pádraig Mac Piarais's 'Fornocht do chonac thú'.[25] Likewise, the poem 'An tAngelus' (*MC* p. 62) is heavily dependent on Seán Ó Ríordáin's 'Siollabadh'.[26] Similarly, the influence of Máirtín Ó Direáin's poetry is very evident throughout the collection — for example, compare Ó Searcaigh's 'Is táimse fearacht gach haon;/dualta do thuismeá dearóil na sráide' (*MC* p. 24; *'And I am like everyone;/chained to the bleak horoscope of the street'*) with Ó Direáin's vision of city life in 'Ár ré dhearóil' (1962; *'Our bleak times'*):

> Tá cime romham
> Tá cime i mo dhiaidh,
> Is mé féin ina lár
> I mo chime mar chách[27]

> *A convict in front of me*
> *A convict behind,*
> *And I in among them*
> *A convict like all.*

I do not wish to dwell too much on this, as the same cannot be said of our poet's more recent and more definitive collections (beginning, for me, with the publication of *Súile Shuibhne* in 1983), in which the offending poems have been completely reworked or dropped altogether. Nevertheless, the point is to be made that his early imitation of the work of poets such as these is indicative of the effect they had on the formation of his craft — and no assessment even of his more recently published work will be complete if it fails to take account of these early influences.

This is because, even after he has begun to speak self-confidently in his own authentic voice, he is still composing — at least in part — within the tradition founded by the likes of Ó Ríordáin and Ó Direáin. If this were otherwise, he would never speak of the latter as 'an fuascailteoir a ghríosaigh is a threoraigh .../éirí amach na bhfocal' ('*the liberator who incited and directed .../the uprising of the words*'), who freed them 'ó dhaorsmacht' ('*from slavery*') so that they are now 'saoránaigh .../.../i bpoblacht do dháin' ('*citizens ... in your poetic republic*').[28] Ó Searcaigh belongs in this particular 'poetic republic' in a very real sense, since Ó Direáin is widely credited with liberating modern Irish poetry from exclusive dependence on traditional metres.

Although Ó Searcaigh may be composing within this tradition, however, his post-1970s work rarely draws directly on the work of other twentieth-century Irish language poets. One exception to this has already been noted — his conscious echoing of Ó Direáin's poetry of exile by using the phrase 'oileán rúin'. His use of the word 'dán' in all its shades of meaning might also be seen as an instance of Ó Direáin's influence, since this word was first employed to effect in the latter's poetry. To these might be added his reworking from our sister language, Scottish Gaelic, of poems by Ruaraidh MacThòmais as 'Cailíní na scadán' (*S* p. 58), 'Cuimhne' (*NBB* p. 55) and 'Caoirigh' (*NBB* p. 57).

Nevertheless, the point is to be made that this more recent work is not composed in splendid isolation from other contemporary Irish language poets. That this is so is shown — if evidence is required — by the fact that he dedicates many of his best poems to the likes of Michael Davitt (*S* p. 47), Liam Ó Muirthile (*S* p. 60), Gréagóir Ó Dúill (*S* p. 64), Gabriel Rosenstock (*S* p. 92) and Nuala Ní Dhomhnaill (*S* p. 121). It is also shown by the way he often interacts with their work, engaging with it in what Ó Dúill, in another context, calls a 'poetic dialogue'.[29] When he does this, he does it in such a way that both his own poem and the poem with which he is, as it were, in conversation benefit and are given new depth. To illustrate what I mean by this, let us look at some examples of him sharing a theme or an image with Nuala Ní Dhomhnaill. Compare his

> B'ise mo mhaoinín, b'ise mo Ghort an Choirce
> mise a thug a cuid fiántais chun míntíreachais
>
> *She was my darling. She was my Gort an Choirce.*
> *It is I who brought her wildness to a cultivated state*

in 'Súile Shuibhne' (*S* p. 115) with these lines from her 'Amhrán an Fhir Óig':

> Osclaíonn trínse
> faoi shoc mo chéachta.
> Nuair a shroisim bun na claise
> raidim.
>
> Mise an púca
> a thagann san oíche,
> an robálaí nead,
> an domhaintreabhadóir.
> Loitim an luachair mórthimpeall.
> Tugaim do mhianach portaigh
> chun míntíreachais.[30]
>
> *A trench opens*
> *under my ploughshare.*
> *When I reach the furrow's extremity*
> *I give.*
>
> *I am the* púca
> *who comes in the night,*
> *the raider of nests,*
> *the one who ploughs deep.*
> *I spoil the rushes all round.*
> *I bring your wild quality*
> *to a cultivated state.*

The overt sexuality of Ní Dhomhnaill's poem helps to clarify what Ó Searcaigh is hinting at in his — specifically, to clarify what he seems to mean by 'mise a thug a cuid fiántais chun míntíreachais'. And then we might look again at the way our poet speaks of his people singing 'mórdhán an mhíntíreachais' in 'Anseo ag stáisiún Chaiseal na gCorr' (see above), and ask whether his use of the word 'míntíreachas' there also constitutes the introduction of sexual imagery to describe the relationship between man and land. In return, the comparison with 'Súile Shuibhne' helps to bring out the fact that, like Ó Searcaigh, Ní Dhomhnaill is talking — at least in part — of man's urge to shape his physical environment, to tame a virgin land and make it bloom. It directs our attention as readers to the word-play at the heart of Ní Dhomhnaill's poem in 'domhaintreabhadóir', which can mean (literally) either *deep-plougher*' or *'world-plougher'*.

To take another example of what I mean, we find that reading Ó Searcaigh's 'Ceist! Cé a tharrthálfadh dán?' (*S* p. 91, and see above) alongside Ní Dhomhnaill's 'Ceist na teangan'[31] will enrich the reader's appreciation of both poems. We have already seen that our poet's concern here is what becomes of a poem of his after he has composed it, and that he compares his poem to an abandoned child to show that he feels his direct responsibility for it ceases once he has brought it into the public domain. He has brought his poem into the world; it is now up to others to care for it. He brings his point home by comparing himself to Moses' mother:

> Is fágaim é cuachta ar Níl na cinniúna —
> Maois beag an cheana.
>
> *And I leave him wrapped up on the Nile of fate —*
> *darling little Moses.*

Ní Dhomhnaill's imagery is identical. She too compares her poem to Moses, and herself to his mother entrusting him to the protection afforded by the bulrushes:

> féachaint n'fheadaraís
> cá dtabharfaidh an sruth é,
> féachaint, dála Mhaoise,
> an bhfóirfidh iníon Fhorainn?

*to see where the current might take him,*
*to see if, as happened with Moses,*
*Pharaoh's daughter will come to the rescue.*

The difference between the two poems is thematic. Whereas both poets are concerned with the relationship between poet and poem and audience, Ní Dhomhnaill differs by adding the question of translation to this mix; her poem's saviour, her Pharaoh's daughter, is the English language.[32] Comparing the two poems with each other might suggest that what Ó Searcaigh is abandoning responsibility for, is — at least in part — whether or not his poem is to be translated into the dominant language, or, conversely, that Ní Dhomhnaill's concern is not just the question of translation but also her audience's role in giving her poem meaning. The point that is to be made here is not that either poet need necessarily have read the other's composition (though it is likely that they have); what matters for present purposes is that they are drawing on a pool of shared experience in these poems, and that the range of interpretative possibilities is opened up for the reader by a comparison of both.

To take just one more example, similar possibilities are presented to the reader by a comparison of Ó Searcaigh's 'Duine corr'[33] with Ní Dhomhnaill's 'Dubh'.[34] I will also add Michael Davitt's 'Ó mo bheirt Phailistíneach'[35] to the mix here in order to widen the debate. And it is not unreasonable to characterise the interaction between these three poems as a debate. The parallels between them are many. All are reactions to genocidal slaughter in faraway places — 'Dubh' to the fall of Srebrenice in 1995, 'Duine corr' more vaguely to 'an mharfach/atá ag gabháil ar aghaidh, thall,/i mBosnia agus i Serbia' ('*the carnage/that is going on over there/in Bosnia and in Serbia*'), and Davitt's poem to the 1982 Sabra/Shatila massacres in Beirut. All three poets are in their home environments when the terrible news reaches them. All three are concerned with the way these tales of slaughter impinge on their own lives and with the moral or emotional implications for themselves. All imply — or reject — a social role for the poet.

The debate, however, lies in the differing reactions to these tragedies. Davitt's poem — one of the best in modern Irish — brings home the horror of the television pictures projected into his sitting room by projecting them further onto the peaceful life of his suburban home. Ní Dhomhnaill too projects the blackness of what has happened onto the everyday sights of her peaceful Irish day; for her, everything she sees around her is 'dubh' ('*black*') because Srebrenice, 'cathair an airgid,/"Argentaria" na Laidne' ('*the silver city,/called "Argentaria" in Latin*') is 'bán' ('*white*' or '*emptied of people*'). The contrast between these reactions and Ó Searcaigh's could not be greater. Enjoying his own company at home by the fire in Mín a' Leá, he is disturbed by friends who have witnessed terrible scenes on the television and are 'ar bís/le gníomh a dhéanamh láithreach' ('*impatient/to do something immediately*'). However, he knows little about these distant disputes, and even if he did he wouldn't feel able to help. He prefers to return to reading love poems from China and Japan. When the fighting starts in China or Japan, he tells us, he will be at home by the fire in Mín a' Leá reading love poems from Bosnia and Serbia.

It might be said that 'Dubh' squanders much of its moral force by being so long-winded. It certainly suffers at an artistic level by comparison with 'Ó mo bheirt Phailistíneach', in which not a word is wasted. For me, it also suffers by comparison with 'Duine corr', whose low-key yet brutal honesty makes Ní Dhomhnaill's response seem over the top to the point of being disingenuous. Alternatively, in light of the contrast with the other two poems, we might ask ourselves if this is how Ó Searcaigh really feels. Might he just be holding up a mirror to his reader? Do his opinions on this really make him a 'duine corr'? Or is his main concern to show that the poet's primary duty is to his muse rather than the outside world? Whatever the reader's answers might be, the debate has succeeded simply by posing these questions. Again, what matters for present purposes is the very fact that a debate is taking place between these contemporary Irish language poets, and that Ó Searcaigh is taking part in this debate — that he not only draws on the older literary tradition but also interacts with his fellow heirs to it.

As I stated at the outset, my concern here has been with three specific aspects of where Ó Searcaigh is coming from. I must add that, by attempting to place him in the context of his homeland, his people and the Irish literary tradition, I do not mean to suggest that he is limited to these. Indeed, we know that he sometimes feels alienated from his home place or from his people, that his reading is not confined to Irish language literature, that he often looks elsewhere for inspiration, that he has other 'foinsí'. However, I will leave these issues for other contributors to explore.

## Notes

1    Author's note: I would like to thank Professor Cathal Ó Háinle, Professor Damian McManus, Mr Eoghan Ó Raghallaigh and Ms Mary Hassett for comments on an earlier draft of this contribution. I bear sole responsibility for any errors. Except where otherwise expressly stated, all translations in what follows are my own.

2    'Cor úr', S p. 30; Fitzmaurice's translation, ABB p. 87.

3    'Cuisle an chaoráin', NBB pp. 48–49; 'Mountain pulse'.

4    T. F. O'Rahilly, Early Irish history and mythology (Dublin: Dublin Institute for Advanced Studies, 1946), pp. 14–15.

5    See, for instance, G. Ó Dúill, 'An File is dual. Filíocht Chathail Uí Shearcaigh: I dtreo anailís théamúil', Comhar 52, no. 12, 1993, 35–41 (p. 36); A. J. Hughes, 'Cathal Ó Searcaigh, file', in A. J. Hughes (ed.), Cathal Ó Searcaigh, Le chemin du retour/Pilleadh an deoraí (La Barbacane: Fumel, 1996), pp. 12–33 (p. 26).

6    A. M. Freeman (ed.), Annála Connacht: The annals of Connacht (Dublin: Dublin Institute for Advanced Studies, 1944), p. 222; 'And after Feidhlimidh ... had lain with (i.e. married) the province of Connacht, his foster-father waited on him that night in the manner remembered by the old men and recorded in the old books; and that was the most splendid kingship-marriage ever celebrated in Connacht down to that day'.

7    All translations up to here from this poem are Ó Laoire's (ABB p. 207).

8    Hughes, op. cit., p. 24; S. Ó Ríordáin, Eireaball spideoige (Dublin: Sáirséal/Ó Marcaigh, 1952), pp. 78–83.

9    G. Rosenstock, Preface to Suibhne, p. 5.

10    G. Ó Dúill, 'Cathal Ó Searcaigh: A negotiation with place, community and tradition', Poetry Ireland Review 48 (Winter 1996), 14–18 (p. 17).

11    S. Heaney, Death of a naturalist (London: Faber and Faber, 1966), pp. 12–13.

12    Hughes, op. cit., p. 22.

13    Hughes, op. cit., pp. 20–21.

14 O. Bergin (ed.), *Irish bardic poetry* (Dublin: Dublin Institute for Advanced Studies, 1970), pp. 145–6.

15 G. Ó Dúill, 'An File is dual', p. 39.

16 On a 1996 Radio Ulster programme broadcast soon after the publication of *Na buachaillí bána*.

17 L. Ó Laoire, 'Dearg dobhogtha Cháin/The indelible mark of Cain: Sexual dissidence in the poetry of Cathal Ó Searcaigh', in É. Walshe (ed.), *Sex, nation and dissent in Irish writing* (Cork: Cork University Press, 1997), pp. 221–34 (p. 229).

18 L. Mac Cionnaith (ed.), *Dioghluim dána* (Dublin: Oifig an tSoláthair, 1938), pp. 215–7; 'I am between two minds'.

19 J. Carney, *The Irish bardic poet* (Dublin: Dolmen Press, 1967), p. 113.

20 S. Ó Tuama (ed.) and T. Kinsella (transl.), *An duanaire, 1600–1900: Poems of the dispossessed* (Dublin: Dolmen Press, 1981), p. 252.

21 Or, in some versions, 'is mo chúl le balla ...'. See D. de hÍde (ed.), *Abhráin agus dánta an Reachtabhraigh* (Dublin: Foilseacháin Rialtais, 1933), p. 26; 'with my back against a wall'.

22 See, for instance, D. Sealy, [review of *An Bealach 'na Bhaile/Homecoming*], *Comhar* 52, no. 6, 1993, pp. 21–2 (p. 22); Ó Dúill, 'An File is dual', p. 40 and 'Cathal Ó Searcaigh· A negotiation with place, community and tradition', p. 18; Hughes, op. cit., p. 22.

23 Ó Laoire, op. cit., pp. 226–30; see also *ABB*, pp. 22–30.

24 G. Ó Dúill, 'Mórfhile le teacht?' [review of *Miontraigéide cathrach*], *Comhar* 35, no. 12, 1975, 17–18 (p. 18).

25 F. O'Brien, *Duanaire nuafhilíochta* (Dublin: An Clóchomhar, 1969), p. 28.

26 Ó Ríordáin, op. cit., p. 111.

27 M. Ó Direáin, *Dánta 1939–1979* (Dublin: An Clóchomhar, 1980), pp. 80–83.

28 From the poem 'An fuascailteoir', *S* p. 88.

29 Ó Dúill, 'Cathal Ó Searcaigh: A negotiation with place, community and tradition', p. 14.

30 N. Ní Dhomhnaill, *Féar suaithinseach* (Maynooth: An Sagart, 1984), p. 28; 'The song of the young man'.

31 N. Ní Dhomhnaill, *Feis* (Maynooth: An Sagart, 1991), p. 128; 'The language question'.

32 As though to emphasise this point, the bilingual collection of her poetry in which 'Ceist na teangan' first appeared is entitled *Pharaoh's daughter* (Oldcastle: Gallery Books, 1990).

33 *NBB* pp. 53–4. Although 'Duine corr' (which could be translated as 'Eccentric') is based on a poem by a Serbian poet, I take it to reflect Ó Searcaigh's own opinions.

34 N. Ní Dhomhnaill, *Cead aighnis* (An Daingean: An Sagart, 1998), pp. 15–16; 'Black'.

35 M. Davitt, *Bligeard sráide* (Dublin: Coiscéim, 1983), p. 29; 'O, my two Palestinians'.

## (as) OíCHE

Bhí gach cead agam, an oíche úd, ar do chaoinchorp caomh;
ar ghile cúr séidte do bhoilg; ar do bhaill bheatha
a ba chumhra ná úllaí fómhair 'bheadh i dtaisce le ráithe;
ar mhaolchnocáin mhíne do mhásaí, ar bhoige liom go mór iad
faoi mo láimh, ná leithead d'éadaigh sróil, a mbeadh tomhas
den tsíoda ina thiús ... Anois agus mé 'mo luí
anseo liom féin i leabaidh léin an díomhaointis
tá mé ar tí pléascadh aríst le pléisiúr ... le tocht

ag cuimhneamh ortsa, a ógánaigh álainn, deargnocht
a d'aoibhnigh an oíche domh ... ocht mbliana déag ó shin, anocht.

(*OO* 90)


## (from) NIGHT

that night    I could do anything with your slender
smooth body    your belly bright as a foaming wave
and below    more tempting than autumn apples
in store    mine were the rolling drumlins of your cheeks
soft under my hand and light as the scantiest silk
now    alone    on a no-such-lucky bed    in pain
in joy    I remember you    beautiful    naked

transforming my night    eighteen years ago    tonight

(trans. Frank Sewell)

36

Mitsuko Ohno

## In Female or Male Voice:
## What Difference Does it Make?

### 1

Considering the advancement of the status of women in Irish society, to which the poems, for example, of Eavan Boland and Nuala Ní Dhomhnaill have contributed a heralding voice, gay men have been noticeably slower to speak out and be heard there than elsewhere in the Western nations. Or, it may be more accurate to say that just as it has taken time for feminist issues such as women's sexuality to come out into the open, similarly, more time has been, and is, required for gay male voices to emerge from the shadows. In a review of Gregory Woods' *A History of Gay Literature: the Male Tradition*, Colm Tóibín writes that gay people

> grow up alone; there is no history. There are no ballads about the wrongs of the past, the martyrs are all forgotten [...] The discovery of a history and a heritage has to be made by each individual as part of the road to freedom.[1]

Here, Tóibín is not confining his comments to Ireland, yet when he adds that 'the idea that gay writing has a tendency to deal in the tragic and unfulfilled [...] has echoes in Irish writing', he must be acutely conscious that gay writing in Ireland may be doubly fraught with tragedy, lack of fulfilment; and even danger.

It is necessary to state here that some of Cathal Ó Searcaigh's poems offer themselves as models of gay writing in the Irish language, even though his first selected poems, *Homecoming/An Bealach 'na Bhaile*, published in 1993, did not overtly disclose the author's homosexuality. Gabriel

Fitzmaurice, editor of this dual language text, notes in his Preface that Ó Searcaigh 'writes as much as a woman as a man — not as androgyny but as one in whom the yin and yang of Chinese dualistic philosophy find expression, complementing each other and informing not only his poetry but his life' (p. x). This reminds one of the tone of Máire Mhac an tSaoi's introduction for Ní Dhomhnaill's *Rogha Dánta/Selected Poems*,[2] and might make one suspect that the time-gap between the publication of Ní Dhomhnaill's and Ó Searcaigh's books (1986 and 1993, respectively) could indicate an equal gap or delay between the general acceptance of women's rights and gay rights in Ireland.

It is, therefore, notable that Lillis Ó Laoire appears only to inadvertently mention the homosexual inclination of the poet in his introduction for the same book: 'Cathal adapts the song to his own experience, dealing with homosexual love, a theme which has until now seldom appeared in Irish language literature' (*ABB* p. 28). One example cited by Ó Laoire is the poem 'Ceann Dubh Dílis/My Blackhaired Love' (*ABB* p. 140):

> A cheann dubh dílis dílis dílis
> d'fhoscail ár bpóga créachtaí Chríosta arís,
> ach ná foscail do bhéal, ná sceith uait an scéal:
> tá ár ngrá ar an taobh tuathail den tsoiscéal.

> *My blackhaired love, my dear, dear, dear,*
> *Our kiss re-opens Christ's wounds here;*
> *But close your mouth, don't spread the word:*
> *We offend the Gospels with our love.*

Despite obvious allusions to homosexual love such as that above, the diversity of the personae employed by Ó Searcaigh in *Homecoming/An Bealach 'na Bhaile* blurs the sexual orientation of his many masks or speakers in poems.

However, when much later volumes appeared, *Na Buachaillí Bána* (1996) and *Out In The Open* (1997), it must have been not only because of the cover paintings of the naked male adolescent bodies but because of the candid content that the collections 'received more media coverage than any other volume of verse published in the Irish language in recent years'.[3] Acknowledging Ó Searcaigh's brave challenge against homophobia, but without adding more to the sensationalism which accompanied the publication of these volumes, I would like to switch my focus directly to the poet's use of gendered masks.

Cathal's adopted son, Prem Timalsina with poets Joan and Kate Newmann, Teileann Bay, Donegal, 2001 (photo: Cathal Ó Searcaigh)

The question of the gender of any poet, translator and reader obviously bears implications for the appreciation of poetry, especially if that poetry is written in a minority language such as Irish and is thus destined to be read in translation by readers outside, in this case, the Irish-speaking community. Since Ó Searcaigh and Ní Dhomhnaill write in Irish, a reader outside that language community encounters their work primarily through English language translations. It is notable that in Ní Dhomhnaill's case, the translation is not limited to female poets,[4] but Ó Searcaigh's poems have largely been translated by male poets, with the exceptions of Sara Berkeley and Joan McBreen in *Homecoming/An Bealach 'na Bhaile* and Heather Allen and Anna Ní Dhomhnaill in *Out In The Open*. In order to see whether the poet's/translator's sexual identity makes any difference in giving the love poem a gendered voice, or if the language employed by the translator gives different impressions concerning the gender of the poet, I attempted a small experiment with some English Department colleagues (a mixed group comprised of males and females, Japanese and native English speakers, none of whom specialise in Irish literature).

I selected and randomly assembled English language translations of four short love poems — two each by Ó Searcaigh and Ní Dhomhnaill. Providing no indication as to the name or gender of the poet and/or translator in each case, I asked my colleagues to identify the gender of the poet/s. It was suggested that they should base their judgement on their first reading rather than on careful scrutiny, but as each reply was returned after a different lapse of time, this part of the experiment was by no means strictly adhered to.

The poems selected were full of sensual and erotic imagery: Ó Searcaigh's 'A Mhianta m'Óige'/'Passions of My Youth' (*OO* p. 132) and 'Rúnsearc'/'Secret Love' (*OO* p. 92), translated by Frank Sewell; and Ní Dhomhnaill's 'Blodewedd' and 'Póg/Kiss',[5] translated by John Montague and Michael Hartnett, respectively. As anticipated, most people found it difficult to assert that any of the poems were written by a male poet because all of the poems seemed to be addressed to a male lover, and no indication of the possibility of homosexual love had been made beforehand.

However, some perceptive readers identified certain signs, which suggested that the poet could either be male or female. A specialist of Renaissance English poetry pointed out rightly that the invocation at the beginning of the first Ó Searcaigh poem 'A Mhianta m'Óige/Passions of My Youth' —

> Taraigí agus glacaigí seilbh orm, a mhianta m'óige.
> Le bhur mbriathra míne cealgaigí mo cheann críonna, le ceol fuiseoige
> bhur ndíograis, cuirigí meidhir mearaidh fá mo sheanchroí támh.

> *Passions of my youth, come over me.*
> *Turn my wary head soft-wards*
> *and make merry with your larks*
> *my stoned and heavy heart.*

— appeared to her to follow the convention of male poets, and did not sound to her like a woman's writing. Another judged that the speaker's was a male voice, because he thought that the term 'pit-stop' which appears in the second stanza is normally associated with male conduct.

'Secret Love' — which begins with the lines

> Agus fiú mura dtig liom treacht ar an té atá le mo mhian,
> mura dtig liom a chuid gruaige, a shúile, a bheola a lua i gcomhrá [...]

> *and even if it's forbidden to refer to the one I'm after*
> *to casually mention his eyes, his lips, his hair [...]*

> (OO p. 92)

— is also highly sensually charged in 'scent and flavour', but one reader did not miss the subtitle 'after C.P. Cavafy'. Aware that Cavafy was a homosexual Greek poet, she concluded that the insertion only made sense if the poet was male. She also interpreted the eroticism and the actuality of the sensation described in the poem 'Kiss' as that of a female:

Ach nuair a chuimhním
ar do phógsa
critheann mo chromáin
is imíonn
a bhfuil eatarthu
ina leacht.

*But when I recall*
*your kiss*
*I shake, and all*
*that lies*
*between my hips*
*liquifies*
*to milk.*

Nevertheless, these were exceptionally acute perceptions after quick reading, and most readers presented a view that all poems might possibly have been written by a woman.

I am not concerned here with the interpretative skills or perceptive ability of my colleagues, nor am I insisting that there are no clear linguistic gender registers in the English language to support our interpretation of the poet's sexual identity. What is at issue here is the fact that Ó Searcaigh's love poems (when read without his male signature) 'appear' to be written in the persona of a woman. But for what purpose?

Transvestism in poetry, or a male poet wearing a female mask, was never an entirely eccentric act in the tradition of English poetry, and in modern Irish literature one can immediately recall the examples in this century of Patrick Pearse's 'Mise Éire'/'I am Ireland', Austin Clark's 'The Young Woman of Beare', and W.B. Yeats's Crazy Jane poems, to name just a few. However, Ó Searcaigh seems to defy easy analogy with his predecessors. Although the Donegal poet has inherited their task as a translator (a modern 'bearer across') of the Irish language tradition,[6] he is obviously not concerned with the patriotic nationalism which is at the core of Pearse's poem, nor is his poetry in alignment with Clarke's efforts to 'express sensuality through imagery based on pagan and Irish mythology'.[7] Ó Searcaigh's female mask, in a way, is more akin to that of Yeats's Crazy Jane, in the sense that its central challenge is a forthright utterance on sexuality and politics. However, while Yeats lets an unabashed woman defend her sexuality against denunciation from the Bishop, the sexual identity of Ó Searcaigh's 'female' remains ambiguous, leaving room for the reader to interpret according to her/his sensitivity. Yeats, in the female mask of Crazy Jane during the era of censorship, had to face accusations of obscenity, but he was not a target for homophobic suspicion. After all, Yeats tried to reclaim the female voice from the erotic tradition of Gaelic literature, rather than to use it as a homo-erotic mask.[8] In fact, strong hostility against homosexuality in Ireland lasted long after Oscar Wilde became the victim of the Criminal Law Amendment Bill of 1885, and gay writing was banned along with other 'sensitive subjects' then seen as a threat to public morality. To quote Colm Tóibín, gay writers in Ireland particularly, until very recently, were only able to deal with the 'forbidden territory' of their sexuality in 'secrecy' and 'fear' with the result that gay readers were left to explore their texts for covert signs.[9]

In such a context, Ó Laoire's comment that the theme of homosexual love 'has until now seldom appeared in Irish language literature' bears a clearer and stronger significance. It appears, for example, that Ó Searcaigh's ambivalent 'female' mask has inevitably resulted from an intrinsic need for protection against the hostile renunciation of homosexuality in the Irish speaking community. This strategy did not come out of a void, nor is it peculiar to the Irish language, but seems to have a source that has not really been fully explored. However, Judith Butler, in *Bodies That Matter: On the Discursive Limits of Sex*, writes about the difficulty surrounding the 'destabilization of masculine and feminine identifications within homosexuality' and argues that 'there is no one femininity with which to identify, which is to say that femininity might itself offer an array of identificatory sites'. She further affirms that 'the non-academic language historically embedded in gay communities is here much more instructive'.[10] This, I believe, can be seen to be the case in the poetry of Ó Searcaigh.

Yet it still comes as a surprise that Ó Searcaigh can brave the taboo, even ahead of English speaking contemporaries in Ireland, and one is compelled to explore further how his use of gendered masks affords emotional identification with the new ethic of sexuality.

## II

If Ó Searcaigh's female mask in love poems such as 'Ceann Dubh Dílis/Dear Dark-Haired Love' (*OO* p. 112) is seen as a protective guise of gay writing, the case of the female protagonist in 'Gort na gCnámh/Field of Bones' (*OO* pp. 66–76), however, requires further analysis. In this poem, the poet adopts the mask of a victimised woman; he uses the female first person's voice to depict a horrifically oppressed and broken life in order, it seems, to condemn the hypocrisy of 'the idyllic Irish rural life' (even more grimly and firmly than Ní Dhomhnaill does in poems such as 'Táimid Damanta, A Dheirféaracha/We Are Damned, My Sisters'[11]):

> Ach bhí m'athair ariamh dúranta agus dall,
> an beathach brúidiúil!

> *But my father*
> *was always dull and dour, the brutal fucker [...]*

> Éisean a rinne an éagóir. Éisean a tháinig idir mé agus suan
> séimh na hoíche;
> idir mé b'fhéidir agus coimirce Dé, cé gur réidh mo spéis
> sna déithe.
> Cha raibh mé ach trí bliana déag nuair a réab sé geasa an
> teaghlaigh
> is léim isteach i mo leabaidh. Oíche i dtús an tsamhraidh a
> bhí ann, sé seachtainí
> i ndiaidh bhás mo mháthara.

> *The fault was his. He came between me and night's peace,*
> *between me and, perhaps, God's love — whatever that is.*
> *Early in the Spring of my 13th year, 6 weeks after mother*
> *had died, he violated me, our home and family [...]*

and:

Ansin bhí sé 'mo mhullach, ag slóbairt is ag slogaireacht
[...]

*Then he was on top of me, mounting and mauling.*

(*OO* pp. 66–76)

Above are the passages which, resentfully and movingly, describe and convey the shocking violation of a young daughter by her own father, and her subsequent misery. As a female reader and admirer of Ó Searcaigh's previous poetry, I must confess that I had a strong sense of unease when I first encountered this poem. My initial shock as a reader came from the utter horror of the girl's experience, her total disgust followed by despair at having no escape from the life to which she is subjected. I felt similarly repulsed and indignant years ago when I read the first few pages of Alice Walker's *Color Purple*. Now, however, aware of Ó Searcaigh's homosexuality, my discomfort was replaced by a curiosity as to why he had employed the mask of a victimised woman in this poem. In other words, the poem, I believe, not only astonishes the reader as a protest against the ill treatment of women in the rural community (something which contemporary Irish women writers have been bringing to the attention of readers) but also challenges the sympathetic reader to wonder why a male poet has employed such a mask. Is Ó Searcaigh trying to articulate his own emotional affinity with the woman in the poem? Does the gender guise of the poem have any strategic merit for describing homosexual experience? Before answering these questions, it is necessary to consider the background from which the poem emerged.

The poem seems to be related to, and to depict, real occurrences in rural Ireland. Even if the events described in the poem might seem to make for a very extreme example, similar tragic cases have actually occurred, although they often remained unreported until recent years when the media started to draw attention to such problems. In poverty-stricken farmlands with remotely dispersed housing, where families are isolated geographically and psychologically, and no one minds other people's business, people's private life can be far from idyllic, especially for women. For example, what is called 'the child murderess tradition' in Irish folklore serves as evidence of grave conditions and predicaments for women in rural Ireland.[12]

When modern incidences of this sort received attention from the media, conscientious minds, feminist or otherwise, responded, and some writers felt compelled to write about such events, and the diverse ways that these subjects inspired or provoked them. The violation of a young girl, her unwelcome pregnancy, and her desperate infanticide became themes for a number of poems: Seamus Heaney's 'Limbo' describes just such an occurrence, and makes the personal tragedy of it transcend to the level of universal Christian faith; Paula Meehan makes the statue of the Virgin Mary weep in compassion with a dying girl/mother in her poem 'The Statue of the Virgin at Granard Speaks'; and Nuala Ní Dhomhnaill's 'Thar mo chionn/There But for the Grace' presents a similar tragedy in a folkloric manner with both terror and compassion. These are only a few examples of works dealing with this issue.

Cathal and Seamus Heaney at Harvard, 1984 (photo: Rachel Giese Brown)

To represent one such girl's desperation, Heaney writes that 'she waded in under/the sign of her cross', but to describe the actual moment of violence, he uses more concrete imagery: 'she stood in the shallows/ducking him tenderly/till the frozen knobs of her wrists/were dead as the gravel'.[13] In 'Gort na gCnámh/Field of Bones' Part V, Ó Searcaigh writes:

> Agus na réaltóga ag dó is ag deargadh mar chocaí cocháin
>     ar thinidh
> i gconlaigh glas fhuar na spéire, rinne mise fómhar beag
>     mo bhroinne
> a mhúchadh le mo mhéara marfóra [...]

> *the stars flamed*
> *like straw on fire in the cold stubble-field of sky*
> *as I extinguished the harvest of my womb*
> *with one finger.*

However, the two female poets Meehan and Ní Dhomhnaill are more allusive, rather than descriptive, about the moment. On a similar tragedy, Meehan lets the speaker of her poem (the Virgin Mary) put the blame for the girl's tragic fate on herself: 'and though she cried out to me in extremis/I did not move,/I didn't lift a finger to help her'.[14] Meanwhile, Ní Dhomhnaill's approach is to make a compassionate acknowledgement that she herself could have ended up in the young girl's predicament or place:

> do tháinig fuarallas orm,
> do phléasc na deora tríom
> is mo ghraidhin í an créatúirín,
> an cailín beag cúig mbliana déag
> a chuaigh ag cur cúraim linbh di i gcoill
> in aice le 'grotto'.

> *cold sweat broke out,*
> *and I burst into tears,*
> *for that poor little thing,*
> *fifteen years old,*
> *who went into the woods*
> *to give birth at a grotto.*[15]

Despite the different styles of approach to the issue, these poems all try to see the reality of rural life from a woman's viewpoint, one which shows another side of rural life which can be repressive and hopeless. The mood of these poems is generally one of helplessness, while the tone strains to offer also some atonement for the victims.

One other aspect of the poem 'Gort na gCnámh/Field of Bones' calls for the reader's attention. Ó Searcaigh's poem appears to contain an echo of Heaney's early poems. However, the echo only makes the contrast between the two poets' concerns more vivid. For Heaney as a son, in the poem 'Digging', potato-picking is an action lovingly and proudly recalled for its positive associations with family love, unity and tradition:

> he rooted out tall tops, buried the bright edge deep
> to scatter new potatoes that we picked
> loving their cool hardness in our hand.
>
> By God, the old man could handle a spade.
> Just like his old man.[16]

However, in Ó Searcaigh's 'Gort na gCnámh/Field of Bones', the family bond is violently shattered by sexual abuse so that representation of the potato-picking father in the latter poem naturally and drastically differs in tone. The daughter/narrator in Ó Searcaigh's poem, for example, 'follows' her father's footsteps with pathetic detachment:

> Seo anois mé ag leanstan lorg a spáide de choiscéim mhall,
> smug le mo shoc, scifleogach, ag piocadh préataí faoi lom
>     na gaoithe
> agus eiseann ag briseadh chraiceann tiubh na hithreach ar
>     nós na réidhe,
> ag brú chun tosaigh go tíorónta, ag foscladh roimhe agus
>     ina dhiaidh.
>
> *So here I am following the traces of his spade,*
> *slowly, snot in my nose, ragged, picking potatoes*
> *under a barrage of wind while he indifferently parts*
> *the thick-skinned soil, thrusting ahead, opening it*
> *up before and after him [...]*

In Heaney's 'Digging', the wet soil is a source of sonic delight:

> The cold smell of potato mould, the squelch and slap
> Of soggy peat, the curt cuts of an edge
> Through living roots awaken in my head.

However, in 'Gort na gCnámh/Field of Bones', the act of potato-picking represents nothing more than sordid endurance of the burden of life. The woman-narrator of Ó Searcaigh's poem perceives the act of potato-picking as silent despair in sombre monotone:

>                                       [...] is beag
>     nach mbriseann mo chroí
> le cumhaidh; ach seo mé ag piocadh liom ó dhruil go druil, síos
>     agus aníos go tostach
> ag coinneáil m'airde ar rithim bhuile na spáide. Mothaím
>     trom torrach
> leis an tocht atá á iompar agam gach uile lá beo, tocht dorcha dochiallach
>     ag lorg urlabhra.

>                                     *[...] my heart*
> *aches for a home but I keep on picking through drills*
> *in silence to the spade's rhythm, weighed down by hurt*
> *deeper and darker every day beyond expression.*

>                                   (*OO* p. 72 and p. 76)

Whereas Heaney's poem reaches for the promising conclusion of 'between my finger and my thumb/the squat pen rests./I'll dig with it', Ó Searcaigh writes:

> Ba mhór an méadú misnigh domh dá bhféadfainn
> an brú seo a ghineadh i mbroinn m'aigne a ionchollú i mbriathra,
>     a thabhairt slán.
> Ach nuair a fhosclaím mo bhéal lená shaolú, lena scaoileadh
>     saor, i dtólamh
> théid sé i bhfostú i mo sceadamán, stiúcann sé ar mo theangaidh [...]

*Could I conceive and flesh that burden in new-born words,*
*what courage I would have! But when I open my mouth*
*to free it, it always sticks in my throat, clamps my tongue [...]*

Finally, the poem is closed off, or in, by silence: 'fate has narrowed/its eyes and left me dumb in the Field of Bones' (*OO* p. 76). Therefore, when Heaney describes his aged father in the field years later, in 'Follower', he can communicate the satisfaction and pathos of having outgrown his father as part of the natural and gratifying course of male life:

I was a nuisance, tripping, falling,
Yapping always. But today
It is my father who keeps stumbling
Behind me, and will not go away.[17]

Yet, the father remains the son's hero, and even in the more recent poem 'The Errand', Heaney recalls him once again with the line 'still he was glad, I know, when I stood my ground', reconfirming his unwavering attachment to his parent. Contrastingly, for the girl in Ó Searcaigh's poem, her father stands as the fatal enemy, while her mother has failed to provide a positive role-model for her. In this poem, women are made victims of the rudeness and brutal violence of the dominant male:

> An créatúr gan choir, cha raibh sí
> in araíocht ag an tsaol
> a leagadh amach dithe. 'Cuirfidh mise geall go ndéanfaidh mé
> an cailín Domhnaigh
> a dhreasú asat, a chlaitseach gan úsáid,' a deireadh sé léithe,
> ag ardú a láimhe
> is á greadadh timpeall an tí.

*Poor gentle mother, hardly cut out for the life he led her.*
*'I'll knock the airs and graces out o' ye, ye useless slut,'*
*he'd tell her, raising his hand and beating her about the house.*

(*OO* p. 68 and p. 74)

The field presented as rich fertile soil in Heaney's 'Digging' is supplanted in Ó Searcaigh's poem by the burial ground — a barren soil where life is denied and hope lost. The female victim of sexual abuse in the poem is deprived of the means of escape. The field, where 'silence veiled [her] shame' remains forever a battlefield for father and daughter. The only difference between the mother and her daughter in the poem is that the latter is stronger in the sense that she learns to fight back against the threat of the paternal power and abuse. However, she still chooses to stay confined to the field of despair rather than to brave the challenges of the world outside.

This section of *Out in the Open* containing 'Gort na gCnámh'/'Field of Bones' opens with a quotation from a poem by the American poet Adrienne Rich — 'grief held back from the lips, wears at the heart' — which alerts the reader to the possibility that the poem might have a wider agenda than one might at first suspect. The reference to Rich reminds the reader that the problem of sexual abuse involves complex factors of gender, class and education. The lines of 'Gort na gCnámh'/'Field of Bones' are testimony to Ó Searcaigh's observation of the darker side of rural life which is dominated by patriarchal power politics. Once conscious of the specific allusions to Heaney's poems, and sensitive to the destructive violence and apathy that prevail in the poem, the reader begins to wonder whether the poem is really about women.

In effect, the scenario is as follows: the father who is expected to be the guardian of a child turns into her/his abuser. The hidden text for this violation of the incest taboo could be interpreted as the tale of a child rejected by a parent, a father-figure who condemns and threatens a daughter or son whose sexuality could possibly violate a sexual taboo by, for example, opposing the heterosexual mores of the patriarchal system. Such a father could denounce a child so brutally that the shattered son or daughter may from then on yearn in vain for parental acceptance and love. In the poem 'Gort na gCnámh/Field of Bones', the fate of the raped daughter is most severe but, in her case, the victim has, at least, been granted a voice (as also, for example, in work by Ní Dhomhnaill and other contemporary women poets).

The fate of a gay youth, however, may yet be more severe, especially if he/she has to continue to bear her/his grief alone and silently: 'grief held back from the lips wears at the heart'.[18]

Even if he/she attempts an escape, the outside world would probably not provide her/him any help or solace, as it is dominated by homophobia and gay-bashing. Even in supposedly more liberated American society, homosexual love has to remain closeted 'in the increasingly homophobic atmosphere of public discourse since 1985'.[19]

There are other images employed in 'Gort na gCnámh/Field of Bones' that also seem to support such a reading. The poem's tone of disgust, despair and remorse appears to reject any possibility of the reproduction of life within the boundaries, at least, of the 'field of bones'. For example, the field is cultivated in order to 'make it rich' so that it will yield a crop for human survival but we are also told that the field 'claimed all I had; my flesh and blood, my child'. Also ironically, although the 'fault was his [the father's]', it was the young girl who was 'deflowered' by the parent's act of spreading 'his seed in the clay of [her] womb', and it was she who in return 'extinguished the harvest of [her] womb'. Thus the soil fails to support life, and instead absorbs grief and death. The daughter/narrator names the bogland the 'Field of Bones', and it is finally inhabited only by a listless old man and a barren woman whose heart 'aches for a home'. The dark background of the poem could be said to correspond with the situation for gay writers and readers. Tóibín has written that 'happiness for homosexuals was a serious transgression', something which he believes has 'echoes in Irish writing', especially where 'there is a dead father or a dead child'.[20]

Ultimately, 'Gort na gCnámh/Field of Bones' could be read as a love poem where, by implication, a son or daughter placed or pushed onto 'the wrong side of a gospel' (OO p. 113) or taboo, seeks reciprocity of love between a father-figure and themselves, or between society and themselves. However, the patriarchal ethos of a society may deny tolerance, and even expression, to the stigmatised existence or offspring in a spiral or cycle of worsening rejection and violence. The strategy of the female mask can, therefore, be seen as a disguised means of expressing a yearning for the familial and societal love that is not readily granted to the marginalised, including, for example, the homosexual or lesbian.

Meanwhile, however grim the depiction of the victim's psychology is in 'Gort na gCnámh/Field of Bones', the reader is deeply moved by the poet's remarkable empathy. This is the power of Ó Searcaigh's poem, and of his poetry in general.

## III

Sherry Simon in her *Gender in Translation* quotes John Florio's equation that all translations are 'reputed females' and concludes that 'the femininity of translation is a persistent historical trope'.[21] However, in the argument regarding the adoption or use of gendered positions in translation theory, Simon notes the subversive role of a new type of translator: 'the feminist translator affirms her role as an active participant in the creation of meaning. She affirms the provisionality of meaning, drawing attention to the process of her own work'.[22] Certainly, like the feminist translator, Frank Sewell (main translator of Ó Searcaigh's second bilingual volume, *Out in the Open*) draws the reader's attention to the process of his work. When he uses the English slang such as 'the brutal fucker' (*OO* p. 73) to translate Ó Searcaigh's 'an beathach brúidiúil' (*OO* p. 66), for example, the reader notes a strong contrast in tone with Ó Searcaigh's other poems which are often more pleasant, optimistic and full of subversive jokes.

Is this what Sewell means when he writes in the Preface that:

> bearing each of these poems across the borderlines between Irish and English, I found that they struck up a conversation as if following the maxim that *giorraíonn beirt bóthar*/two shorten a road. I also found that to reach roughly the same destination, they had to approach it by divergent means (*OO* p. 13)?

The complexity that issues of language and gender (both the poet's and the translator's) bestow on a poem such as 'Gort na gCnámh/Field of Bones' may not be entirely deliberate, but by directing the reader to an awareness of this complexity, the poem, translation and, in this case, their layout[23] certainly engage the attention of readers and critics alike.

Further, by following Ó Searcaigh's poems as they move between languages, and from issues of gender (of the poet and/or speaker and/or translator) to those of sexuality, the active reader is made to think seriously about her/his own attitude towards homo/sexuality. Thus, the reader is absorbed in some central concerns of our contemporary society, namely 'hybridization of diasporic culture and the mobility of all identities, including gender' and sexuality.[24]

In this sense, Michael Cronin is wrong to claim that, in translation, 'it is the original poet rather than the translator who becomes invisible'.[25] In 'Gort na gCnámh/Field of Bones', for example, Ó Searcaigh adopts a female mask to transgress the gender barrier, while Sewell's translation, in turn, transgresses (for non-Irish language readers) a linguistic barrier. Awareness, however, of the original poet's homosexuality and also of the problems surrounding gay literature in countries such as Ireland, still manages to compel the reader to actively respond to the message of the *source* language, i.e. that of the original poet, through, if necessary, the *target* language, i.e. that of the translator. Cronin does, however, usefully point out that, in Ireland, translation itself has become 'a privileged mode of interrogation' in a modern cultural context where increasingly 'fixed identities were [and are] being questioned' and explored.[26]

## Notes

1    Colm Tóibín, 'Roaming the Greenwood', a review of *A History of Gay Literature: the Male Tradition* by G. Woods (1998), in *London Review of Books*, Vol. 21, No. 2, 21 January 1999, 12–16.
2    In her introduction to Nuala Ní Dhomhnaill's *Rogha Dánta/Selected Poems*, 3rd edn (Dublin: Raven Arts Press, 1991), Mhac an tSaoi seems to have carefully avoided terms with ideological implications in spite of the obvious 'feminist' aspects and agendas of the book presumably because, in her opinion, these might not have enhanced the reputation of the book or of the young woman poet at that time.
3    See the 'Biographical Note' on Ó Searcaigh in *Out in the Open*.

4    Most of Nuala Ní Dhomhnaill's *Selected Poems/Rogha Dánta* is translated by Michael Hartnett except for a small section translated by Ní Dhomhnaill herself; among her other bilingual volumes, *Pharaoh's Daughter* is translated by 13 poets, male and female; and *The Astrakhan Cloak* is translated solely by Paul Muldoon.

5    Ní Dhomhnaill, *Pharaoh's Daughter*, p. 116; and *Rogha Dánta/Selected Poems*, p. 38, respectively.

6    Some of Ó Searcaigh's love poems, for example, are retellings of old songs from Irish folk tradition. See 'Introduction', *ABB* pp. 27–30.

7    Robert Welch, ed., *The Oxford Companion to Irish Literature* (Oxford: Clarendon Press, 1996), p. 100.

8    For related gender discussion of Yeats' work, see Adrian Frazier's 'Queering the Irish Renaissance: The Masculinities of Moore, Martyn, and Yeats', in *Gender and Sexuality in Modern Ireland*, ed. by A. Bradley and M.G. Valiulis (Amherst: University of Massachusetts Press, 1997).

9    Tóibín, op. cit.

10   Judith Butler, *Bodies That Matter: on the Discursive Limits of Sex* (New York: Routledge, 1993), pp. 239–240.

11   Ní Dhomhnaill, *Rogha Dánta/Selected Poems*, pp. 14–17.

12   A. O'Connor, 'Women in Irish Folklore: the Testimony Regarding Illegitimacy, Abortion and Infanticide', in *Women in Early Modern Ireland*, ed. by M MacCurtain and M. O'Dowd (Edinburgh University Press, 1991), pp. 304–312.

13   Seamus Heaney, *New Selected Poems: 1966–1987* (London: Faber and Faber, 1990), p. 37.

14   Paula Meehan, *The Man Who Was Marked by Winter*, 3rd edn (Loughcrew: Gallery Press, 1994), pp. 40–42 (p. 42).

15   Ní Dhomhnaill, *Féar Suaithinseach* (Maigh Nuad: An Sagart, 1984), pp. 72–74 (p. 73). Translation by Angela Bourke, 1993.

16   Heaney, *New Selected Poems*, pp. 1–2.

17   Heaney, *New Selected Poems*, p. 6.

18   Quote from Adrienne Rich used by Ó Searcaigh as an epigram to introduce the poem 'Gort na gCnámh/Field of Bones'. See *OO* p. 65.

19   Eve Kosofsky Sedgwick, *Epistemology of the Closet* (Berkeley, Los Angeles: University of California Press, 1990), p. 21.

20   Tóibín, pp. 14–15.

21   Sherry Simon, *Gender in Translation: Cultural Identity and the Politics of Transmission* (London, New York: Routledge, 1996), p. 1.

22   Simon, *Gender in Translation*, p. 29.

23   The English language translation of the various sections of 'Gort na gCnámh/Field of Bones' is not printed side by side with the original Irish version as is the case with other poems, but begins after the entire poem has been presented in Irish, as if the original and translated version were almost independent.

24   Simon, *Gender in Translation*, p. 135.

25   Michael Cronin, *Translating Ireland: Tradition, Languages, Cultures* (Cork University Press, 1996), p. 177.

26   Cronin, *Translating Ireland*, p. 169.

## A Chavafy, a chroí

Cheiliúraigh tusa an grá seo i do dhánta
Gan scáth folaigh, gan eagla. Ar feadh blianta,
Cheiliúraigh tú bogstócaigh do shamhlaíochta
I do chuid filíochta: buachaillí bána an cheana
Lena ngéaga téagartha is a mbeola maotha meala
Ag imirt a mbáire baoise ar léana do leapa
Go háthasach. Ach anseo i gCloich Cheann Fhaola
Agus an mbeifeá ag súil lena athrach -
Tá an Grá Gréagach mínáireach, mínádúrtha:
I nDuibhlinn, i nDroim na Tineadh, i Maigh Rátha,
I gCaoldroim, i gCollchéim agus i mBaile an Átha
Níl ann ach ábhar magaidh agus masla.
Ach, a Chavafy, neartaigh, neartaigh m'fhocla!
Ná lig daofa imeacht ar fán
I na gciflí ceo a chaillfear go deo
I ngleannta gaofara seo na gcnoc
I dir an tArd Ramhar agus an tÉadan Bán:
A Chavafy, buanaigh iad i mo dhán.

(*ATLS* 211)


## To Constantin Cavafy

In your poems, you celebrated this love, openly and fearlessly.
For years, you immortalised the young bucks of your dreams
in poems: lovely, loving lads with strong limbs and soft sweet
lips,
happily fooling around the four corners of your bed. But here,
in Cloich Cheann Fhaola - if you expected anything different -
Greek love is considered shameful and degenerate: in Duibhlinn,
Droim na Tineadh, Maigh Rátha, Caoldroim, Collchéim
and in Baile an Átha, it is mocked and abjured. But Cavafy,
strengthen, strengthen my words! Don't let them melt away
like clouds of mist lost forever in the windy glens between
Ard Ramhar and Éadan Bán: Cavafy, let them live in my poems.

(trans. Frank Sewell)

Frank Sewell

## Between Staisiún Chaiseal na gCorr and Stantzia Zimá: The Poetry of Cathal Ó Searcaigh

Ariamh níor dhiúltaigh [mé] solas
Ó na ceithre hairde nuair tháinig.

*I never knocked back light*
*from anywhere when it came*[1]

In his illuminating essay 'Words and the Word', W. H. Auden wrote: 'give me a list of the names in your life, and I will tell you who you are'.[2] Reading Cathal Ó Searcaigh's first collection, *Miontraigéide Cathrach*/'A Minor City-tragedy' (1975), and particularly the introduction, it is easy to build up a profile of the fledgling poet based on the masters, named and unnamed, who were beginning to infiltrate his consciousness.

Ó Searcaigh recalls his father's recitation of poems by Robert Burns as his first, youthful introduction to the then unintelligible, but still magical, sound of poetic speech. The rest of the introduction, however, judging from the number of quotations and references, makes it clear that Ó Searcaigh's main mentor in poetry at the time (the early to mid-1970s) was T. S. Eliot. There is nothing strange in this (many poets have been influenced by Eliot) except that Ó Searcaigh seems to refer to Eliot as a contemporary with whom he is in almost complete agreement. For example, instead of developing, updating or challenging Eliot as, say, MacNeice did,[3] Ó Searcaigh is content simply to agree with, and repeat, Eliot's 'furies' in *Murder in the Cathedral* for whom 'man's life is a cheat and disappointment' (*MC* p. 11), especially in the city, which he terms a 'reilig bheo'/'living graveyard' or, in Eliot's phrase, 'the dead land'. The influence of Eliot with regard to form, at least, was more open-ended: Ó Searcaigh clearly adopts Eliot's definition of free verse as 'a preparation for new form or for the revival of the old' (*MC* p. 14). This left the young poet himself free to follow and extend the traditional line along the contours of his own time, topic, and individual talent.

There is another unacknowledged but conspicuously obvious presence clearly influencing Ó Searcaigh in the introduction to *Miontraigéide Cathrach*: Seán Ó Ríordáin is omnipresent in the apologetic tone as well as in the religious language with which Ó Searcaigh tries to define (and, initially, write) poetry. The introduction itself, including its layout, with the repeated question 'cad is filíocht ann?'/what is poetry?, is based on the same in Ó Ríordáin's first collection, *Eireaball Spideoige* (1952). The latter referred openly to Eliot's objective correlative. Ó Searcaigh does not do so but, at least, develops the concept by mingling the ideas of the two earlier poets:

> Tá mé ag ceapadh gurb é atá i bhfilíocht ná sraith de chodarsnachta a bhfuil gaol gairid eatarthu agus a fhreagraíonn dá chéile ar bhealach a dheimhníonn teorainn an limistéir ag a dtarlaíonn gníomh diamhair amhail Apacailiops ag a cheartlár éiginnte. Tá an Apacailiops seo, mar a déarfá, i riocht geit.[4]

> I think that in poetry you get a series of contrasts that are closely related and mirror each other in a way that affirms the sphere where a mysterious act like an Apocalypse happens at its uncertain centre. This Apocalypse [...] is something which startles

Another unacknowledged source for Ó Searcaigh's early ideas on poetry, is Máirtín Ó Direáin. Referring to the elusiveness of any all-encompassing definition of poetry, Ó Searcaigh mocks the would-be pursuer of such a definition with a metaphor from Ó Direáin's poem 'Gasúir'/Children:

> Criathar chun tobar le gasúir
> Nó gad chun gainimh go síor,
> Obair nach follas a thoradh
> Cé ard a torann go fíor.[5]

*Boys bringing a sieve to the well*
*or a noose to sand for ever,*
*a means to a too obscure end*
*despite all the palaver.*

Furthermore, Ó Searcaigh's perception of the poet-figure as an emancipator and restorer of the word in its purest form, is inextricably associated in his mind with the achievement of Ó Direáin. A prose paragraph on page eleven of *Miontraigéide Cathrach*, in fact, later resurfaces as a poem in honour of Ó Direáin in *ABB*:

Is tusa an fuascailteoir
a ghríosaigh is a threoraigh le do theacht
éirí amach na bhfocal.

As daingne díchuimhne
shaoraigh tú iad ó dhaorsmacht
le heochair d'inchinne.

*You are the Emancipator,*
*Who fired and steered with your coming*
*The Rising of the Words.*

*From the fortress of amnesia,*
*You loosed them from bondage,*
*With your cerebral key.*[6]

Ó Direáin, together with Eliot, may also have confirmed Ó Searcaigh in his distaste for cities. At times, in this first, and premature, collection, the Donegal poet's sympathy for city people crosses the border of unintended insult:

daoine gan spionnadh, gan seannadh, is cúram mar nasc ar gach béal [...] ag tnúth go héadóchasach le réiteach; — ag feitheamh lena nGodot [...] fágtar an duine ina chorpán bheo, stoite ina aonarán, seachranach, i Haceldama na linne seo.[7]

'Dispirited, inconstant people, with worry like a muzzle on every mouth [...] waiting hopelessly for a solution; for their Godot [...] Left like a Zombie, uprooted, single, astray like a modern Haceldama'

Cathal, barman in the Ox & Gate, Cricklewood, London, 1975 (photo: Cathal Ó Searcaigh)

While this one-dimensional, Kafkaesque view of the city and its inhabitants dominates Ó Searcaigh's early work, his more mature oeuvre includes several poems which expand to share some of MacNeice's more urban and urbane outlook.[8] In 'Is Glas na Cnoic/Faraway Hills', for example, Ó Searcaigh takes a much more positive look at the urban landscape, concluding: 'don chéad uair braithim sa bhaile i gcéin'/'for the first time I feel at home abroad' (*ABB* p. 206). However, he feels more 'at home' because he makes himself more at home, turning the traffic metaphorically into a flock of sheep, and office-blocks into mountains. In Ó Searcaigh's case, beauty certainly is in the eye of the beholder since he must first 'naturalize' the cityscape before he can compliment it or feel 'at home' in it — his highest term of praise. The development marked in this poem, therefore, is not the attainment of a less leafy, or less pejorative, view of the city, but the poet's growing self-confidence, and the transgressive manner in which his personal stereo, boldly and symbolically, picks up and re-mixes new blends or combinations in poetry of diverse languages and cultures:

Anois piocaim suas Mín a' Leá agus Mayfair
ar an mhinicíocht
mhire mhíorúilteach amháin i m'aigne
sa *bhuzz* seo a mhothaím i mBerkley Square;
agus mé ag teacht orm féin le dearfacht
nár mhothaigh mé go dtí seo
mo *vibe* féin, mo rithim féin,
rithim bheo na beatha ag borradh agus ag *buzzáil*
i bhféitheacha mo bhriathra.

*Now I pick up Mín a' Leá and Mayfair*
*On the same mad miraculous*
*Frequency in my mind*
*In this buzz I feel in Berkeley Square;*
*While I discover myself with a positiveness*
*I haven't already felt*
*My own vibe, my own rhythm*
*The exciting rhythm of life increasing and buzzing*
*In the arteries that are my words.*

(ABB p. 206)

Finally, there is one other presence overshadowing Ó Searcaigh's first volume, *Miontraigéide Cathrach*, another great master whose influence had not yet been completely absorbed by the young poet: Yevgeny Yevtushenko. Ó Searcaigh's Russian studies in Limerick led him to the discovery of Yevtushenko but his own personal and poetic temperament (they are inseparable) are what led him to identify with this Russian exemplar. What do they have in common?

Peter Levi and Robin Milner-Gulland point out in their introduction to his *Selected Poems* that, in Yevtushenko, man and poet are indivisible: 'when asked about his early life, Yevtushenko is apt to refer the questioner to his poetry'.[9] Ó Searcaigh could easily do the same for he, too, belongs to the school of Yevtushenko who once famously declared that 'a poet's autobiography is his poetry [...] if the poet tries to split himself in two between the man and the poet, he will inevitably commit suicide as an artist'.[10] Consequently, what draws some readers to Ó Searcaigh's work is the freshness of a real human voice talking about real things, real encounters and experiences which the surreal language and imagery of his poems come tantalisingly close to re-creating, re-experiencing through language.[11]

However, this somewhat old-fashioned poetic stance (of the poet *as*, in most poems, speaker) makes for a rather public persona, and poetry that tends to seek after truth.[12] Recently, the tendency for so-called post-modern poets has been to follow Auden's view that 'the truest poetry is the most feigning',[13] and to retreat behind ironic masks and put-on voices, in the manner, say, of Paul Muldoon. Nevertheless, the direct, personal approach (more common in Russian and Irish language poetry) can still be seen to be effective. For example, from a poet's and a reader's perspective, identification of the 'I' of the poems with that of the author, is not necessarily limiting. In practice, both the 'I' (poet-speaker or poet *as* speaker) and the poetry, can be continually stretched or broadened to accommodate, what Joyce called, the reality (and diversity) of experience which it encounters.

Meanwhile, assumption, in *most* poems by Yevtushenko and Ó Searcaigh, of the combined role and voice of 'poet-speaker' is also part and parcel of an ideological insistence on 'honesty'.[14] Levi and Milner-Gulland wrote of Yevtushenko, for example, that 'the central stronghold of the poems is a rock-like absolute of integrity'.[15] I interpret this integrity not just as candour but also as a sense of readiness and willingness to encounter and absorb the outside reality (pleasant and unpleasant) that the 'I' confronts.

Yet, all of this has repercussions for the poet. He/she, as in the case of Seán Ó Ríordáin and, particularly, Máirtín Ó Direáin (who shared Yevtushenko's rock-like integrity and pursuit of truth), can become, in Derrida's terms, a centred structure whose 'free play' is grounded and limited in order to master the anxiety of feeling at stake in the 'game' of life, and in the enquiry into life which their work constitutes.[16] Levi and Milner-Gullard's comments on Yevtushenko (below) could actually refer to Ó Searcaigh, Ó Ríordáin or any such mask-less poet:

> The whole of Yevtushenko's life is at stake in this inquiry and therefore also his belief in the society in

which he lives, and in the source of his poems. Since everything stands or falls together in his writing, his fundamental realism about experience involves him at the same time [...] in an entire galaxy of accurately observed *sensibilia*, which he records with a tension that expresses his own solitude and tension, and in a searching humanist inquiry into Russian society. This combination of intimate moral stature with an implacable public voice and the attractive personal mannerisms of a likeable poet works itself out in differing proportions in different poems, but it is always present.[17]

Significantly, however, Ó Searcaigh seems to get round the truth-seeking limitation and possible grounding (noted by Derrida), as well as Levi and Milner-Gullard's notion of everything standing or falling together in his writing, by bringing to bear on his past, his home and himself, visions and values that sometimes clash radically with them, and by re-enacting the very struggles and motivations that drove him from his home in the first place. This, in Marshall Berman's terms, is what 'distinguishes modernism from sentimentalism'[18]; and it is also, in my opinion, what has helped to make Ó Searcaigh the prolific and popular, international poet that he is today.

From the outset, Ó Searcaigh has shown a great ability to adopt and adapt methods and techniques from a select international array of mentors with whom he identifies: these clearly include the verbal, sexual and mystical free-wheeling of the American Beat poets[19] but also the public voice of the Siberian small-town boy, Yevgeny Yevtushenko. For example, in *Miontraigéide Cathrach*, Ó Searcaigh notes that Yevtushenko (like himself) came from a 'baile beag tuaithe'/small country town (*MC* p. 65). A geographically, linguistically and even sexually marginalised young writer, Ó Searcaigh surely identified with Yevtushenko when he read that the latter 'is a peasant boy who has come to the city — and for whom his remote birthplace continues to hold a deeply felt significance; vigorously sensual, often regarded by his elders as a destructive and degenerate influence (though in reality he is a passionate seeker after truth and moral justice) ...'[20]

Yevtushenko hails famously from Stantzia Zimá (literally, 'winter station', a small junction on the Trans-Siberian Railway, near Lake Baikal). Note how the Soviet poet lets the station itself send him off at the end of his early, but far-reaching, poem 'Zimá Station', named after his home town:

> 'You're not the only one,
> like you now in the world,
> who is searching, scheming, struggling.
> It's OK, son, that you didn't answer
> the particular question asked of you.
> Be patient, look about you, listen.
> Keep searching the whole world over.
> Yes, truth is fine, but happiness is better,
> though without truth, you'll never be happy.
> Go through life with your head held high.
> Be up-front [...]
> Love people — for love looks after its own.
> Remember. —
>        I'm keeping you in mind.
> It won't be easy — but you can always come back to me ...
> Go on!'
>     I went.
>        And I am still going.[21]

It is interesting that Ó Searcaigh also hails from an area quite close to a (former) rail-stop: Stáisiún Chaiseal na gCorr, celebrated in one of his best-known poems:

> Anseo braithim go bhfuil éifeacht i bhfilíocht.
> Braithim go bhfuil brí agus tábhacht liom mar dhuine
> is mé ag feidhmiú mar chuisle de chroí mo chine
> agus as an chinnteacht sin tagann suaimhneas aigne.
>
> *Here I feel the worth [value, importance, effectiveness] of poetry.*
> *I feel that I have meaning and significance as an individual*
> *as I work [function, operate] like the pulse [beat] of my people's heart*
> *and from that certainty comes peace of mind.*

In this poem, 'Anseo ag Stáisiún Chaiseal na gCorr'/Here at Caiseal na gCorr Station (*ABB* p. 94), Ó Searcaigh repeats some of the themes and concerns that are evident in the poetry, and biography, of Yevtushenko: the importance for these individual poets of feeling at one with, and as one functioning part of, their community; the acknowledgement of taking pride in, and inspiration from, their home region and people; and finally, the sustaining solace and sure-footing that 'home' holds out both for setting off and for return/homecoming, 'an bealach 'na bhaile'.[22]

Cathal and Swedish poet Tomas Transtomer, Cape Cod, Provincetown Arts Centre, 1984 (photo: Rachel Giese Brown)

Ó Searcaigh, therefore, follows not only Irish tradition but a world-wide tradition that includes Yevtushenko, in trying to celebrate the essence, the 'truth' of his homeland and people. In his *Precocious Autobiography*, for example, Yevtushenko shares the most important piece of advice which he claimed to have ever received: 'find the truth in yourself and give it to others, and find it in others and store it up in yourself'.[23] The Russian poet was given this advice by an old factory worker, a Soviet version of Ó Searcaigh's wise old woman character, Bríd, in the poem 'Bean an tSléibhe'/'Mountain Woman' (*OO* p. 22).

Ó Searcaigh recounts that Bríd was never 'gruama nó grusach linn/gruff or gloomy with us', comparing her to an apple-tree of knowledge: 'mar shíolta thitfeadh a briathra in úir mhéith m'aigne/her words fell like seeds into the welcoming earth of my mind'. Her words quoted in the poem do, indeed, have an ancient ring of poetic, but earthy and proverbial, wisdom: 'sa tír seo, tugtar na *crusts* is cruaidhe don té atá mantach/in this country, the hardest crusts are given to those with least teeth'. Commemorating this old woman, her ways and expressions, Ó Searcaigh follows the advice given to Yevtushenko to find, store and share the truths he finds in himself and in others. Such storing and sharing allows a kind of eternity to be achieved through which the present (and even the future) can be illuminated by the light of knowing something of ourselves and those around us, past and present. This knowledge can be passed on again quietly and respectfully in poems: 'is fearr cogar sa chúirt ná scread ar an tsliabh'/a whisper in the court is better than a roar on the moor.

Yevtushenko, in a 'lament against destruction' which is typical both of his own and of Ó Searcaigh's poetry, has written that 'no people are uninteresting./Their fate is like the chronicle of planets'.[24] Similarly, when Ó Searcaigh celebrates or sings the lives or fates of local friends and neighbours, he does not approach such people or their language as does, it is suggested,[25] the 'anthropologist or alien invader', or even the 'remembering exile' of, say, contemporary British poetry — certainly not since he moved back to have a permanent base among his own people ['mo dhaoine'/'mo mhuintir'] in Donegal. Instead, Ó Searcaigh's relationship with them is always personal. The poems make clear that he himself had to be consumed by, for example, the warmth and wisdom of local characters before he could allow, or redirect, the same warmth and homely wisdom to radiate out to readers. Therefore, in 'Oícheanta Geimhridh', Ó Searcaigh illumines his current 'Winter Nights' by re-calling former heartening times in the company of Neddie Eoin, a local seanchaí/storyteller:

> Tá sé corradh le fiche bliain anois
> ó chuaigh a thinidh as, i mbarr na Míne Buí
> ach istigh anseo i gcigilt mo chuimhne
> drithlíonn beo nó dhó den tinidh adaí
> is leáfaidh na drithleoga sin an dubhacht
> a mhothaím anocht i bhféitheoga an chroí.

*His fire is out these twenty years*
*or more at the top of Mín Bhuí*
*but here in the banked hearth of my memory*
*a live coal or two from that fire sparkles,*
*and those sparks will dissolve the gloom*
*I feel in my heart tonight.*

(*ABB* p. 115)

By convincing the reader that the fiery spell of Neddie Eoin's talk, alive and glowing with songs by Burns and lays of the Fianna, has heartened *him* as an individual (the artist himself 'as a young man'), Ó Searcaigh proves the value of such things for one and all, confirming Yevtushenko's point that 'only in a sharply outlined individual can that which is common to many be combined and fused'.[26]

Another point where the tracks of Yevtushenko and Ó Searcaigh meet, is in their concept of audience. Again in his *Precocious Autobiography* (a favourite book of Ó Searcaigh's), Yevtushenko recounts a lesson that he learnt from experience, but firstly from Kirsánov:

> a poet has only one indispensable quality: whether he is simple or complicated, people must need him. Poetry, if it's genuine, is not a racing car rushing senselessly round and round a closed track, it is an ambulance rushing to someone's aid.[27]

For Yevtushenko, this 'aid' takes the form of restoring people's 'faith in life', in their own, and their country's, worth. He shares and, no doubt, encouraged Ó Searcaigh's view that poet and people are mutually dependent; that the poet is not only a microcosm of the people but an essential element of the larger organism. Such thinking moved Ó Searcaigh to produce the poem 'Portráid den Ghabha mar Ealaíontóir Óg'/A Portrait of the Blacksmith as a Young Artist (*ABB* p. 84) in which he likens the essential, communal craft of the blacksmith to that of the poet (*and vice versa*).

At times, the relationship between poet and people may become a strained one[28] but for Ó Searcaigh (and Yevtushenko), the nature of that relationship is necessarily such that it always involves a two-way exchange: for example, story-telling neighbours such as the seanchaí Neddie Eoin taught the young Ó Searcaigh to say 'more than his prayers' (*ABB* p. 28) but, in return, he numbers such anti-heroes in his poems/songs, casting them (like a sculptor) in the 'clay of memory':

> ach gurb é gur chan mé thú i mo dhán, a dhuine,
> rachadh d'ainm i ndíchuimhne ...
>
> *only I number you in my song,*
> *your name would go into oblivion ...*[29]

As if to further illustrate the two-way nature of the relationship between the poet and her/his community, Ó Searcaigh also lets the old man commemorated in the above poem do some of the singing himself, quoting him directly and vividly in his own earthy, Rabelaisian words:

> Agus nuair a d'fhiafróchainn dó caidé mar a bhí rudaí deireadh sé, "buíochas le Dia, tá mé ag mún, ag cac is ag feadalaigh".
>
> *And when I asked how things were going, he'd say,*
> *"thanks be to God, I'm pissin', shittin', an' whistlin'".*
>
> (OO p. 30)

Ó Searcaigh shares with Yevtushenko a deep enjoyment of his native tradition of poetry, songs, proverbs and folklore, and also an eagerness to incorporate the tradition and language (both pure *and* 'earthy') of the countryside into his verse. Yevtushenko, for example, wrote that

> it was through [village] songs and proverbs, always full of metaphors and aphorisms, that I first discovered the many-faceted beauty of Russian. There in the country, as though sheltered by the *taiga* [Siberian virgin forest] from the pollution of the towns, the language was pure. Language is like snow — covered with factory soot in the town, and only in the country virginally fresh. The songs and ballads I collected had the very smell of the *taiga*. Almost unconsciously I slipped into the habit of writing verses in the folklore manner.[30]

As in the above quotation, however, poets from more rural areas, who have a deep appreciation of country style and wordhoard, often begin with an overly negative view of the town, and an under-appreciation of its particular styles. Ó Searcaigh, for example, throughout his first collection, contrasts images from nature with the 'unnatural' imagery of the city, dressing the urban wolf in sheep's clothing and, thereby, one could argue, sacrificing some of the wolf's otherness:

> Cois Life
> Deimheas-ghaoth Shamhna
> Ag lomadh na gcrann
> Ag breith lomra na ngéag
> Go seolshruth na Life.

(MC p. 22)

> *By The Liffey*
> *A shearing November wind*
> *clips the trees,*
> *bears fleece from limbs*
> *to the slipstreams of the Liffey.*

The poem finally crowns the Liffey 'teachtaire áilleachta/Trí dhoiléireacht cathrach', a messenger of beauty/through city-murk. Unused to the city, the young poet appears to have given in to the temptation of painting it in the dark light of his own isolation.

Urban life and landscape come under extreme and, in my view, exaggerated criticism in Ó Searcaigh's early work. The first title poem in *Miontraigéide Cathrach* (strangely, there are two consecutive poems by the same name) dramatises a female figure in exile in the city. There are some startling images: for example, the pubs which 'feed like worms on the surrounding loneliness',[31] and the television aerials which travesty holy crosses[32]; however, the apparent fate of city-people, including the poem's Magdalene-like heroine, is to suck alcohol, for comfort, out of bottles and bars that, in turn, suck life and fertility out of them. Meanwhile, relationships are portrayed as in Part Four of Eliot's 'The Wasteland', and life as a death-march (a recurring image). Who is the early Ó Searcaigh's 'rún'/secret darling, his Magdalene exiled from the bare hills of home? The poet's soul? And what city is this? Is it as black as it is painted, or just looked at through grime-tinted glasses?

I don't want to be too pedantically critical of this very early poem or of others in the collection which have often formed the basis of much-improved later work in which disillusionment gives way to illumination, but it is disappointing that Ó Searcaigh's early response to the multifaceted and fascinating urban environment was comparatively one-dimensional compared even to Yevtushenko's metaphorical double-take in his mid-career poem 'The City of Yes and the City of No':

Everything is deadly,
                everyone frightened,
                                in the city of No.
It's like a study furnished with dejection [...]
Every portrait looks out suspiciously.
Every object is frowning, withholding something [...]
Typewriters chatter a carbon copy answer:
'No-no-no...
        No-no-no...
                No-no-no ...' [...]

But in the town of Yes - life's like the song of the thrush [...]
Lips ask for yours, without any shame,
softly murmuring: 'Ah - all that nonsense ...' -
and daisies, teasing, are asking to be picked [...]
And water, faintly murmuring, whispers through the years:
'Yes-yes-yes ...
        Yes-yes-yes ...
                Yes-yes-yes ...'
Only to tell the truth, it's a bit boring, at times,
to be given so much, almost without any effort,
in that shining multicoloured city of Yes ...

Better let me be tossed around
                to the end of my days,
between the city of Yes
                and the city of No!
Let my nerves be strained
                like wires
between the city of No
                and the city of Yes![33]

Ó Searcaigh had, like the younger Yevtushenko before him, further to travel before reaching this plane of awareness or dual perspective. However, there is also a formal irony surrounding Ó Searcaigh's early 'déistin'/disdain [*disgust*][34] at the urban landscape: the sprung rhythms and line-spacings featured above, for example, and which Ó Searcaigh borrows in poems such as 'Miontraigéide Cathrach [2]'/'Minor City-Tragedy [2]' and 'Éag'/'Death',[35] date back (from before Yevtushenko) to Mayakovski who, like the Cubists, actually based his art on his vision of contemporary *urban* life around him:

> The poetry of Futurism is the poetry of the city, of the contemporary city. The city has enriched our experiences and impressions with new city elements, unknown to the poets of the past [...] Telephones, aeroplanes, express trains, elevators, moving machines, sidewalks, factory chimneys, stony heaps of buildings, soot and smoke are the elements of beauty in the new nature of the city. We see electric lights more than we see the old romantic moon. We city dwellers do not know forests, fields, flowers — we are acquainted with the tunnels of streets with their movement, noise, rumbling, flickering, and eternally-turning wheels [...] The flowing, tranquil rhythm of the old poetry does not correspond to the psyche of the contemporary city dweller. Feverishness is what symbolizes the tempo of the contemporary world. In the city there are no flowing measured curved lines; angles, fractures, zig-zags, characterize the picture of the city. Poetry ... must correspond to the new elements in the psyche of the contemporary city.[36]

Thus the city had enriched the life of the very art through which Ó Searcaigh was now attacking the city as dead and deadly.

In Russia, they say that in taste and colour, there are no comrades. Yet, Ó Searcaigh's fault may be that he was all too faithful a disciple of Mayakovski and Yevtushenko in speaking out so vehemently. One of Yevtushenko's most famous poems begins:

Half-measures
can kill.[37]

There is indeed nothing half-measured about Ó Searcaigh's complaints against the cities which he blames for his feelings of homesickness, alienation and despair:

Bogaim liom
'Mo chiaróg ghortach
I ngráscar beatha
Le seangán séirse
Na síorghnó
Mé ag truailliú
Is ag fáil truaillithe
Mé ag rámhaíocht
In aghaidh an easa
Ag fí duain
Go tútach
Go mantach
Ar bhuairt-sheol m'anama.

('I gCathair'/'In a City', *MC* p. 27.)

*I move on,*
*a hungry beetle*
*in the dregs of life*
*with tireless ants,*
*fouling and fouled,*
*going against the grain,*
*spinning yarns of poetry,*
*crudely and coarsely,*
*from sorrow, my soul's loom.*

Significantly, however, Ó Searcaigh's early work also sometimes conveys the poet's sense of alienation even from fellow country people, though rarely from the countryside itself. In 'Deoraí'/An Exile (*MC* p. 32), he refers to himself as 'Im thuatalán deorach/I measc daoine tuatha',[38] but still relies on images drawn from nature to illustrate this condition, comparing himself to 'Órdhuilleoigín Samhna/Cois róid ag rince/Dearmadta ag sodar/An ghuairneáin daonna'.[39] Another poem, one of the best in *Miontraigéide Cathrach*, 'Do m'Athair'/For My Father, contrasts his parent's time-honoured integrity, labour and language, with the ways of

urban 'hollow men' among whom the poet significantly
includes himself:

> Chuimhníos airsean aréir
> I gciréib dheabhaidh na sráide
> Airsean nár chleacht riamh cathair
> Ná béasa gonta claona [...]
>
> Chonacthas a aoibh faoi chuing
> Cruachan gnáth na gnoc
> Is shantaíos an uaisleacht ait
> I dtréanas ríghin a chleacht.
>
> Ach táimse gan an dúthracht chiúin
> A chlóigh do scealp is seascán dúr
> Is táim mar chách ag séanadh gnáis
> Faoi bhuarach bhaoth na sráide.

(MC p. 30)

> *I thought of him last night*
> *in the rat-race of the street;*
> *how he never took to the city's*
> *short shrift and cool conceit [...]*
>
> *I saw him smile under the strain*
> *of his usual uphill graft,*
> *and envied the strange dignity [nobility]*
> *of his stern unworldly craft.*
>
> *But I lack the quiet devotion*
> *to take on rock and bog;*
> *like everyone else, I swap customs*
> *for street cred and newer gods.*

Cathal in Nepal – Pemba Thamang on right (photo: Cathal Ó Searcaigh)

Despite the strong echoes of Ó Direáin,[40] the more personal note and stronger focus of this poem make it stand out above the generalised expressions of preference for the country over the city elsewhere in this first collection.

Finally, it is with some relief that one finds Ó Searcaigh's juxtaposition of country-angels with city-devils occasionally qualified or, indeed, breaking down. In 'Teachtairí na mBláth'/Flower People (*MC* p. 60), some country inhabitants are portrayed as narrow-minded and deeply flawed when they fail to recognise 'Sóiscéal Chríost i samhlaoid Róis'/the Gospel of Christ in the symbol of each rose handed round by 'Hippies' whom the locals look upon as junkies. San Francisco is, after all, the city compared favourably to (San) Falcarragh in the later and superior version of the poem when it resurfaced in *Suibhne* (1987):

> Ní fhaca muid le samhail ná le súil, muidne
> a thaithíonn go maíteach
> an tAifreann deasghnáth, dea-mhéin
> Chríost in abhlann bhláth.
> Ní fhaca muid ansiúd os comhair an phobail
> ach, 'diamhaslóirí an diabhail,'
> is chúlaigh Críost roimh sciúirsí ár súl
> siar isteach ina shoiscéal.

> *Faithful, in public, to the Mass ritual,*
> *neither our minds nor imaginations*
> *saw Christ's blessing in the flower*
> *communion. All we could see*
> *were 'anti-Christs' and so Christ*
> *died away again under the scourge*
> *of our eyes, back into his gospel.*[41]

This poem marks the early beginning of Ó Searcaigh's adoption of a more public voice, prepared (like Yevtushenko) to speak out against repressive aspects of society, such as puritanism. Conformity to a hypocritical and sanitised schema was already attacked by Ó Ríordáin who said it could lead to 'charging the birds with lust/and filling the world with shame'.[42] Yet, neither Ó Ríordáin nor the young writer of 'Cathú'/Conflict[43] and 'An Clochar'/The Covenant, were free of the burden of mainly sexual guilt:

> Ach d'airíos ansin ag caolú as m'aigne,
> Smaointe i riochtaibh péist [...]

> *And then I felt them crawling out of my mind,*
> *thoughts in the shape of worms [...]*

(*MC* p. 44)

One most revealing early Ó Searcaigh poem is 'Máchail'/'Blemish' (*MC* p. 37) in which the poet openly dramatises his inability to be sexually aroused by a female. The tone is tragic. The poet feels exiled even from nature with which he generally identifies: he feels 'ar an uaigneas i measc duilliúr'/'alone among leaves' and 'in éad/Leis an earrach drúiseach'.[44] The poet-speaker's non-arousal is movingly portrayed as a fault or deficiency: 'Ó táimse stoite de bharr m'easnamh/De shíor i bhfeighil mo léin'.[45] A recent, revised version of the poem, published in *Lesbian and Gay Visions of Ireland*,[46] now reads much more assuredly and unapologetically as 'Geasa'/'The Bond':

> [...] Ach tráthnóna teann teasbhaigh
> a bhí ann agus bruth na hóige i mo chuislí;
> ag breathnú uirthi, ag baint lán
> mo dhá shúl, as a corp álainn, éadrocht,
> chan ise a bhí romham sínte,
> chan ise a bhí mo ghriogadh
> ach bogstócach mo shamhlaíochta
> agus é mo bheophianadh ...
> Ach b'fhada go gcasfaí orm é ina bheatha,
> b'fhada go bhfaighinn sásamh
> óna chneas álainn fionnbhán,
> óna chumthacht tharnocht
> ach amháin ...
>> i mo dháin ...

> *On a hard hot afternoon,*
> *youth bubbling in my veins,*
> *my eyes full drunk*
> *on her bright beautiful body ...*
> *Only it wasn't her stretched out before me,*
> *not her turning me on,*
> *but a slender youth I imagined,*
> *burning me alive ...*
> *It would take years to meet him in the flesh,*
> *years to satisfy my wish*
> *for his pale, wonderful skin,*
> *his clear, naked form -*
> *but sometimes ...*
>> *in poems ...*

(*OO* p. 78)

It is worth noting that in the later version, Ó Searcaigh still links the 'bond' placed on him (homosexuality) with poetry. His current celebration of this bond[47] is in sharp contrast to the martyrology of his first collection:

> ... An fhírinne a d'fholaíos
> I dtaiseadach focail,
> Is m'anam ar tinneall
> I bhfanntais dhá shaoil,
> Ag impí an chéasta
> Mar éiric a pháise.

(MC p. 64)

> ... *the truth I hid*
> *in a shroud of words,*
> *my soul ready to fall*
> *between two worlds,*
> *begging crucifixion*
> *as a payment for passion.*

There is a definite link between Ó Searcaigh's early appreciation of Yevtushenko's honesty and/or courage (*MC* p. 72) in speaking out against racism, lies and hypocrisy in Soviet society, and the Irish poet's own *increasingly* vocal and open stand against puritanical intolerance directed against the gay, or any non-conforming or ill-used community (including women).[48] In his first collection, for example, Ó Searcaigh paid Yevtushenko the homage of carefully selected translation.[49] The poems which the Donegal poet chose to translate were 'Babii Yar', 'Conversation with an American Writer' and 'The Sigh' (*MC* pp. 65–74). The first, in the absence of any official monument, marks the site where Nazis slaughtered thousands of Jews during the Second World War. In this poem, Yevtushenko directly identifies with Jewish victims of the Shoah, and ironises that the hatred borne him by every Russian anti-semite (who might see him as a Jewish sympathiser and, therefore, as a kind of Jew) is what actually makes him a true internationalist and, therefore, a 'true-Russian'. Ó Searcaigh's version begins: 'carn cuimhne níl ar Babii Yar'/there is no monument to Babii Yar — none, of course, until Yevtushenko's poem which caused so much trouble/'racán' upon its first publication in *Literatúrnaya Gazéta*[50] that the poem itself was not republished in Russia for twenty-three years.[51]

While neither I nor Ó Searcaigh himself would compare the uniquely diabolical persecution of the Jewish people to the suffering inflicted on any other group, I am suggesting that the poets Yevtushenko and Ó Searcaigh do, in fact, share a similar sense of indignation and natural revulsion towards evils such as racism, (sectarian) exclusivism and (sexual) intolerance. They also share the same habit of getting into trouble when they do speak up, and out, about such evils: Ó Searcaigh's recent poem 'Gort na gCnámh'/Field of Bones (which highlights incidents and effects of incest, rape and infanticide) brought down on him, for example, in a very different political and cultural context, the wrath of the Catholic church[52]; while other, openly gay love poems have prompted walk-outs among some American audiences.

The second Yevtushenko poem which Ó Searcaigh translated in *Miontraigéide Cathrach*, is 'Comhrá le Scríbhneoir Meiriceánach'/Conversation with an American Writer in which the latter observes that Yevtushenko has much 'courage' in speaking out against cowardice, hypocrisy and falsehood in *Soviet* society (*MC* p. 72). Yevtushenko disagrees on the grounds that future generations will look back in shame at the 'strange time' when bare honesty or plain-speaking was deemed 'courageous'. However, the final translation from Yevtushenko's poetry, 'An Osna'/The Sigh (*MC* p. 73), acknowledges recurring problems and difficulties in speaking out with what Ó Searcaigh translates as 'macantacht lom'/bare honesty. The poem tells of two friends, each burdened with an unspeakable, or unspoken, grief which wells up in each one of them into the 'sigh' of the title. Ó Searcaigh's revised version of the only subsequently reprinted translation concludes:

> A sheanchara sheachantaigh,
> A sheanchara dhoicheallaigh,
> Suímís síos mar ba ghnáth
> Is líonaimis gloine dá chéile
> Thart ar thinidh na féile
> Is ligimis Osna,
>     An t-am seo le chéile.

> *My old, distant friend,*
> *my old churlish friend,*

> *let's sit down as we used to*
> *and drink each others' health*
> *around a hospitable fire*
> *and let's sigh*
> > *This time together.*[53]

Something unspoken or unspeakable has separated or divided the two friends, each kept apart in their own stanza. The fact that the later version of the poem (above) is placed in the 'love' (and/or 'unrequited love') section of *An Bealach 'na Bhaile/Homecoming* suggests that the wordless, dividing (but potentially unifying) sigh may be caused by what Oscar Wilde referred to as 'the love that dare not speak its name'. Crucially, however, this particular poem's importance for Ó Searcaigh is in the fact that it rehearses a theme central to his work: the difficulty of putting thoughts into words,[54] the unfreedom (even in 20th/21st century Ireland) of utterance:

> A bheith i ngrá le fear:
> Sin scéal nach bhfuil na focla agam go fóill
> lena insint, lena rá
> amach os ard, sa dóigh nach mbeidh sé 'mo chrá.
>
> Ba mhaith liom
> teangaidh a thabhairt don tost seo
> a thachtann mé;
> a phlúchann mé achan lá.
>
> *To be in love with a man:*
> *that's a tale I haven't the words for yet,*
> *to tell it, to say it out*
> *in a way that won't come back on me.*
>
> *How I would like*
> *to loosen the tongue of this silence*
> *that chokes me;*
> *that smothers me every day.*[55]

Many Ó Searcaigh poems (themselves written in a minority language often pronounced prematurely 'dead') enact a struggle against the stranglehold of silence[56] so that each realised, full-born poem represents a symbolic victory over such things as the 'grief held back from the lips'[57] which 'wears at the heart':

Ba mhór an méadú misnigh domh dá bhféadfainn
an brú seo a gineadh i mbroinn m'aigne a ionchollú
        i mbriathra, a thabhairt slán.
Ach nuair a fhosclaím mo bhéal lena shaolú, lena
scaoileadh
        saor, i dtólamh
théid sé i bhfostú i mo sceadamán, stiúcann sé
        ar mo theangaidh,
agus cha saolaítear ach marbhghin gan mhothú agus théid
sé
        i dtalamh
anseo idir claí agus clasaidh [...]

*Could I conceive and flesh that burden in new-born words,*
*what courage I would have! But when I open my mouth*
*to free it, it always sticks in my throat, clamps my tongue,*
*a still-birth between hedge and ditch [...]*[58]

In an earlier poem, 'Caoineadh'/Lament (*ABB* p. 208), Ó
Searcaigh wished that his language, Irish, would let out 'liú
amháin gaile — liú catha/one war-cry, one battle-cry'. Instead,
Ó Searcaigh's entire oeuvre is not so much a war-cry[59] as a love
call ('liú searcach'[60]) from a poet (like Yevtushenko) standing
firmly not only on the side of light, and of life[61] but also on the
side of love:

Agus fiú mura dtig liom trácht ar an té atá le mo mhian [...]
mura dtig liom a chuid áilleachtaí a chanadh os ard
faoi mar is dual don té atá i ngrá [...]
beidh siad anois agus i dtólamh
ag tabhairt blais agus bolaidh do mo bhriathra
is cuma cén smaoineamh a nochtaim, is cuma cén dán a
chumaim.

*And even if it's forbidden to refer to the one I'm after [...]*
*even if I'm not allowed to sing his praises in the open air*
*like anyone else who loves [...] they*
*will always scent and flavour my words, whatever thought*
*I lay bare, whatever poem I concoct.*

(*OO* p. 92)

The above poem written 'after C. P. Cavafy' reminds Ó
Searcaigh's readers of the wide range of sources and
influences, from Donegal to Nepal and the Urals, that have

assisted Ó Searcaigh in speaking out openly, 'go macnasach, mórchroíoch .../as croí an tsléibhe ...'.[62]

Gradually, Ó Searcaigh has put Staisiún Chaiseal na gCorr on the same literary map as Stantzia Zimá. The Irishman has established a direct line with world-class poets such as Yevtushenko and Cavafy by adding his own 'laments against destruction'[63]; by his adoption of diverse forms, and production of original, startling work such as the phantasmagoric, nightmare-like narrative of 'Dreimire/Ladder' (*OO* p. 232); and lately, by writing a poem that *had* to be written, one that was needed like 'an ambulance rushing to someone's aid'.[64] The poem is 'Gort na gCnámh'/Field of Bones (*OO* pp. 65–76) in which, consciously or not, Ó Searcaigh has actually risen to the challenge laid down by Eiléan Ní Chuilleanáin in her essay 'The borderlands of Irish poetry':

> the events which shocked the consciences of Southern [Irish] people in the middle 1980's had nothing to do with a war between Catholics and Protestants. They were the discovery of an infant's body in Kerry and the subsequently published story of a local girl who falsely confessed that it was hers and that she had murdered it. Later a public inquiry found that, while the original baby could not have been hers, she had indeed had a child which died at birth. A few months later a schoolgirl was found dead outside a church in Co. Longford, having given birth there to a dead child [...] While nobody has yet written a great poem about Joanne Hayes or Ann Lovet, who with their children were the victims of these episodes just mentioned, the public wants somebody to do it. The public would probably like the job done with simplicity and directness.[65]

Ó Searcaigh's poem 'Gort na gCnámh' does the job, I believe, although it does not deal specifically with the cases mentioned, choosing instead to relate to them not by name but as part of a wider and continuing legacy of guilt and hypocrisy about sexual issues. 'Russian poets have always been the spiritual government of their country', Yevtushenko declares in his autobiography[66]; perhaps, with power and respect slipping from the hands of priests and politicians in Ireland, it is for poets, such as Heaney and Ó Searcaigh, to maintain (as they have done) responsible citizenship, and to turn, occasionally, from the 'private Japanese garden of poetry'[67] to attack the weeds and dangerous growth, for example, of injustice and of reluctance to face home truths, hidden realities and contradictions which dominant and dominating ideologies (or sexualities?) deny or deem inadmissible. Yevtushenko once wrote: 'we had flutes in plenty, what we needed now was the bugle',[68] the bugle to drive people not from failed faith to no faith, but to new faith in the necessary 'struggle for the future'.[69] One thing I have noticed about Ó Searcaigh's work and its reception is that it gives people hope.[70] It does so not by being childishly naïve or fanatically positive but by facing the dark, the 'duibheagán' or abyss, head on in the same way that it faces the sun.[71]

'Mórfhile le teacht?'[72]/'A great poet on the way?', Gréagóir Ó Dúill once entitled an article on Ó Searcaigh. He has not only reached but passed that stage by 'keeping going' like Heaney and by leaving us work, like Yevtushenko, that itself is 'still going'.[73] At home or on the road, the contradictions he encounters are not so much 'cancelled on the spot'[74] as held simultaneously in an all-inclusive vision that can unearth a daisy in a cracked London pavement (*OO* p. 166), the best clay-pipes in the most deadly of enemy country (*ABB* p. 198), and a friend whose life was 'chomh díreach lena mharbh/as straight as his death' (*OO* p. 34).

Blake believed that without contraries there is no progression;[75] Ó Searcaigh has progressed far on the zig-zag tracks, the '*qui vive*, weaving and dodging'[76] between the unwalled 'city of Yes and the city of No', the 'city of No and the city of Yes'. Like Yevtushenko at 'Zimá Station', he may not have *the* answer but he keeps us alive and alert in the middle of the question. And what is the question?

> Is bás, dar liom fós, freagairt,
> Is beatha fiafraí.
>
> *And death, for me, is answer;*
> *life — asking.* [77]

# Notes

1 Máirtín Ó Direáin, 'Solas'/'Light', *Craobhóg Dán* (Dublin, An Clóchomhar, 1986), p. 23.

2 W. H. Auden, *Secondary Worlds* (London, Faber and Faber, 1968), p. 123.

3 'But yet there is beauty narcotic and deciduous/In this vast organism [the city] grown out of us'. Louis MacNeice, 'An Eclogue for Christmas', in *Collected Poems*, 2nd edn (London, Faber and Faber, 1979, repr. 1986), pp. 33–36 (p. 35).

4 (*MC* p. 9). Ó Searcaigh uses Ó Ríordáin's term 'geit'.

5 Máirtín Ó Díreáin, *Cloch Choirnéil* (Dublin, An Clóchomhar, 1966), p. 32.

6 'An Fuascailteoir'/'The Liberator' (*ABB* p. 187).

7 (*MC* pp. 12–13).

8 See note 3, above.

9 Yevgeny Yevtushenko, *Selected Poems*, ed. by R. Milner-Gulland and P. Levi, S. J. (Middlesex: Penguin Books, 1962, repr. 1964), p. 9.

10 Yevtushenko, *A Precocious Autobiography*, translated by A. R. Mac Andrew (Harmondsworth: Penguin Books, 1965), p. 7.

11 'Re-creating' in Ó Ríordáin's sense that a poem is a being, not a telling (*ES* p. 11); and 're-experiencing' satisfying Adrienne Rich's wish that poems should *be* experiences, not *about* them. See Eavan Boland, 'Outside History', in *Object Lessons: The Life of the Woman and the Poet in Our Time* (London: Vintage, 1996) pp. 123–153 (p. 131).

12 'Poetry is a jealous woman who will not forgive untruth. Nor will she forgive anything less than the truth'. Yevtushenko, *A Precocious Autobiography*, p. 7.

13 W. H. Auden, *W. H. Auden: Collected Poems*, ed. Edward Mendelson (London: Faber and Faber, 1976), pp. 619–621.

14 See, for example, Ó Searcaigh's translation of a Yevtushenko poem, 'Comhrá Le Scríbhneoir Meiriceánach'/Conversation with an American Poet (*MC* p. 72).

15 Yevtushenko, *Selected Poems*, p. 16.

16 Derrida, J., 'Structure, Sign and Play in the Discourse of the Human Sciences', in R. Rylance (ed.), *Debating Texts: A Reader in Twentieth Century Literary Theory and Method* (Milton Keynes: Open University Press, 1987, 1990), p. 124.

17 Yevtushenko, *Selected Poems*, p. 16. The 'accurately observed sensibilia' which Ó Searcaigh records with a similar tension includes 'An Lilí Bhándearg'/The Pink Lily (*OO* p. 236); his own 'searching humanist enquiry' into *Irish* society is evidenced by controversial poems such as 'Gort na gCnámh'/Field of Bones (*OO* p. 66) which confronts the realities of incest, rape and infanticide; finally, his moral stature, public voice and personal mannerisms are to the fore in poems such as 'Briathra agus Bráithre'/Brotherly Words (*OO* p. 36) and 'Ceann Dubh Dílis'/Dear Dark-Haired Love (*OO* p. 112) which challenge inequalities and intolerance.

18 I am paraphrasing what Marshall Berman says 'distinguishes modernism from sentimentalism' in M. Berman, *All That Is Solid Melts*

*Into Air: The Experience of Modernity* 2nd edn (London: Verso, 1983, repr. 1995), p. 333. Regarding Ó Searcaigh in this context, see 'Bó Bhradach'/A Braddy Cow (*ABB* p.126) and 'Déagóir ag *Drift*eáil'/Drifting (*OO* p. 152).

19    'Do Jack Kerouac'/Let's Hit the Road, Jack (*OO* p. 180), 'Ma Bohème' (*ABB* p. 62) and 'Déagóir ag *Drift*áil'/Drifting (*OO* p. 152).

20    Yevtushenko, *Selected Poems*, p. 13.

21    My translation; for an alternative version, see Yevtushenko, *Selected Poems*, p. 51.

22    'I rely often on this ordinary thought:/near Lake Baikal my own town waiting for me'. From 'Zimá Station', Yevtushenko, *Selected Poems*, pp. 19–51 (p. 19).

23    Yevtushenko, *A Precocious Autobiography*, p. 124.

24    Yevtushenko, *Selected Poems*, pp. 85–86. For an example from Ó Searcaigh's work, see 'Do Narayan Shrestha' (*OO* pp. 188–193).

25    *The Penguin Book of Contemporary British Poetry*, ed. Blake Morrison and Andrew Motion (London: Penguin, 1982), p. 12.

26    Yevtushenko, *A Precocious Autobiography*, p. 10.

27    Ibid., p. 74. Semyón Isaákovich Kirsánov was a poet born in Odessa in 1906. He was Jewish, a member of the Left Front in literature — a Futurist movement; and was close to Mayakovski.

28    As noted in Ó Searcaigh's poem 'An Díbeartach'/Outcast (*OO* p. 48) where the poet-speaker feels misunderstood by his community but still offers the gift of song.

29    These lines refer to a farming neighbour of Ó Searcaigh's. See 'Cré na Cuimhne'/Cast in Clay (*OO* p. 26).

30    Yevtushenko, *A Precocious Autobiography*, pp. 21–22.

31    '... tábhairní cíocracha a bheathaíonn/Mar chnuimh ar an aonarachas timpeall'. See 'Miontraigéide Cathrach', *MC* pp. 16–18 (p. 16).

32    This image is borrowed from Yevtushenko.

33    Translated by Tina Tupkina-Glaesner, Geoffrey Dutton, and Igor Mezhakoff-Koriakin in *Twentieth Century Russian Poetry: selected with an introduction by Yevgeny Yevtushenko*, ed. by Albert C. Todd and Max Hayward with Daniel Weissbort (London: Fourth Estate, 1993), pp. 809–810.

34    'Gladstone Park' (*SS* p. 11).

35    *MC* pp. 19–21 and pp. 41–42, respectively.

36    Vladimir Mayakovsky quoted by Lawrence Leo Stahlberger in *The Symbolic System of Majakovskij* (The Hague: Mouton and Co., 1964), p. 45.

37    Todd and Hayward (eds), *Twentieth Century Russian Poetry*, pp. 818–819.

38    'An exiled misfit/among country people'.

39    'A golden leaf/dancing by the road/forgotten in a whirl of people'.

40    See, for example, 'Stoite' and 'Ár Ré Dhearóil' in Máirtín Ó Direáin, *Dánta 1939–1979* (Dublin: An Clóchomhar, 1980), p. 30 and p. 80, respectively.

41    *'If You're Going to San Falcarragh, be sure to wear your rosary beads in your hair '* (*S* p. 79).

42  'Do chuirfeadh coir na drúise in intinn na n-éan/Is do líonfadh le
    náire an domhan'. Seán Ó Ríordáin, 'Cnoc Melleri'/Mount Mellery,
    *Eireaball Spideoige*, 2nd edn (Dublin: Sáirséal Ó Marcaigh, 1952, 1986),
    pp. 64–67 (p. 66).

43  *MC* p. 40. The title could also mean 'Temptation' or 'Regret'.

44  'Alone among leaves' and 'envious of lustful Spring'.

45  'I am cast aside [literally 'stoite'/'uprooted', making his own of Ó
    Direáin's term] for this lack/into eternal grief'.

46  Íde O'Carroll and Eoin Collins (eds.), *Lesbian and Gay Visions of
    Ireland: Towards the Twenty-first Century* (London: Cassell, 1995).

47  See, for example, 'Gorm'/Blue (*OO* p. 102), 'Oíche'/Night (*OO* p. 90),
    'Rúnsearc'/Secret Love (*OO* p. 92).

48  See, for example, 'Teachtairí na mBláth'/Flower-People [Messengers],
    *MC* pp. 60–61; and also the later version 'If you're going to San
    Falcarragh …' (*S* pp. 79–80). See also 'An Peann Luaidhe'/The Pencil
    (*SS* p. 42), 'Scrúdú Coinsiasa roimh Dhul chun Suain'/Examination of
    Conscience before Going to Bed (*ABB* p. 132), and 'Briathra agus
    Bráithre'/Brotherly Words (*OO* p. 36).

49  See the three poems 'Babii Yar', 'Comhrá le Scríbhneoir
    Meiriceanach'/Conversation with an American Writer, and 'An
    Osna'/The Sigh (*MC* pp. 65–74).

50  19 September 1961.

51  Yevtushenko's collected poems, in Russian: E. Evtushenko, *Sobranie
    sochinenii v treh tomah* (Moskva: Hudozhestvennaya Literatura, 1984).
    'Babii Yar' appears in Volume 1. In 1962, Shostakovich used the
    words of the poem in his 13th Symphony, Part 1 of which is actually
    entitled 'Babii Yar'.

52  Nuala Ní Dhomhnaill, 'Tidal Surge: 1990–1999', in *Watching the River
    Flow: A Century in Irish Poetry*, ed. by Noel Duffy and Theo Dorgan
    (Dublin: Poetry Ireland, 1999), pp. 219–225 (p. 223).

53  Cumha na gCarad'/Lament for Friendship [The Longing/Loneliness
    of the Friends], *ABB* p. 172. This seems to be the translation from
    Yevtushenko which is closest to Ó Searcaigh's own concerns as a
    writer.

54  Idir an smaoineamh agus an briathar/tá dúichí oighir agus ceo' (ABB
    p. 184). In English, 'between the thought and the word/[there] are
    regions of ice and fog'.

55  Ó Searcaigh, 'Buachaill Bán' (*OO* p. 82).

56  'Umhlaigh'/Submit (*OO* p. 56), 'Rúnsearc'/Rúnsearc (*OO* p. 92),
    'Gort na gCnámh'/Field of Bones (*OO* p. 66), 'Buachaill Bán' (*OO* p.
    82), 'D'Ainm'/Your Name (*OO* p. 100), 'Ceann Dubh Dílis'/Dear
    Dark-Haired Love (*OO* p. 112).

57  Adrienne Rich, quoted by Ó Searcaigh (*OO* p. 65).

58  'Gort na gCnámh'/Field of Bones (*OO* p. 72).

59  See 'Duine Corr'/Odd Man Out (*OO* p. 60).

60  Even Ó Searcaigh's name seems to derive from the word 'searc'
    which is pronounced like 'shark' but actually means 'love' or
    'beloved one'.

61  'Do Isaac Rosenberg'/For Isaac Rosenberg (*OO* p. 240).

62   'Wildly, wholeheartedly .../from the heart of the mountain ...'. From 'Cuisle an Chaoráin'/Mountain Pulse (*OO* p. 40).

63   Yevtushenko, *Selected Poems*, pp. 85–86. For an example from Ó Searcaigh's work, see 'Do Narayan Shrestha'/For Narayan Shrestha, (*OO* pp. 188–193).

64   Yevtushenko, *A Precocious Autobiography*, p. 74.

65   Eiléan Ní Chuilleanáin, 'The borderlands of Irish poetry', in *Contemporary Irish Poetry: A Collection of Critical Essays*, ed. by Elmer Andrews (Houndmills: MacMillan Press, 1992), pp. 25–40 (pp. 34–35).

66   Yevtushenko, *A Precocious Autobiography*, p. 99.

67   Ibid., p. 100.

68   Ibid., p. 104.

69   Ibid., p. 137.

70   Ó Searcaigh even explained his editorial policy for the anthology *Watching the River Flow* as follows: 'the ten poems I have selected represent man's spirit coming to terms with the anguish of being. They all aspire, either openly or covertly, to the redemptive and affirmative condition of boundlessness'. See Ó Searcaigh, 'In a State of Flux: 1980–1989', in *Watching the River Flow: A Century in Irish Poetry*, ed. Duffy and Dorgan, pp. 185–186.

71   See, for example, 'Sú Talun'/The Red Heart (*OO* p. 168), 'An Duibheagán'/The Abyss (*OO* p. 228), 'Na Píopaí Créafóige'/The Clay-Pipes (*ABB* p. 198) and 'Fiacha an tSolais'/The E.S.B. or Light Bill (*ABB* p. 120).

72   See Gréagóir Ó Dúill, 'Nótaí'/'Notes', in 'Filíocht Chathail Uí Shearcaigh', *An tUltach* (Eanáir 1993), p. 19.

73   Seamus Heaney, 'Keeping Going', *The Spirit Level* (London, Faber and Faber, 1996), p. 10; Yevtushenko, *Selected Poems*, p. 51.

74   As suggested in 'Anseo ag Staisiún Chaiseal na gCorr'/'Here at Caiseal na gCorr Station' (*ABB* p. 96).

75   William Blake, 'The Marriage of Heaven and Hell', in *Blake: Complete Writings*, ed. Geoffrey Keynes (London, Oxford University Press, 1966), pp. 148–160 (p. 149).

76   Heaney, 'Squarings' Part 4, *xliii*, *Seeing Things* (London, Faber and Faber, 1991), p. 103.

77   Ó Ríordáin, 'Guí', *Brosna* (Dublin, Sáirséal and Dill, 1964, 1987), p. 16.

## (as) Laoi Cumainn

Is tusa mo laoch, mo thréan is mo neart,
mo Chú na gCleas agus níl fhios agam i gceart
cé acu an luan laoich é seo
    atá ag teacht ó do chneas
nó gríos gréine. [...]

Anocht má tá cath le fearadh agat, a ghrá,
bíodh sé anseo i measc na bpiliúr:
Craith do sciath agus gread do shleá,
    beartaigh do chlaíomh
go beacht. Lig gáir churaidh as do bhráid.
Luífidh mé anseo ag baint sásamh súl
    as a bhfuil den fhear
ag bogadaí ionat, a dhúil, go ndéanfaidh tú do bhealach
    féin
a bhearnú chugam fríd pluid agus piliúr.

(ABB 166–68)

## (from) HOUND OF ULSTER

My solace, my defence, my fortress,
Playful Hound, how can I tell
is it the valour-halo
    which emanates from your skin
or sun-glow? [...]

Tonight, sweet soul, should you declare battle
let it be here among pillows:
let your shield shudder, aim your spear
    let your sword be ready
and true. Shout loud your war-cry.
Here I'll lie, my eyes entranced
    as your manliness
moves and - darling - I lie in the breach,
in the theatre of linen.

(trans. Gabriel Rosenstock)

James E. Doan

CATHAL Ó SEARCAIGH:
GAY, GAELACH AGUS GALÁNTA/GAY, GAELIC AND GORGEOUS[1]

Cathal Ó Searcaigh, who has been identified as a leading gay, Irish-language poet, expresses male homoerotic love, as well as masculine beauty, within the continuum of traditional Irish verse. His poetry also expresses a strong sense of the transgressive nature of the love he experiences within the context of Irish Catholic, especially rural Donegal, society: a society which is moreover under increasing pressure from the English-speaking world and Euro-American tourism. Since there are few precedents for this type of poetry in the Irish language, (though some have argued for the existence of a homoerotic bond between Irish tribal rulers and their chief poets before the sixteenth century),[2] Cathal has adapted heterosexual Gaelic love poetry to a new use. This is not entirely new, since cross-gendered lyric voices are possible within the song tradition, i.e. male singers performing traditionally female songs and vice versa. As Lillis Ó Laoire, one of Cathal's translators and himself a *sean nós* or traditional singer, has pointed out to me,[3] this allows a gay Gaelic performer to encode his love for a member of his or her own sex within a seemingly heterosexual context.

Cathal views himself as working within the mainstream Irish poetic tradition, stretching over more than a millennium, as seen in his collection, *Homecoming/An Bealach 'na Bhaile*,[4] with English translations by twelve Irish poets. The first poem, entitled 'An Tobar'/'The Well', is dedicated to the pre-eminent Irish woman poet, Máire Mhac an tSaoi (b. 1922), one of the first to adapt traditional themes to a modern consciousness. Here Cathal also invokes the image of *sean-Bhríd* ('old Bridget'), who represents the ancient Irish goddess of poets and patron of men of learning, and also an early Irish saint (herself therefore bridging the pagan Irish and Christian traditions). In the first stanza, in a gesture linked with the bestowal of the gift of poetic inspiration, itself a traditional theme in Irish verse, Bríd offers the poet a

> ...babhla fíoruisce...
> as an tobar is glaine i nGleann an Átha.
> Tobar a coinníodh go slachtmhar
> ó ghlúin go glúin, oidhreacht
> luachmhar an teaghlaigh...

> *...bowl of spring water...*
> *from the purest well of Gleann an Átha,*
> *a well that was tended tastily*
> *from generation to generation, the precious*
> *heritage of the household...*

(ABB pp. 42–43)

Cathal with Irish language poet Maire Mhac an tSaoi at Wake Forest, North Carolina, USA, 1984 (photo: Rachel Giese Brown)

However, she decries the fact that now 'among my people/the springwell is being forgotten'; in other words, that English has crept more and more into their speech and poetic traditions. In the final stanza Bríd tells the poet to 'seek out your own well, my dear,/for the age of want is near: There will have to be a going back to sources' (45). I believe Cathal here links Máire Mhac an tSaoi, as a sort of poetic foremother, with the ancient goddess, Bríd, suggesting as well a strong feminine matrix in his own approach to writing in Irish. The placement of the poem, first in the collection, is certainly not coincidental, and seems to represent his symbolic birth as a poet.

In the third work in the collection, a prose-poem entitled 'Lá de na Laethanta'/'On Such a day', the narrator encounters the goddess of poetry once again. In a concatenation of images which mark him as both postmodern and traditional (the two do not appear to be mutually exclusive), Cathal adapts the theme of the Muse appearing on a hilltop to give the future poet the divine gift of poetry:

> Casadh sruthán orm a bhí ag fáil bháis leis an tart. Thosaigh mé ag caoineadh is tháinig sé chuige féin go tapaidh. Thóg mé cnoc beag a bhí ag siúl ar thaobh an bhealaigh. Dúirt sé go raibh sé ag déanamh cúrsa i dtarrtháil sléibhe. Is cuimhneach liom gur fhág sé a chaipín ceo ina dhiaidh sa charr.
>
> Ach dúirt an ghaoth liom a casadh orm i mbarr an Ghleanna go raibh sí ag gabháil an treo sin níos déanaí is go dtabharfadh sí an caipín ceo arís chuige. An ghaoth bhocht. Tháinig mé uirthi go tobann. Bhí sí nocht. Ach chomh luath agus a chonaic sí mé tharraing sí an t-aer thart uirthi féin go cúthalach agus labhair sí liom go séimh [...]
>
> Agus tháinig an oíche 'na bhaile i mo chuideachta, a corp slim sleamhain ag sioscadh i mo thimpeall; spéarthaí dubha a gúna ag caitheamh drithlí chugam. Mheall sí mé lena glórthaí.
>
> *I chanced upon a stream that was dying of thirst. I began to cry and it recovered quickly. I picked up a small hill that*

*was walking by the wayside. It said it was doing a course in mountain-rescue. I remember it left its cap behind in the car.*

*But the wind I met at the top of the Glen said she was going that way later and would return the cap to him. The poor wind! I came upon her suddenly. She was sunning herself at the top of the Glen. She was naked. But the instant she saw me, she drew the air shyly around her and spoke gently [...]*

*And night came home with me, her sleek and slender body rustling about me; the black skies of her dress twinkling all around me. She enthralled me with the sound of her voice...*

(*ABB* pp. 49–51)

Much of Cathal's poetry has a strong sense of place, another traditional feature which goes back to the ancient *dinnsheanchas* (placename lore). His love of his own district — the hills, lakes and bogs of Gort a' Choirce (Gortahork) in Northwest Donegal — is paramount in poems such as 'Cor Úr'/'A Fresh Dimension'. In this poem he literally undresses the landscape:

Féachann tú orm anois go glé
le lochanna móra maorga do shúl
Loch an Ghainimh ar deis, Loch Altán ar clé,
gach ceann acu soiléir, lán den spéir
agus snua an tsamraidh ar a ngruanna.

Agus scaoileann tú uait le haer an tsléibhe
crios atá déanta as ceo bruithne na Bealtaine
scaoileann tú uait é, a rún mo chléibhe,
ionas go bhfeicim anois ina n-iomláine
críocha ionúine do cholainne ...

*You see me truly*
*in the majestic lakes of your eyes --*
*Loch an Ghainimh on the right, Loch Altán on the left,*
*both plainly visible, full of sky,*
*the complexion of summer on their cheeks.*

*And you loosen to the mountain air*
*your girdle of the hazy heat of May;*
*you loosen it, my love,*

*that I may wholly see*
*the beloved boundaries of your body ...*

(*ABB* pp. 86–87)

Then, in a traditional yet modern form of paronomasia connecting the human body and the land, he lists places such as 'Log Dhroim na Gréine... Alt na hUillinne... Malaidh Rua' and 'Mín na hUchta ...'. As Ó Laoire points out in his introduction to the collection:

> *Log Dhroim na Gréine* becomes the hollow of the sunny ridge. *Droim* is also the ordinary Irish word for back. Similarly *alt* can mean a hillock or stream as well as a joint while *uilinn* is an elbow. *Malaidh* can be a brae or a brow, *ucht* is a slope or the human chest. The idea of the earth goddess as the lover of the king is an archaic and a tenacious one in Gaelic poetry so much as to render it forbidden territory to modern poets in search of an original voice. Ó Searcaigh again transforms this idea into an extremely personal response to the returning emigrant while still retaining the age-old resonances (*ABB*, p. 35).

Cathal himself, in a reading (21 July 1998) at the annual meeting of the International Association for the Study of Irish Literatures (IASIL), held at the University of Limerick, which he once attended, spoke about the possible meanings of various placenames in his native locale. He whimsically interpreted the names of two townlands in the Mt. Errigal region (Baile an Geata and Caiseal na gCorr) as 'Gaytown' and 'Fort of the Queers', stating that 'if I hadn't been born, the land would have produced me', thereby 'queering' the landscape. In an homage to Robert Frost, he added that he had come to a fork in the roads and chosen the one less travelled — sodomy — thereby foregrounding the homoerotic element in his work. The first clearly homoerotic poem in the collection, actually the first one in Part III, which contains most of the gay verse, is based on a traditional heterosexual love song, 'Ceann Dubh Dílis'/'My Blackhaired Love', with which it shares its title. Cathal closely adapts the metrical form and images of the original song, which tells of the male poet's desire for a particular woman, despite the fact that other girls are pursuing him:

Tá cailíní ar an mbaile seo ar buile 's ar buaireamh,

ag tarraingt a ngruaige 's á ligean le gaoith,
ar mo shonsa, an scafaire is fearr ins na tuatha,
ach do thréigfinn an méid sin ar rún dil mo chroí.

*There are girls in the town enraged and vexed,*
*they tear and loosen their hair on the wind*
*for the dashingest man in this place -- myself!*
*But I'd leave them all for my secret heart.*[5]

In Cathal's poem, the subject of the poem, rather than the speaker, becomes the object of desire, thus transferring a heterosexual female-directed lyric to a homoerotic male-directed one, though, as mentioned earlier, this is entirely possible within the folksong tradition itself through coding. In the stanza of the poem analogous to the one cited above, the speaker says to the beloved:

Tá cailíní na háite seo cráite agat, a ghrá,
's iad ag iarraidh thú a bhréagadh is a mhealladh gach lá;

ach b'fhearr leatsa bheith liomsa i mbéal an uaignis
'mo phógadh, 'mo chuachadh is mo thabhairt chun aoibhnis.

*You plague the local belles, my sweet,*
*They attempt to coax you with deceit*
*But you'd prefer my lonely kiss,*
*You hugging me to bring to bliss.*

Both lyrics focus on the mouth (*béal*) and the kiss (*póg*). In the first and third stanzas of the folksong the speaker refers to the beloved's 'honey mouth' (*bhéilín meala a bhfuil boladh na tíme air*) 'that smells of thyme'. In Cathal's reworking of this, however, the speaker tells the beloved

d'fhoscail ár bpóga créachtaí Chríosta arís;
ach ná foscail do bhéal, ná sceith uait an scéal:

tá ár ngrá ar an taobh thuathal den tsoiscéal.

*Our kiss re-opens Christ's wounds here;*
*But close your mouth, no detail break --*
*We offend the Gospels with our love.*

(*ABB* pp. 140–41)

The sense of transgression remains salient throughout Cathal's poem, in which he questions conservative Irish Catholicism and rural Irish mores regarding homosexuality. The injunction to 'close your mouth', of course, echoes Oscar Wilde's defence of the 'love which dares not speak its name,' probably the most passionate defence of homosexual love in the Irish or Anglo-Irish tradition. In the course of the poem the speaker breaks through his reservations, though, proclaiming at the end of the third stanza his rejection of his boyhood religion:

> ní fhosclód mo bhéal, ní sceithfead an scéal
> ar do shonsa shéanfainn gach soiscéal.
>
> *I'd close my mouth, no detail break --*
> *I'd deny the Gospels for your sake.*

(ABB pp. 140–41)

Cathal with Scottish Gaelic poet, Sorley McLean (photo: Rachel Giese Brown)

The next poem in this section, dealing with abandonment by his beloved ('Tá mé ag Síorshiúl Sléibhe'/'Wandering the Mountainside'), echoes one of the most widespread Gaelic songs, found throughout Ireland and Gaelic Scotland, 'Dónall Óg'/'Young Dónall'. In the original song (which John Huston used in his film adaptation of James Joyce's 'The Dead', though it is not found in the original short story in *Dubliners*), the speaker (a woman) pleads with her lover to take her with him. In the final stanza, probably one of the most powerful in Gaelic poetry, she proclaims:

> Do bhainis soir díom is do bhainis siar díom,
> do bhainis romham is do bhainis im dhiaidh díom,
>
> do bhainis gealach is do bhainis grian díom,
> is is ró-mhór m'eagla gur bhainis Dia díom.[6]
>
> *You took the East from me and you took the West from me,*
>
> *you took before and you took behind from me,*
> *you took the moon and you took the sun from me,*
> *and I greatly fear that you've taken God from me.*

(My translation)

Cathal's poem suggests an even greater derangement of the speaker, reminiscent of the mad women of traditional Irish saga and poetry.[7] In the first stanza the male speaker proclaims:

> Tá mé ag síorshiúl sléibhe ar feadh na hoíche
>
> Ó Mhalaidh na Gaoithe suas go barr Mhín na Craoibhe,
> is ó thréig tú aréir mé - cé shamhlódh é choíche -
>
> tá mo shaolsa níos loime na blár seo an tsléibhe.
>
> *From Malaidh na Gaoithe to the top of Mín na Craoibhe*
> *Since last night you left me - oh most unhappy chance -*
> *My life is barer than this mountainous expanse.*
> *I am wandering the mountainside all night long and grieving .*

The final stanza more closely echoes 'Dónall Óg' in its intensity and in its rejection of Catholic dogma:

Bhéarfainnse a bhfuil agam agus flaitheas Dé lena chois
ach mé a bheith sínte anois idir tusa agus saol na ngeas.
Ó, a cheann dea-chumtha agus a chorp na háilleachta,
b'fhearr amharc amháin ort anocht ná solas síoraí na
bhFlaitheas.

*I'd offer my possessions and all of Heaven too*
*To be stretched between my loved one and the world of taboo.*
*O lovely head and body, I'd prefer one single night*
*Of you this night than Heaven, than everlasting light.*

(ABB pp. 142–43)

The word Cathal uses for 'taboo' (in Irish, *geasa*) again takes us
back to the world of the early Irish sagas, such as *Togail
Bruidne Dá Derga* ('The Destruction of Da Derga's Hostel') or
*Táin Bó Cuailnge* ('The Cattle-Raid of Cooley'), in which the
hero must overcome a series of taboos in order to reach a
particular goal or destiny. The poet here is quite conscious of
his transgressive behaviour (*ach mé a bheith sínte anois idir tusa
agus saol na ngeas*: 'To be stretched between my loved one and
the world of taboo') and the realization that he is making a
choice between his lover and 'Heaven ... everlasting light', at
least within the traditionally constructed Catholicism of his
youth.

In the following poem in the collection, 'Tá mo Chéadsearc i
Londain'/'To my Heart's Desire in London', Cathal uses two
themes found in traditional Irish verse and saga: *grá éagmaise*
('love from afar', or a longing desire for one separated by
distance) and secret or forbidden love. He recontextualizes
these to fit the facts of emigration to London and the need to
keep homosexual desire secret from neighbours, family and
perhaps the beloved himself. The speaker finds himself alone,
since his beloved has been in London for the past twenty-one
months. Linking himself with the empty land, in a form of the
wasteland theme, he states:

Inniu is mé ag siúl mar a dtéimis i gcónaí Dé Domhnaigh
Suas Malaidh na Míne is amach droim Loch an Ghainimh,

Bhí cuma bheag chaillte ar sheanbhailte bánaithe na gcnoc
Is a hoiread leo siúd, ó d'imigh tú uaim, níl gnaoi ar mo
shaol.

*Today, like all Sundays, I'm out taking the air,*
*Up by Malaidh na Míne, way beyond the Sandy Lake,*

*The villages are all empty, windswept and bare*
*As though they had died in their sleep for your sake.*

The revelation of secret desire has caused the beloved to emigrate, and the speaker fears that he will never see him again. The poem ends on a note reminiscent of the Old Irish dream vision poems such as *Aislinge Óenguso* ('The Dream of Óengus'), in which a man dreams of a beautiful woman from the Otherworld,[8] who then leaves him, after which he searches throughout the world for her:

Mar an ghealach sin a shleamhnaigh isteach fuinneog an dín
Is a ghoid codladh na hoíche uaim ó mo leabaidh shuain,
Aniar aduaidh a tháinig an grá orm, aniar aduaidh is isteach i mo chroí,
Is é a sciob uaim mo stuaim is a d'fhág folamh mé choíche.

*Like the moon that is furtively paling my room*
*Stealing my dreams and keeping me awake,*
*Love comes from afar, from a distant gloom*
*And shimmered awhile like one cloud on a lake.*

(*ABB* pp. 144–45)

The prohibition on revealing the beloved's name is found in the next poem, 'D'ainm'/'Your Name', in which the speaker indicates that he tried to obey the beloved's injunction:

Gan d'ainm a lua níos mó ...
Ach níl leoithne dá dtig
Nach gcluintear an crann seo ag sioscadh ...
Joe ... Joe.

*Never again to utter your name ...*
*But the slightest breeze that cares to blow*
*Ruffles that tree, whispers ... Joe... Joe...*

(*ABB* pp. 146–47)

Thus, memory and the act of poesis cause the poet to violate the injunction.

In the following work, 'Soinéad'/'Sonnet', adapted from the English poetic genre, the poet again relies on memory to recreate the absent beloved in a Wordsworthian passage:

> In albam na cuimhne atá siad taiscithe
> an ceann catach, na súile macánta
> agus tráthnónta galánta na Bealtaine [...]
> sin a bhfuil iontu, a bhuachaill na Bealtaine,
> samhailteacha nach dtéann i ndíchuimhne.
>
> *In memory's album they are stored,*
> *the curly head, the gentle eyes*
> *and those beautiful evenings in May [...]*
> *That's all they are, my Bealtaine boy,*
> *images that don't go away.*

The second stanza repeats the scene with the addition that these memories will provide the source for his future poems:

> agus dhéanfaidh mé iad a aeráil i mo dhánta,
> do cheann catach, do shúile macánta
> agus tráthnónta galánta na Bealtaine.
>
> *and I will air them in my poems,*
> *your curly head, your gentle eyes*
> *and those beautiful evenings in May.*
>
> (*ABB*, pp. 148–49)

One of the most erotic poems in the collection, 'Searmanas'/'Ceremony', uses religious imagery to suggest the intensity of the speaker's passion and the transgressive, even idolatrous, nature of the love. Anatomizing the beloved as he works his way down the body, he says:

> Ar altóir na leapa
> ceiliúraim do chorpsa anocht, a ghile,
> is deasghnátha mo dhúile.
> Gach géag ghrástúil, gach géag mhaighdeanúil
> sléactaim rompu go humhal ...
>
> *On the altar of the bed*
> *I celebrate your body tonight, my love,*
> *with the rites of my desire.*
> *I humbly kneel before*
> *each graceful limb, each virgin limb ...*

Building up to the climax he concludes:

> Is de réir mar a théann
> an searmanas i ndéine is i ndlúthpháirtíocht
> tá mo bhaill bheatha ar crith
> ag fanacht le míorúilt mhacnais
> is tiocfaidh, tiocfaidh go fras
> nuair a bhlaisfead diamhrachtaí do ghnéis --
> cailís an mhiangais
> tiocfaidh, áthas na n-áthas
> ina shacramint, ina thabhartas,
> ina theangacha tine an eolais.
> Tiocfaidh
> réamhaisnéis na bhflaitheas.

> *And as the ceremony intensifies*
> *in solidarity*
> *my body trembles*
> *expecting the miracle*
> *which will come voluptuously*
> *when I taste the mystery of your sex --*
> *the chalice of desire.*
> *It will come, joy of joys,*
> *a sacrament, a gift,*
> *the fiery tongues of knowledge*
> *and I will have*
> *intimations of heaven.*

(*ABB* pp. 156–57)

Another type of knowledge is suggested in the next poem, 'Fios'/'Knowledge' (*ABB* p. 159), which alludes to the legendary hero, Fionn mac Cumhaill, who obtains wisdom from a magical salmon, though here the 'salmon of knowledge' (*bradán feasa*) is the beloved's tongue, which 'tonight will swim in me' (*ag snámh ionam anocht*).

In 'Crainn'/'Trees,' the speaker is a 'cherry tree', surrendering in his pink dress to the beloved, an 'oak, manly and generous'. Then, using a theme found in such tales as 'The Romance of Tristan and Iseult' or the ballad of 'Barbara Allen', the poet describes them as two trees on a hill:

Ár gcinniúint adeir tú bheith deighilte ó luan go luan.
Amaidí! Tá ár gcuid rútaí ag muirniú a chéile go buan.

*It's fate that parts us loin from loin.*
*Nonsense! Our roots caress till the end of time.*

(*ABB* pp. 160–61)

'Laoi Cumainn'/'Hound of Ulster' makes use of the figure of Cú Chulainn (literally, the Hound of Culann), the hero of the Old Irish saga, *Táin Bó Cuailnge*, who defends the province of Ulster at times single-handedly against the armies of Queen Medb. The poet speaks to his beloved of their sparring in bed, in scenes perhaps suggested by the famous 'Pillow Talk' episode of the saga • a debate between Queen Medb and her husband Ailill over which is the wealthier and more powerful. Here the sparring takes on sexual overtones:

Anocht má tá cath le fearadh agat, a ghrá,
bíodh sé anseo i measc na bpiliúr:
Craith do sciath agus gread do shleá,
      beartaigh do chlaíomh
go beacht. Lig gáir churaidh as do bhráid.
Luífidh mé anseo ag baint sásamh súl
      as a bhfuil den fhear
ag bogadaí ionat, a dhúil, go ndéanfaidh tú do bhealach féin
a bhearnú chugam fríd plúid agus piliúr.

*Tonight, sweet soul, should you declare battle*
*let it be here among pillows:*
*let your shield shudder, aim your spear,*
      *let your sword be ready*
*and true. Shout aloud your war-cry.*
*Here I'll lie, my eyes entranced*
      *as your manliness*
*moves and -- darling -- I lie in the breach,*
*in the theatre of linen.*

(*ABB* pp. 166–67)

As Ó Laoire states about this poem:

Ó Searcaigh achieves the greatest synthesis of the layers of tradition ... It is a rich and joyful celebration of physical love. The text in the original contains many echoes and allusions for the skilled reader of Irish literature. In this respect it is strongly reminiscent of the poetry of Nuala Ní Dhomhnaill, particularly 'Mo Mhíle Stór' [literally, 'My Thousand Treasures', her title adapted from another Gaelic folksong]. In this poem she juxtaposes some of the most memorable phrases from the corpus of women's poetry in Irish, but her achievement goes far beyond well-crafted pastiche. The associations set off by such allusions in the reader's mind acquire added significance at the poem's end. Her recalling of the Gaelic voice reappropriates an eroticising of male beauty.[9]

Cathal's poem also appropriates elements from two traditional songs, 'Bean an Fhir Rua' ('The Red-haired Man's Wife') and once again, 'Dónall Óg', including the whole range of associations connected with them.[10] One point to mention here: Cathal is familiar with the songs from both published and oral sources, having heard many of them from his friend and neighbour in Gortahork, Lillis Ó Laoire. He seamlessly weaves these lines into his verse, linking his work both with the older Gaelic tradition epitomised by *The Táin* and with the living stream.

As a final note, the poet's sense of displacement from his own culture and his native land may be seen in the poem, 'An Díbeartach' ('The Outcast'), with the epitaph: 'An tír seo bheith ag fonóid, faoi gach rabhán dá ndéan tú de cheol' ('This country to be mocking every spasm you create in song'). This poem was not included in the *An Bealach 'na Bhaile/Homecoming* collection, though it is found in *Out in the Open*, perhaps because its bitter tone was at odds with most of the poems found in the earlier collection. In this work, which seems one of his most confessional and which he read quite movingly at the 1998 IASIL meeting in Limerick, Ó Searcaigh states:

> (i)
> Ní thuigeann siad an buachaill seanchríonna
> a bhíonn ag cumadh ar feadh na hoíche
>
> thuas i gcnoic Bharr an Ghleanna.
> Tá a bhfuil ar siúl aige amaideach
> a deir siad thíos i dtigh an leanna --

macsamhail an mhadaidh bháin
a bhíonn ag cnaí chnámh na gealaí
i bpolláin uisce ar an bhealach.

Ach fós beidh a chuid amhrán
ina n-oileáin dúchais agus dídine
i bhfarraigí a ndorchadais.

(ii)
Ní duitse faraor
dea-fhód a dhéanamh den domasah
ná an Domhnach a chomóradh mar chách
ná grá na gcomharsan lá na cinniúna
ná muirniú mná faoi scáth an phósta
ná dea-chuideachta an tí ósta.

Duitse faraor
dearg dobhogtha Cháin
a bheith smeartha ar chlár d'éadain.

(i)
*They don't understand the ageing boy*
*who composes all night long*
*above in the hills of Barr an Ghleanna.*
*All he does is foolish*
*they say below in the pub --*
*resembling the white dog [i.e. a parasite]*
*who gnaws the bone of the moon*
*In the small water pools on the road.*

*But his songs will yet be*
*islands of hope and shelter*
*in the seas of their darkness*

(ii)
*Not for you sadly*
*to turn the peaty earth into good land*
*nor the celebration of Sunday like the rest*
*nor the love of neighbours on the day of tragedy*
*nor the cherishing of woman in the protection of marriage*
*nor the good company of the inn.*

*For you sadly*
*the indelible mark of Cain*
*smeared on your forehead.*[11]

# Notes

1    Earlier versions of this paper were read at the 6th Annual Lavender Language and Linguistics Conference, Washington, D.C., September 1998, and at the International Association for the Study of Irish Literatures meeting in Barcelona, July 1999. My thanks for all those who shared insights on this poetry with me at those venues.

2    See Brian Ó Conchubhair's essay, 'Cathal Ó Searcaigh: Teip agus Téagar na Teangan — Falling Down and Falling Back on Language' in this volume for a further discussion of this issue.

3    Personal communication, 26 July 1998. Ó Laoire also mentions this in 'Dearg Dobhogtha Cháin/The Indelible Mark of Cain: Sexual Dissidence in the Poetry of Cathal Ó Searcaigh' in *Sex, Nation and Dissent in Irish Writing* (ed. Éibhear Walshe), Cork University Press, 1997, pp. 221–34 (p. 226).

4    Cló Iar-Chonnachta, Indreabhán, Conamara, 1993. Unless otherwise indicated, citations refer to this edition.

5    *An Duanaire 1600–1900: Poems of the Dispossessed* (ed. Seán Ó Tuama and tr. Thomas Kinsella), Dolmen Press, Mountrath, in association with Bord na Gaeilge, 1981, pp. 284–85

6    *An Duanaire*, p. 292.

7    See Angela Partridge (Bourke), 'Wild Men and Wailing Women', *Éigse: A Journal of Irish Studies*, 18 (1980), pp. 25–37, and Mary Helen Thuente, 'Liberty, Hibernia and Mary Le More: United Irish images of women' in *The Women of 1798* (eds. Dáire Keogh & Nicholas Furlong, Four Courts Press, Dublin, 1998, pp. 9–25, for further examples.

8    See James E. Doan, Introduction to *The Romance of Cearbhall and Fearbhlaidh*, Dolmen Press, Mountrath, in association with Humanities Press, 1985, pp. 11–34, for further examples.

9    Ó Laoire, 'Dearg Dobhogtha Cháin,' pp. 228–29.

10   Ó Laoire, pp. 229–30.

11   Ó Laoire, pp. 231–32.

## (as) BUACHAILL BÁN

A bheith i ngrá le fear:
Sin scéal nach bhfuil na focla agam go fóill
lena insint, lena rá
amach os ard, sa dóigh nach mbeidh sé 'mo chrá.

Ba mhaith liom
teangaidh a thabhairt don tost seo
a thachtann mé;
a phlúchann mé achan lá. [...]

(OO 82–4)

## (from) BUACHAILL BAN

To be in love with a man:
that's a tale I haven't the words for yet,
to tell it, to say it out
in a way that won't come back on me.

How I would like
to loosen the tongue of this silence
that chokes me;
that smothers me every day. [...]

(trans. Frank Sewell)

Kieran Francis Kennedy Jr.


'OIRFÉAS AS GACH *ORIFICE*'[1]
THE IRISH LANGUAGE QUESTION, GLOBALIZATION AND
HOMOSEXUALITY


I

Cathal Ó Searcaigh's emergence as the first openly gay poet
writing in the Irish language[2] was facilitated by a significant
transformation in the sexual values of the Irish state. Ó
Searcaigh was the first Irish-language poet to claim the
political importance of identifying himself as a gay man.
Furthermore, this self-identification bears directly on the
reception of his poetry because it provides a clear context for
reading his love poetry as homoerotic, although Ó Searcaigh's
work tends not to explore the connections between sexual and
national identity directly.

A first generation of Irish gay rights activists emerged in the
early 'seventies, drawing their inspiration from the Stonewall
Rebellion.[3] From the 1970s to the early 1990s Senator David
Norris spearheaded a successful campaign to decriminalize
homosexuality. In an exuberant speech celebrating the passage
of the relevant bill, he situated the victory in the context of
Ireland's history as a former British colony. For Norris, the
new state of affairs wiped 'the lingering shame of British
imperial statute from the record of Irish law'.[4] If the Republic
of Ireland has managed to release itself from the imperial
construction of homosexuality as a criminal pathology, how
successful have Irish poets been in elaborating a discourse of
male-male eroticism? Cathal Ó Searcaigh reluctantly uses the
English term 'homosexuality' when he discusses the love
content of his poetry because, he states, there is no such term
in Gaelic. Does this usage amount to a capitulation to scientific

modes of fixing homosexuality, or does it rather acknowledge such modes while retaining the option of articulating as yet unnamed practices in Gaelic culture?

As an Irish-language poet, Ó Searcaigh celebrates a thriving literary tradition that has persisted in spite of the aftershocks of sustained effort under the British Empire to eradicate the language permanently. This status as a representative of a minority language could easily conflict with his willingness to express same-sex love since this expression draws its inspiration from identities formed in the imperial metropolis, London. In other words, linguistic purists could accuse Ó Searcaigh of betraying the heritage of Gaelic culture by incorporating elements that are alien to that culture. In particular, they could argue that the politics of gay identity comes from a culture that in the past fundamentally threatened the rights of a Gaelic culture to exist at all.

Ngugi Wa Thiongo has written that 'the domination of a people's language by the languages of the colonising nations was crucial to the domination of the mental universe of the colonised'.[5] Certainly, the curbing of the Irish tongue was an integral part of British imperial domination in Ireland. The nineteenth century saw the installation of an educational system that systematically stamped out the use of Gaelic and replaced it with English. This loss of the indigenous language had far-reaching consequences for the Irish political psyche:

> It is evident that the wholesale adoption of the English language by the Gaelic-speaking Irish – sometimes voluntary, more often enforced by atrocious pressures – carries with it a psychological heritage, a recriminatory history of scandal, betrayal and shame, the last of these most indelibly associated with poverty and the trauma of the Famine.[6]

Writers within the Gaelic literary tradition today have to contend with this psychic heritage.

Ó Searcaigh's conception of a Gaelic literary tradition striving for organic continuity within itself, while incorporating influences from other literary traditions, complements his view of the Gaelic language itself.[7] He understands the language as being in need of renovation from outside and asserts that the capacity to adapt and change and to incorporate external influences is a sign of the strength of a language[8]: 'a language that cannot survive change is probably not an adequate language' (*File an Phobail*).[9] This comment makes more sense if one reads it as an implicit critique of the conservative attitudes and beliefs of native speakers who respond xenophobically to external influences.

Cathal, Prem and singer Brian Kennedy in Dublin (photo: Cathal Ó Searcaigh)

In the documentary, *File an Phobail*, the critical judgements of the poet's high school English teacher and Irish-language scholars at the University of Ulster, Coleraine, serve to establish his success as a creative artist in the modern world. They also fortify the connections between the rural poet and the state. The title of the documentary itself suggests Ó Searcaigh's representativeness as the poet of the people and also plays off the insurrectionary nationalist and leftist overtones of the term, *an pobal*, root of *Poblacht* ('Republic'). The critics praise Ó Searcaigh's choice to re-establish his roots and to demonstrate that he can 'succeed' as a poet in a provincial, rural setting. The documentary plays heavily on the bucolic, tranquil, and unchanging aspects of Ó Searcaigh's home landscape. By focussing primarily on his local context, the documentary neglects the significance of the poet's international connections and identifications. Travel actually produces the awareness that enables Ó Searcaigh to celebrate the distinctiveness of his 'home'.

Given the minority status of the Irish language in the Irish state, Ó Searcaigh's gay Gaelic lyrics risk becoming a quaint cottage industry available to the metropolitan gaze of the scholarly linguistic tourist. However, Ó Searcaigh's construction of 'Irishness' does not depend on nationalist claims of insular reunification. Rather, it reaches beyond the geographic boundaries of the island and seeks to be fertilized by other homoerotic writings, such as those of Constantin Cavafy and Jack Kerouac.

The politics of identity and identification are particularly fraught for a gay writer who chooses to write publicly about his sexuality, since gay sexuality, like the language itself, has too often also been the subject of a shameful silence. Furthermore, the norms and imperatives of Gaelic daily life in a sense dominated gay sexuality. To articulate a different sexuality is to challenge this structure of domination. Ó Searcaigh writes that the poet's love for another man is a story that can neither be told as a narrative nor performed as a speech act except as a provisional negative:

> A bheith i ngrá le fear:
> Sin scéal nach bhfuil na focla agam go fóill
> lena insint, lena rá
> amach os ard, sa dóigh nach mbeidh sé 'mo chrá
>
> *To be in love with a man:*
> *that's a tale I haven't the words for yet,*
> *to tell it, to say it out ...*[10]

Ironically, then, Cathal Ó Searcaigh enters the silence surrounding gay male sexuality in the Irish language by interrogating English formations of sexual subjectivity. In other words, he draws on the language associated with the shameful destruction of Gaelic in order to fabricate queer subjectivity in Gaelic.

Ó Searcaigh has published two bilingual collections: *Homecoming: An Bealach 'na Bhaile* (1993) and *Out in the Open* (1997), with the support of the Irish Arts Council.[11] Both are compilations that reconfigure earlier work and present it to readers whose first language is most likely English. Significantly, *Out in the Open* has no Irish title, even though the poems in Irish precede their English translations in the book. This monoglot title acknowledges the poet's sense of indebtedness to English for giving him the terms with which to narrate his own 'coming out' as a gay man and also marks the degree to which discussions of identity, even the identity of an Irish-language speaker, must be mediated through English. As Cronin writes, 'The history of translation in Ireland is the history of encounters'.[12] He notes further that 'as fixed identities were being challenged both north and south of the border, it was not surprising that translation itself became a privileged mode of interrogation'.[13]

Ó Searcaigh left his native Donegal as a teenager in search of a culture that would be more thoroughly supportive of his same-gender attractions. Yet his departure was driven by a wider set of related impulses than a desire to mould a sexual identity. Granted, he could find no role models upon which to base an emergent gay identity in his local community, but he was also concerned that he could not experience there the aesthetic and cultural conditions that he sensed in his limited exposure to popular culture via Radio Luxembourg. Yet, as the title of *Homecoming/An Bealach 'na Bhaile* suggests, the poet ultimately opted to settle in the rural Irish-speaking environment where he was raised in spite of prolonged periods abroad. How, then, does his poetry eventually come to balance the celebration of a local ethos with the integration of mass-cultural elements from a more properly global context? After all, gay globalization has its perils. It can obfuscate, as Martin Manalansan puts it, 'hierarchical relations between metropolitan centers and sub-urban peripheries'.[14] Ken Plummer also writes with some sense of foreboding about the global/local dialectic:

Along with globalization comes an intensification of the local. Indeed, with the process of globalization comes a tendency towards tribalism: fundamentalism winning over difference, a politics that separates rather than unites.[15]

The predicament of the rural gay man, drawn towards the sexual opportunities of metropolitan life, yet attached also to his place of origin, gets mapped in linguistic terms in 'Cainteoir Dúchais'/'Native Speaker'. A new language of lived gay experience and a subculture of gay identities became available to Ó Searcaigh in English. In this poem, an Irish-speaking gay man cleans his apartment in London prior to going cruising in the hopes of finding another Irish speaker:

> Bhí sé flat-out, a dúirt sé
> i gcaitheamh na maidine.
> Rinne sé an t-árasán a *hoover*eáil,
> na boscaí bruscair a *jeyes-fluid*eáil,
> an *loo* a *harpick*áil, an *bath* a *vim*eáil.
> Ansin rinne see an t-urlár a *flash*áil
> na fuinneoga a *windolene*áil
> agus na leapacha a *eau-de-cologne*áil.
>
> Bhí se shagáilte, a dúirt sé
> ach ina dhiaidh sin agus uile
> rachadh sé amach a *chruise*áil;
> b'fhéidir, a dúirt sé, go mbuailfeadh sé
> le boc inteacht
> a mbeadh Gaeilge aige.
>
> *He was flat-out, he said,*
> *after the morning.*
> *He had the place all hoovered,*
> *the bins jeyes-fluided,*
> *the loo harpicked, the bath vimmed.*
> *Then he flashed the mop over*
> *the floor, windowlened the windows*
> *and eau-de-cologned the beds.*
>
> *He was shagged-out, he said,*
> *but even so, he was all set*
> *to go out cruising;*
> *you never know, he said,*

*he might run into someone*
*with a* cúpla focal.

(OO pp. 134–35)

One assumes that, like Ó Searcaigh, the protagonist came to London as a refugee from rural homophobia seeking access to popular culture and a queer community. However, as an Irish-speaking immigrant, integration into another community was far from automatic. This poem correlates the exploration of sexual identity with the interdependence of nationhood and language. The man's obsessive hygiene and cleaning corresponds to his desire for ethnic purity figured as linguistic authenticity. He becomes an ironic figure in the poem, however, because he's clearly no purist in the language he uses. He moulds the English brand-names of cleaning products into Irish verbs and nouns, and names his exhaustion in English: 'Bhí sé flat-out', 'Bhí sé shagáilte'. The translator finds an ingenious way to mimic the strategy of borrowing from English by using the Irish phrase '(someone with a) cúpla focal'; this expression literally means 'a few words,' but it is also an idiom used to describe a degree of competence in using Irish. The juxtaposition of English and Irish vocabularies and idioms interrogates the distance between the 'peripheral' and 'central' sites of identity and investigates the resonances of each cultural space within the other. His landscapes of same-sex love exemplify the hybridization of Gaelic-speaking culture in the contact zone of modernity. The protagonist's cravings — for sexual satisfaction abroad and reintegration into his culture of origin — are at least in part satisfied by his articulation as the subject of this poem.

The purity of the native speaker reveals itself to be an impossible dream in the metropolis where languages meet, mix, and affect each other. Furthermore, the cleaning spree in the poem complicates the traditional gender roles usually assigned in rural Ireland. The blurring of domestic duties and social roles manifests itself as an effect of more fluid modern identities. Ó Searcaigh also comments on the ubiquity of market values in all aspects of life. The brand names borrowed from English suggest the sterility of commodification and make a parallel between the market in products and the market in bodies. By studying the figure of the Irish-speaking gay man within the social structures of the metropolis, Ó Searcaigh's poetry considers the possible losses and gains of the construction of modern gay male identity in global capitalism.

II

'An Tobar'//'The Well' seizes on the trope of well water as a way of moralizing the impact of modernization on a rural community. The five-stanza poem begins and ends in the present with the words of 'sean-Bhríd'//'old Bridget' who extols the vital, energizing qualities of the long-lost well water. In the intervening three stanzas the poet recalls how in his youth every family proudly maintained a well. The water from these wells is praised for its refreshing quality and the satisfaction it provided to agricultural workers in the summer. The well water, 'Uisce beo bíogúil, fíoruisce glé'//'Lively, lively water, pellucid spring-water', contrasts with the piped water that now can be found in every kitchen and is 'uisce lom gan loinnir'//'mawkish, without sparkle' (*ABB* pp. 44–5). The poet presents the onslaught of modernity as an abandonment of a purer, more organic connection with nature in favour of a mechanical world of convenience, forgetful of sensual pleasure and stimulation.

The poem concludes with the old woman's advice to the poet, that unveils the well metaphor as an explicit comment on poetic inspiration. The woman's name, Bridget, suggests both the tradition of Celtic spirituality (St. Bridget) and pejorative representations of old Irish women as 'old biddys'. Ó Searcaigh reclaims and valorizes the old woman as the embodiment of a Gaelic tradition organically connected with the land and its abundance. She advises him:

> Aimsigh do thobar féin, a chroí,
> Óir tá am an anáis romhainn amach:
> Caithfear pilleadh arís ar na foinsí.

*Seek out your own well, my dear,*
*for the age of want is near:*
*There will have to be a going back to sources.*

(ABB pp. 44–5)

Cathal's writing table in Mín a Leá (photo: Jan Voster)

Of course, as Derrida has taught us, the source always differs from itself. In Heraclitean terms, you cannot step in the same source twice. In other words, the simple opposition that Ó Searcaigh seems to propose between tradition and modernity gets complicated and, in my reading of his work, ultimately displaced by questions of history, language, and textuality. Poetic sensibility, as figured by the taste for well water passed down from generation to generation, 'ó ghlúin go glúin', can no longer be thought simply from within the temporality of the organic rural community. As soon as the poet gives the date of his adolescence ('i dtús na seascaidí'/*'in the early sixties'*, *ABB* pp. 42–3), the poem becomes complicit with the perspective of modernity. Unavoidably, old Bridget in the first stanza comes under the reader's now anthropological gaze. What has been lost, if we can indeed speak of anything being lost with the advent of modernization, is not so much tradition, but rather the very possibility of a perspective that is unconscious of its traditionalism as such.

This problem of 'going back to sources'/'pilleadh arís ar na foinsí' informs Ó Searcaigh's approach to representing sexuality. 'Geasa'/'The Bond' (*OO* pp. 78–81) returns to a childhood source memory to narrate how the poet became conscious of his sexuality. At one level, the 'bond' of the title denotes the profound connection that Ó Searcaigh experiences between his mode of desire and his artistic expression. He relates how as a youth he watched a naked young woman sunbathing. The first stanza plays with the universally heterosexual expectations of the imagined reader as it builds towards a crescendo of teenage hormones on overdrive. However, these expectations are undercut (quite literally) by the final line of the opening stanza: 'a cneas chomh glé ... //le béal scine' ('*her skin as bright ... //as the edge of a knife*'). The poet goes on to express his youthful feelings of estrangement and inadequacy when he realises that he was more likely to breed poems than children:

> Is ba mhór an crá croí domh
> Na geasa dubha draíochta
> A leagadh orm go síoraí
> As féith seo na filíochta.

> *O, and it hurt so deep,*
> *this black magic bond*
> *placed on me forever*
> *by Poetry.*

(*OO* pp. 80–81)

Poetry serves to fill the void of unrequited longing and provides Ó Searcaigh with a fantasy space where he can imagine satisfying sexual encounters. He conjures a beautiful male body in the final stanza of the poem:

> Ach b'fhada go gcasfaí orm é ina bheatha,
> b'fhada go bhfaighinn sásamh
> óna chneas álainn fionnbhán
> óna chumthacht tharnocht
> Ach amháin ...
>     I mo dhán ...

*It would take years to meet him in the flesh,*
*Years to satisfy my wish*
*For his pale, wonderful skin,*
*His clear, naked form --*
*But sometimes ...*
            *In poems ...*

                                                    (*OO* pp. 80–1)

Ó Searcaigh's homoerotic explorations emerge out of the tension between provincial routine and poetic inspiration. The poet wishes to celebrate his native landscape without idealizing it, yet his fellow glen dwellers are not attuned to the beauty he perceives. He finds himself trapped in the same predicament of which Patrick Kavanagh complained:

The first gay flight of my lyric
Got caught in a peasant's prayer.[16]

While I focus mainly on Ó Searcaigh's attempts to negotiate between Anglo-American expressions of gay identity and Gaelic expressions of male-male love, I want to acknowledge the important role that he gives to the reinterpretation of traditions of love poetry within the Gaelic canon. In 'Laoi Chumainn'/'Hound of Ulster', Ó Searcaigh plays with the celebrated figure of Cú Chulainn to homoerotic ends:

sleánna cosanta do sciathán
mo chrioslú go dlúth
óir is tusa mo laoch, an curadh caol cruaidh
a sheasann idir mé agus uaigneas tíoránta na hoíche.

*Your limbs are swift spears*
*Fending off the world*
*My champion, proud sleek warrior*
*You man the gap between me and night's tyranny.*

                                                    (*OO* pp. 86–87)

In this context, Ó Searcaigh works less to invest the original mythic figure with homoerotic significance and more to elucidate the homoerotic implications already latent in traditional representations of the hero. His poetry suggests that the all-male world of mythic Celtic warriors is already saturated with sexual tension and, by applying the vocabulary of daring feats and combat to homoerotic engagement, he brings this tension to the surface. Ó Searcaigh does not simply surrender the contested conceptual terrain of sexual identity within the Gaelic poetic tradition to purist critics, who might claim that same-sex love is innately alien to poetic writing in Gaelic. His rewriting of an eighteenth-century love poem such as 'Ceann Dubh Dílis' with an explicitly homoerotic 'plot' both reclaims the poetry for a contemporary gay and gay-friendly readership and also implicitly argues that it is a mistake to conclude that homoerotic practices and attractions were nonexistent during a period when they did not find explicit literary expression. In 'Ceann Dubh Dílis'/'My Own Dark-haired Love', he shows that these lyrics, that had assimilated medieval Norman French influences, can be transformed to address the romantic concerns of gay Irish speakers at the end of the twentieth century. The 'original' poem (A) is followed below by the contemporary 'version' (B):

(A)
A chinn duibh dhílis dhílis dhílis,
cuir do lámh mhín gheal tharam anall;
a bhéilín meala, a bhfuil boladh na tíme air,
is duine gan chroí nach dtabharfadh duit grá.

Tea cailíní ar an mbaile seo ar buile 's ar buaireamh,
ag tarraingt a ngruaige 's á ligean le gaoith,
ar mo shonsa, an scafaire is fearr ins na tuatha,
ach do thréigfinn an méid sin ar rún dil mo chroí.

Is cuir do cheann dílis dílis dílis,
cuir do cheann dílis tharam anall;
a bhéilín meala a bhfuil boladh na tíme air,
is duine gan chroí nach dtabharfadh duit grá.

*My own dark head (my own, my own)*
*your soft pale arm place here about me.*
*Honeymouth that smells of thyme*
*he would have no heart who denied you love.*

*There are girls in the town enraged and vexed,*
*they tear and loosen their hair on the wind*
*for the dashingest man in this place--myself!*
*But I'd leave them all for my secret heart.*

*Lay your head, my own (my own, my own)*
*your head, my own, lay it here upon me.*
*Honeymouth that smells of thyme*
*he would have no heart who denied you love.*

(Ó Tuama and Kinsella, pp. 284–85)

(B)

A cheann dubh dílis dílis dílis
d'fhoscail ár bpóga créachtaí Chríosta arís;
ach ná foscail do bhéal, ná sceith uait an scéal:
tá ár ngrá ar an taobh thuathal den tsoiscéal.

Tá cailíní na háite seo cráite agat, a ghrá,
's iad ag iarraidh thú a bhréagadh is a mhealladh gach lá;
ach b'fhearr leatsa bheith liomsa i mbéal an uaignis
'mo phógadh, 'mo chuachadh is mo thabhairt chun
aoibhnis.

Is leag do cheann dílis dílis dílis
leag do cheann dílis i m'ucht, a dhíograis;
ní fhosclód mo bhéal, ní sceithfead an scéal,
ar do shonsa shéanfainn gach soiscéal.

*My dark dear, dear dark-haired love,*
*our kisses open Christ's wounds up;*
*don't open your mouth, don't tell a soul--*
*our love's on the wrong side of the gospel.*

*The local girls are going crazy,*
*trying to win you away from me;*
*but you prefer us on our own,*
*kissing, cuddling till the healing comes.*

*Lay your dark dear, dear dark head,*
*lay your dark head on my breast, dear friend;*
*I won't say a word to a living soul--*
*for you I'd thrice deny a gospel.*

(OO pp. 112–13)

Ó Searcaigh's queering of this lyric keeps the form of the earlier version intact. Indeed, his version mischievously picks up on the unusually explicit emphasis on masculine consciousness. These poems were considered 'men's love-songs' according to the editors of *An Duanaire*. In his deft revision, Ó Searcaigh draws on the available resources of this poem to establish a context for gay romance within contemporary Irish-speaking society. In the folk poem, the narcissistic, attractive male speaker draws back from the fervent attentions of the town's female population in order to protect his secret love, 'a rún dil mo chroí'. In the second stanza of the contemporary version, the narcissistic narrator is displaced by another male voice who articulates their mutual attraction. The conflict between the local girls and the poet's secret love becomes a contest between the prescriptions of normative heterosexuality and the pursuit of homosexual love on the brink of isolation: 'b'fhearr leatsa bheith liomsa i mbéal an uaignis//'mo phógadh, 'mo chachadh is mo thabhairt chun aoibhnis' ('but you prefer us on our own,//kissing, cuddling till the healing comes').

Ó Searcaigh's poem discusses the entanglement of religion and sexuality. Although religion can be a repressive force, the Catholic body becomes a source of spiritual investigation. The poem reclaims a religious space for gay people, revising the biblical condemnations of homosexuality as 'the indelible mark of Cain'.[17] The poem plays on scéal/soiscéal (story/gospel) to challenge the intertext of the bible. Ó Searcaigh uses the bodily imagery of the folk poem to stage the queer body's subjugation to religious homophobia. The 'sweet mouth' of the third and eleventh lines becomes a silenced mouth in Ó Searcaigh's poem: 'ach ná foscail do bhéal, ná sceith uait an scéal://tá ár ngrá ar an taobh thuathal den tsoiscéal' ('don't open your mouth, don't tell a soul--//our love's on the wrong side of the gospel'). Unlike the folk poem, the modern version makes an explicit reference to the passion of Christ: 'd'fhoscail ár bpóga créachtaí Chríosta arís' ('our kisses open Christ's wounds up'), suggesting that the universally heterosexual conventions of love poetry up to this point functioned as a cross upon which to crucify gay people. In the final line of Ó Searcaigh's version, the speaker pronounces the importance of denying all master narratives on behalf of his beloved: 'ar do shonsa shéanfainn gach soiscéal' ('for you I'd thrice deny every gospel').

Rick Rambuss discusses how 'the naked body of Jesus' presides over the devotional poetry of Richard Crawshaw[18]: 'Around this body accrue a sensuous, even sexy thematics of ecstatic rupture, of penetration and its attendant spurting streams ... The fluid permeabilities of Christ's own body become so many openings for identification with his passion and for a passionate, pleasurable union with his saving flesh'.[19] Rambuss details the lengths to which an eminent historian, a celebrated art critic, and several luminary literary critics will go to avoid the homoerotic possibilities of mediaeval representations of Jesus in art and in metaphysical poetry (Crawshaw, Herbert, Donne). He sees in Crawshaw's poetry how 'one merges with Christ, becomes one crucifix with him, through his wounds and what proceeds from out of them — by entering him or being entered by him, and then being engulfed by the salvific streams that flow from the multiple openings in his body'.[20] Rambuss sees in metaphysical poetry a homoerotic love of Jesus 'full of queer excitations to pleasure and devotion'.[21]

Ó Searcaigh concerns himself particularly with the celebration of spaces that enable unfettered poetic utterance. To that end, he contests the authoritative cultural interdictions laid down by the Catholic Church. This challenge parallels the relationship between the poet's writing of gay sexuality in the present and same-sex practices in Gaelic culture of the past. In 'Tearmann'/'Sanctuary', Ó Searcaigh applies the metaphors of religious worship to the rural landscape he inhabits. The sacramental value of nature is held in opposition to the 'brutal piety of the pulpit', and the very architecture of the country chapel is appropriated to celebrate the poet's ritualistic experience of the landscape. The poet challenges the parish priest's authority and the sway he exercises over the sensibilities of his congregants. Patrick Kavanagh's vision of nature 'pouring redemption' stands behind the concluding lines of the poem that demystify the celebration of the eucharist and present the elements of bread and wine in their full materiality as sources of bodily sustenance and pleasure:

> Le gach anáil dá dtarraingím,
> análaím chugam é ar an aer íon
> Chomh friseáilte le harán, chomh fionnuar le fíon.

*With every breath I take*
*I breathe him from the pure air*
*As fresh as new-baked bread, as cool as wine.*

(ABB pp. 46–47)

A strong lineage of romantic influence shows itself in this poem, from Wordsworth through Kavanagh to Ó Searcaigh. The extended metaphor of the mountain hollow as chapel in which the poet wanders recalls 'The Prelude'. The embrace of an Anglophone aesthetic tradition here enables the poet's celebration of homoeroticism elsewhere. The subjective sensuality of the romantics and their pantheistic conception of a non-judgmental God serves Ó Searcaigh's purposes when he turns to the representation of sensual pleasure between men.

In 'Searmanas'/'Ceremony' Ó Searcaigh uses the language of spiritual devotion to lend majesty to an encounter with his beloved:

Ar altóir na leapa
ceiliúraim do chorpsa anocht, a ghile,
Le deasghnátha mo dhúile.

*On the altar of the bed*
*I celebrate your body tonight, my love,*
*With the rites of my desire.*

(ABB pp. 156–157)

The poet appropriates the vocabulary of religious worship: 'kneel', 'prayer', 'the sense's choir', 'hymns', 'trinity', 'sacrament' and 'heaven'. In direct confrontation with the religious prohibitions of the Catholic Church, the poet equates oral sex with partaking in the eucharist: 'nuair a bhlaisfead diamhrachtaí do ghnéis--//cailís an mhiangais' ('*when I taste the mystery of your sex--//the chalice of desire*'). Ó Searcaigh's appropriation of the symbolism of Catholic sacraments is not parodic, because it takes seriously the spiritual dimension of worship and praise at the heart of these rituals. It does, however, contest the authority of the institutional church to regulate the bodily pleasures of Irish people. In fact, it reclaims the sacraments for people who have historically been banished from their administration.

Ó Searcaigh again casts gay sex as a secular sacrament in 'Ag Na Pioctúirí ar na Croisbhealaí'/'At the Pictures on the Crossroads': the poem retells a sexual interlude that occurred on a Sunday night in a movie theatre. It commemorates 'that slender handsome face and strong strapping body'/'an aghaidh chaol álainn sin agus úrghéag chruaidh a cholainne' in a poem:

> saor ó bhaol i mo bhrionglóidí agus anois i ndiaidh trí bliana fichead ar fán
> i mo chloigeann tá dídean faighte acu i ndán

> *and now after 23 years going round and round in my head,*
> *they have finally found sanctuary in a poem.*

(*OO* pp. 104–05)

## III

In importing identity-based notions from Anglophone culture in order to express the possibilities of sexual love between men, Ó Searcaigh's work raises a number of theoretical questions: Where did these possibilities stand before a vocabulary was found to express them? Were they somehow absent from Irish-speaking culture during the period in which they remained unnamed? Or does this new vocabulary make apparent a form of sexuality that existed although the culture failed to recognize it in language? In my opinion, there is no right answer to these kinds of questions. Rather they suggest routes of investigation: as the saying goes, 'd'fhiafraíonn ceist ceist eile', meaning roughly, 'one question leads to another'. Since articulation in language can facilitate the policing and disciplining of bodily practices, do the methods and forms of Ó Searcaigh's poetry provide ways of evading such surveillance?

When Ó Searcaigh emigrated from his birthplace in the Donegal Gaeltacht as a teenager in the early 1970s and went to live in London, he tried at first to write in English, since 'everything that [he] was reading and all that [he] was encountering was in the English language'.[22] However, he quickly 'found that the language that had emotional resonance for [him] was Irish and [he] knew more about the register of language in Irish'. His first collection of poetry in Irish, the title of which translates as *Trivial City Tragedy*, was written during this period heavily under the influence of modernist poetry, particularly T. S. Eliot's *The Wasteland*.[23] Ó Searcaigh has always been fascinated with dealing with the city in Irish, that he sees as 'the language of a rural, agricultural society; all the imagery comes from that background'. His concern to adapt Irish to 'the needs and urgency of living in the modern metropolis' arose in part from the process of self-naming that living in London made possible. The urban counterculture of London in the early 'seventies offered a dazzling vista of sexual possibilities. The second-hand bookstores on Charing Cross road exposed Ó Searcaigh to gay English and American literature in the shape of writers like Walt Whitman, Tennessee Williams, W. H. Auden, and Thom Gunn. Gay Anglo-American literature facilitated a process of self-recognition and self-acceptance that quickly broadened into an interrogation of rural Donegal.

London has at least two contrapuntal roles in Ó Searcaigh's poetry. On the one hand, it offers the creative and sexual liberation of a popular counterculture and, on the other, it represents the drudgery of the work-a-day world in the modern metropolis. The latter is severely accentuated by the racist treatment that Irish immigrants often confront in the British capital. Ó Searcaigh's poetry of exile is full of figures who travel to London with high hopes of economic well-being only to find themselves trapped in positions of menial servitude. The historical consciousness of poverty and dispossession wrought by British imperial occupation of Ireland further aggravates the sense of shame associated with immigrant living conditions in London. 'Ma Bohème' takes up the more optimistic side of the London dialectic: the poet finds the pleasures of free verse as he hitches a lift to the city. However, the precariousness of his situation is captured in the closing lines of the poem:

> O, táimse i m'ór-uige chomh mórluachach le Rí, cé
> go bhfuilimse ar tí bheith i dtuilleamaí na déirce.

*In my cloth-of-gold I have a princely style*
*Although I come close to having to look for hand-outs.*

(*ABB* pp. 62–3)

By contrast, 'Mise Charlie An Scibhí'/'I Am Charlie The Skivvy' takes a far more acerbic look at the conditions of the immigrant worker. The sense of isolation here is specifically one of cultural and linguistic alienation. The protagonist lacks anyone with whom to speak about his memories of 'úrchnoic mo chuimhne'/'the refreshing hills of my youth'. The English language offers only disorientation and spiritual impoverishment. The borrowings from English that crop up in the poem reflect this sense. The darkness of winter evenings is compared to a 'vacuum cleaner' and Charlie voices his frustration in his inner monologue with the phrase, 'fuck this for a lark' (*ABB* pp. 202–05).

London represented gay liberation for the youthful Ó Searcaigh. In 'Tá mo chéadsearc i Londain'/'To my heart's desire in London', the metropolis becomes the place to which the poet's beloved flees after an unfulfilled romance. This poem draws on the traditional elements from Irish verse and saga, such as grá éagmaise ('love from afar') and secret or forbidden love[24]:

> Cion istigh a bheith agam duit is cion amuigh a d'fhág mise ar an bhfaraoir
> Is tú anois i bhfad ó láimh is gan fonn ort bheith i mo ghaobhair;
> Chan bris duit mo bhuairt is chan buaireamh duit mo phian
> Is mar barr ar an donas b'fhéidir gur cuma leat, a mhian.

> *My secret desire that I failed to conceal!*
> *And now you're in London, far from my gaze:*
> *What the eye cannot see the heart cannot feel*
> *And will you ignore me the rest of your days?*

(*ABB* pp. 144–45)

London and rural Donegal are proposed frequently in the poetry as disparate locations that can be brought into the same present tense by language. Linguistic resources tend to flow away from the rural locale to enrich the sense of daily life in the metropolis. The rural area supplies the needs of the city, as in 'High Street, Kensington, 6 P.M.':

> Blaisim ar uairibh
> i maistreadh sráide
> babhla bláiche
> i riocht dáin.

> *There are times I taste*
> *in the street's churning*
> *a bowl of buttermilk*
> *in the shape of a poem.*

(ABB pp. 64–5)

Sensation is subordinated to the temporal imperatives of the city. At tea-time, food manifests itself in the form of a product fit for consumption. And yet, the buttermilk appears to be unavailable on the city streets that churn minds not milk. The poem provides a satisfying replacement for the buttermilk that the poet used to enjoy. The poet's senses and his compositional instincts respond to the demands of the city.

The fear of economic dependence complicates the ambivalent relationship between Ó Searcaigh's Irish-language poetry and English influences. He returns to the figure of the female prostitute to represent the alienation of modern love by commodification. 'Maigdiléana'/'Magdalene' draws an analogy between an isolated prostitute walking the London streets and the Passion. The first stanza of the poem, which consists of two stanzas and a freestanding final line, ends with a reference to crucifixion and the second with a reference to resurrection. Ó Searcaigh's standard opposition between ugly urban life and beautiful nature dominates the opening of the poem: 'I dtrátha an ama a dtachtann sealán aibhléise//aoibh shoilseach na spéire' (*'About the time the noose of electric light chokes//the luminous beauty of the sky'*), lines that recall the violent symbolism of city life that García Lorca explores in *Poeta en Nueva York*. The urban landscape is completely dominated by commodity fetishism, from the prostitute 'agus í ar a *beat* ag *cruiseáil* go huaighneach' ('on her beat cruising lonely') to the advertising on the walls of the 'underground'. The prostitute's isolation resembles that of many figures in Ó

Searcaigh's London landscape. This recurrent motif suggests the poet's sense of linguistic alienation in a city where he is far from an audience that can understand the poetry he creates. Christian myth and consumer products are both reduced to the same lowest common denominator when they both become the subject of marketing. In the underground, the only opportunity of speech seems to be a passive reception of the advertising messages:

> Nuair nach labhraíonn éinne leat, a ghrá,
> thíos ansiúd, dubh bán nó riabhach
> bhéarfaidh na fógraí béal bán duit agus béadán
> i dtuamba folamh an *underground*
>
> nó b'fhéidir scéala on Ghalailéach.
>
> When nobody speaks to you love,
> Down there, black, white or in-between,
> The ads will softsoap you with gossip
> In the empty tomb of the Underground
>
> Or maybe bear tidings of the Galilean.
>
> (*ABB* pp. 66–67)

As in many of Ó Searcaigh's London lyrics, the language of sexual encounter borrows directly from English: 'agus í ar a *beat* ag *cruise*áil go huaighneach'//'on her beat cruising lonely.' 'Piccadilly: Teacht na hOíche'/'Piccadilly: Nightfall' makes a more pointed comment on the connections between the English language and sexual commodification:

> '*You wanta make it, dontcha?'*
> arsa leadhb i ngúna gairid;
> cling-cleaing scipéad airgid
> ina canúint bhréag-Mheiriceánach.
>
> '*You wanta make it, dontcha?'í*
> *says a skimpily clad tart,*
> *the cling-clang of a cash register*
> *in her pseudo-American drawl.*
>
> (*ABB* pp. 70–71)

The English that makes it into the Gaelic text often seems to bear the corrupting mark of the marketplace. In

'Londain'/'London' the poet spots a prostitute: '"I'm Nano//the Nympho" arsa mána gríogach a cíoch' ('"I'm Nano//the Nympho" emblazoned over her breasts'). The figure of the commodified prostitute, which recurs in Ó Searcaigh's work, could be a projective identification.

In Cathal's Gaeltacht, people simultaneously have a connection with the world of rural heritage and the world of the immigrant, generating an ambivalence towards tradition. For example, in interviews Ó Searcaigh freely employs a model of subjectivity, perception and imagination that relies on U.S. pop psychology. When speaking in Irish, he uses English phrases like 'therapy session' and 'psychic connection', the language of mental hygiene and self-development. The integration of queer experience into Irish-speaking culture marks a particularly stark encounter between modernity and tradition. To this end, Ó Searcaigh engages in an outrageous camp reappropriation of those shimmering figures of the Celtic twilight, fairies. He had first heard about *na sí*, as fairies are known in Irish, from his mother when he was a small child. Later in life, he came to diagnose her narrative effusiveness as manic depression, but in the poem 'The Fairy Reel' he envisions the London gay community in terms that preserve the wonderment of a child making a connection with the otherworldly. Fundamentally, this poem repossesses the rural landscape on a journey home:

> I get off the Tube at Tottenham Court Road
> where I wander around Soho from the Square
> to Carnaby Street. This place is enchanting,
> so much more than the hunting of Prochlais Wood.
> Here, the fairies come out from fear's ring-forts
> and the raths of loneliness to cruise the waves of twilight.
> They flow in the frenzied freedom of the street
> with their longings and lusts, with the boutique queens
> and the hashish hustlers, and hipsters blowing their horns.
> They ride the storm, the fairy wind whirling
> toward the street with Love and Affection.
> This is my street!
>
> (*OO* p. 163)

Ó Searcaigh refuses to limit himself to an archaeological dig for a prenational and essential homosexuality, preferring instead to engage in linguistic barter and exchange in the realm of modernity. The gay lyricism of Constantin Cavafy, the preeminent Greek poet, translated into Irish, has unique affinities with Ó Searcaigh's, not least because both poets belong to European island nations on the periphery of modernity. Cavafy figures in Ó Searcaigh's collection as the shadow of a classical Greek homoeroticism rooted in the Mediterranean ancient world and transmitted to the poet through E. M. Forster. This transmission of a classical homoeroticism to a rural, provincial poet from one periphery of Europe to another takes place through the agency of a writer tapped into metropolitan canon-making authority. The desirable gay boys in Cavafy's poems are street trade refigured as ancient Greek heroes. Ó Searcaigh refashions Cavafy's 'thoughts and imaginings' and he hopes that he has done justice to 'the spirit of Greek in this Gaelic body'. In a queerly pentecostal moment, homoeroticism becomes the foreign holy ghost that descends and inhabits the domestic body (the Irish language). Ó Searcaigh also seems to emulate the simplicity, directness, and economy of Cavafy's lyrics. He aspires to a poetic utterance that matches the master in its poised temperament. He draws on Cavafy as an antecedent to support his bold celebration of intergenerational homoeroticism in a rural Irish context.

Ó Searcaigh steers a course between the Scylla of global capitalism and the Charybdis of local fundamentalism. His work challenges any epistemological privileging of the imperial metropolis over the rural periphery. His poetry offers the rural as a locus of enunciation and the metropolis as a locus of the enunciated. However, he refuses to become an antimodernist who blandly rejects modernity in favor of the local. Instead, he integrates the myriad ways that the local and the metropolitan define each other. The relationship between the local and the global, the rural and the metropolitan, is emphatically synchronous. The historical identification of Gaelic with ignorance, underdevelopment and starvation on the one hand, and English with progress, success, and modern integration on the other, gives way in Ó Searcaigh's work to an assertive and independent local voicing of inescapable hybridization.

## Notes

1  I select this title, from 'Do Jack Kerouac', because it proposes a utopian relationship between English and Irish in the representation of gay sex. The coupling of an English- and Irish-language poet (in this case, Kerouac and Ó Searcaigh) captures one of Ó Searcaigh's central aesthetic preoccupations. The full line is 'Rinne muid Oirféas as gach orifice'/'Out of every orifice, we made Orpheus'. Orpheus sought unsuccessfully to retrieve his wife from the underworld and, as Ovid tells it, turned equally to the pleasures of boys and girls in his grief. The overtones of Greek love intensify the poet's imaginary homoerotic coupling with Jack Kerouac, but the phrase suggests a series of acts without the anchoring certitude of an identity.

2  In this respect, his treatment of homosexuality is quite distinct from that of the playwright Frank McGuinness, who searchingly probes the relationship between male-bonding, homosexuality, and the formation of a Protestant national community in *Observe the Sons of Ulster Marching towards the Somme*.

3  Kieran Rose, *Diverse Communities: The Evolution of Lesbian and Gay Politics in Ireland* (Cork: Cork University Press, 1994).

4  Senator David Norris, 'Criminal Law (Sexual Offences) Bill 1993: Second Stage Speech, Tuesday 29 June 1993', reprinted in Íde O'Carroll and Eoin Collins (ed.), *Lesbian And Gay Visions of Ireland: Towards the Twenty-first Century* (London and New York: Cassell, 1995), p. 14.

5  Ngu●gi● wa Thiong'o. *Decolonising the mind. the politics of language in African literature*. London. Currey. 1986, p 16.

6  Séamus Deane (ed.), *Field Day Anthology of Irish Writing* (Derry: Field Day Publications, 1991), p. xxiv.

7  Patrick Pearse wrote 'we would have our literature modern not only in the sense of freely borrowing every modern form which it does not possess and which it is capable of assimilating, but also in texture, tone and outlook. This is the twentieth century and no literature can take root in the twentieth century which is not of the twentieth century' (*An Claidheamh Soluis*, 26 May 1906), quoted in Eoghan Ó hAnluain, ed., 'Irish Writing: Prose Fiction and Poetry 1900–1988', in *The Field Day Anthology of Irish Writing* (gen. ed. Seamus Deane), III, Field Day Publications, Derry, 1991, p. 815.

8  Ó Searcaigh's association of Irish with weakness and English modernity with strength corresponds to how Jews saw Yiddish after the Holocaust. See *A Marriage Made in Heaven: The Sexual Politics of Hebrew and Yiddish* (Berkeley and Los Angeles: University of California Press, 1997). Hebrew was seen as a strong, masculinized language (with Middle Eastern accent) while Yiddish was seen as weak and effeminate (with a European accent), connected also with the construction of an Israeli phallic male who would not be

dominated and humiliated. Ó Searcaigh sees his project in part as restoring virility to a feminized Irish language.

9    The documentary films of Mairín Seoighe and Ciarán Hegarty, *An Bealach 'na Baile/The Road Home* (Scannáin Dobharchú, 1993) and *File an Phobail/Poet of the People* (BBC Northern Ireland, 1994), deal with Ó Searcaigh's work.

10    From 'Buachaill Bán', the title poem of the collection, *Na Buachaillí Bána*, reprinted with a translation in *Out in the Open*.

11    Ó Searcaigh's work has benefited from the Arts Council's efforts to wrestle the representation of 'the Irish image' away from economically driven London publishers. From 1984 onwards, the Arts Council adopted a new policy sponsoring translation to encourage bilingualism. Interestingly, Ireland's growing economic integration into European culture has been accompanied by an increasingly strong sense of Irish cultural difference (Cronin, p. 174). Furthermore, translation into English affects the writing of Irish literary history by increasing the prominence of the translated writer.

12    Michael Cronin, *Translating Ireland* (Cork: Cork University Press, 1996), p. 1.

13    Ibid., p. 169.

14    Martin F. Manalansan IV, 'In the Shadows of Stonewall: Examining Gay Transnational Politics and the Diasporic Dilemma', in Lisa Lowe and David Lloyd (ed.), *The Politics of Culture in the Shadow of Capital* (Durham & London: Duke UP, 1997), pp. 485–505 (p. 486).

15    Ken Plummer, 'Speaking its Name: Inventing a Gay and Lesbian Studies', in Ken Plummer (ed.), *Modern Homosexualities: Fragments of Lesbian and Gay Experience* (London: Routledge, 1992), p. 17.

16    From 'Stony Grey Soil,' in Patrick Kavanagh, *Collected Poems* (New York: The Devin-Adair Company, 1964), p. 82.^

17    For a fuller discussion of Catholicism and homosexuality in Ó Searcaigh's work, see Lillis Ó Laoire's 'Dearg Dobhogtha Cháin/The Indelible Mark of Cain: Sexual Dissidence in the Poetry of Cathal Ó Searcaigh' in *Sex, Nation, and Dissent in Irish Writing* (ed. Éibhear Walshe), Cork University Press, Cork, 1997, pp. 221–34.

18    Richard Rambuss, 'Pleasure and Devotion: The Body of Jesus and Seventeenth-Century Religious Lyric,' in *Queering the Renaissance* (ed. Jonathan Goldberg), Duke University Press, Durham and London, 1994, pp. 253–279.

19    Ibid., p. 260.

20    Ibid., p. 269.

21    Ibid., p. 274. The full quote reads, 'The rhapsodic pinings of Donne, Crashaw, Herbert, and Trelerne for union with Christ are, among other things a form of love poetry written by men that revels in its desire for the male body of Jesus, "that beauteous form," rendered by turns penetrable and penetrating, ravished and ravishing. And as such, the verse of these poets is full of queer excitations to pleasure and devotion'.

22    Unless otherwise stated, quotes are from an unpublished interview which I conducted with the poet in April 1998.

23    Ó Searcaigh is now rather embarrassed by this early collection, which he considers juvenilia; he jokes that although the book is called *Miontráigéide Cathrach* (*Trivial City Tragedy*), the only tragedy about it is that it was published.

24    See James Doan's essay in this volume.

Cathal reading at Irish Fest Milwaukee, Usa, 1990 (photo: Cathal Ó Searcaigh)

Cathal reading Gabriel Garcia Lorca at the Summer Palace, Kilcar, July 2000 (photo: Kate Newmann)

## (as) GORT NA GCNÁMH

## VII

Anois agus soilse beaga sochmhaidh na hoíche á lasadh i dtithe
    teaghlaigh
i bhFána Bhuí, ar an Cheathrúin, i gCaiseal na gCorr is beag
    nach mbriseann mo chroí
le cumhaidh; ach seo mé ag piocadh liom ó dhruil go druil, síos
    agus aníos go tostach
ag coinneáil m'airde ar rithim bhuile na spáide. Mothaím
    trom torrach
leis an tocht atá á iompar agam gach uile lá beo, tocht dorcha
    dochiallach
ag lorg urlabhra. Ba mhór an méadú misnigh domh dá
    bhféadfainn
an brú seo a gineadh i mbroinn m'aigne a ionchollú
    i mbriathra, a thabhairt slán.
Ach nuair a fhosclaím mo bhéal lena shaolú, lena scaoileadh
    saor, i dtólamh
théid sé i bhfostú i mo sceadamán, stiúcann sé
    ar mo theangaidh,
agus cha saolaítear ach marbhghin gan mhothú agus théid sé
    i dtalamh
anseo idir claí agus clasaidh, gan de chloch chuimhne os a
    chionn lena chomóradh
ach grág préacháin nó gnúsachtach madaidh nó gíog
    ó spideoigín beag fán;
ach ó shaobh an chinniúint a súil orm sílim gurb é
    sin mo dhán...

(OO 66–72)

## (from) FIELD OF BONES

### 7.

As soft lights in family houses begin to glow
in Fána Bhuí, on Ceathrúin, in Caiseal na gCorr, my heart
aches for a home but I keep on picking through drills
in silence to the spade's rhythm, weighed down by hurt
deeper and darker every day beyond expression.
Could I conceive and flesh that burden in new-born words,
what courage I would have! But when I open my mouth
to free it, it always sticks in my throat, clamps my tongue,
a still-birth between hedge and ditch with no mourners
but crows and dogs or a stray robin. Fate has narrowed
its eyes and left me dumb in the Field of Bones.

(trans. Frank Sewell)

Celia de Fréine

WHAT'S IN A LABEL?
AN APPRAISAL OF THE WORK OF CATHAL Ó SEARCAIGH

In the editor's preface to *An Bealach 'na Bhaile / Homecoming*, a dual language selection of the poetry of Cathal Ó Searcaigh, Gabriel Fitzmaurice suggests that the poet 'would appear to be a sitting duck for feminist censure, and not without reason' (*ABB* p. x). I am intrigued. What is feminist censure? What is a feminist? Am I one? Whether I am or not, I am impressed by the work of this poet, in particular his most recent publication, his second and updated dual language selected poems, *Out in the Open*.

On first reading this text, what strikes me about it is the overwhelming sense of place; how place informs the poetry; how the language changes when the poet moves from his beloved Donegal to the urban landscape of Dublin or London, and further afield to America and Kathmandu. Seán Ó Tuama writes that it is unlikely:

> that feeling for place [...] is found so deeply rooted, and so widely celebrated, in any western European culture as it is in Irish culture [...] By and large the places revered [...] are rural places.[1]

He goes on to argue that this is due to the fact that the cities and towns 'have historically been the creations and preserves of invading colonists', and due also to 'the consequent sense of alienation of the native population'. I doubt that contemporary city-dwellers like myself feel alienated from our surroundings because of past history but many may perhaps feel at odds with their urban environment because of its fast pace, the on-going self-destruction, and the ways in which this destruction impacts on our daily travails. Perhaps this is one of the reasons why I find the language in Ó Searcaigh's poetry so rooted in place, and why I am so aware of how it changes from the traditional rhythms in poems such as 'Bean an tSléibhe'/'Mountain Woman':

> Bhí féith na feola inti ach fosta féith an ghrinn
> agus in ainneoin go raibh sí mantach agus mórmhionnach
> ní raibh sí riamh gruama nó grusach linn [...]

> *She was fleshy but funny, and though*
> *she swore through the gaps in her teeth*
> *she was never gruff or gloomy with us.*

(OO pp. 22–25)

to the urban tone in poems such as 'Blues na Bealtaine'/'Bealtaine Blues':

> Ar maidin Dé Domhnaigh
> Gheibhimis na paipéirí i gcónaí:
> Tusa an *Times* is an *Tribune*
> Mise na cinn le *Page Three*;
> Is léimis iad sa leabaidh,
> Stravinsky againn ar an *Hi-fi*.
> Ach inniu, tá na paipéirí gan bhrí
> Fiú amháin *page three* [...]

> *On Sundays, we always*
> *read the papers,*
> *your* Times *and* Tribune,
> *mine with* Page Three.
> *We'd read them in bed,*
> *to the sounds of Stravinski,*
> *but today, the papers*
> *are not worth a fuck,*
> *not even* Page Three *[...]*

(OO pp. 126–129)

Ó Searcaigh's most recent collection, *Na Buachaillí Bána*, is divided into four sections. Two of these, 'Na Buachaillí Bána' and 'Scaradh', mainly contain poems of unrequited love, and poems that recall relationships and one night stands. The other remaining sections are 'Gort na gCnámh' and 'I bhFianaise na Bé'. Most of the poems from this volume have been reproduced and translated into English by Frank Sewell for Ó

Searcaigh's second dual language selected poems *Out in the Open*. The latter volume, which is what I intend to discuss in this article, comprises six sections. Part One is culled from poems in earlier collections; the long poem 'Gort na gCnámh' makes up Part Two; Part Three is a fusion of poems from 'Na Buachaillí Bána' and 'Scaradh'; Part Four is a selection from earlier collections and generally has an urban setting; Jack Kerouac, Johnny Appleseed, Narayan Shrestha, and the exotic Kathmandu are evoked in Part Five; Part Six includes, inter alia, poems from 'I bhFianaise na Bé' (in *Na Buachaillí Bána*), other earlier poems, plus poems influenced by writers such as Luigi Pirandello and Roberto Deidier.

*Out in the Open* is a significant book, not least because its translation into English brings it to a wider audience, and facilitates comparison with contemporary Irish poets who write in English. Wonderfully rich in language, themes, and characters, it is written by one of the few Irish language writers who was born, bred, and lives in the Gaeltacht, although somewhat outside the 'community', as suggested in poems such as 'An Díbeartach/The Outcast', 'Coirnéal na Sráide/Corner Boys', and 'Duine Cor/Odd Man Out'.[2] The editing and arrangement of the poems make for a breathtaking read.

Gréagóir Ó Dúill has written of the love poem 'Cor Úr/A Fresh Dimension', in *An Bealach 'na Bhaile*, that 'the landscape takes on the physical form of the beloved'.[3] This metaphor is repeated in 'Ag Faire Do Shuain'/'Watching You Sleep':

> santaím tú a thrasnú ó lochanna scuabacha do shúl
> go leargacha gréine do ghruanna [...]

> *I want to go over you from the sweeping lochs*
> *of your eyes to your sunny sloping cheeks.*
> (OO pp. 136–139)

In 'Cuisle An Chaoráin'/'Mountain Pulse', landscape becomes Muse:

> Chrom sé agus phóg sé
> plobar úscach an tsléibhe —
> cíocha silteacha Bhríde, bandia na gcríoch, Bé:

deoch a bhí lena mhian [...]

Anois nuair a labhrann sé amach
i bhfilíocht, labhrann, mar nár labhair ariamh,
go macnasach, mórchroíoch ...

as croí an tsléibhe ...

*He bent and kissed*
*the wet neck of the mountain,*
*the weeping breasts of Bríd, mountain-goddess, Muse;*
*a drink to his taste [...]*

*Now when he speaks out*
*in poetry, he speaks, as never before,*
*wildly, whole-heartedly ...*

*from the heart of the mountain ...*

(*OO* pp. 40–43)

Prem Timalsina, with Errigal in the background    Prem gardening in Min a Lea
(Photos: Cathal Ó Searcaigh)

Cathal on Kilcloney Dolmen, Ard an Ratha.
'His native airport as he flies into himself'

(Photo: Rachel Giese Brown)

Some elderly neighbours play their part in helping the poet identify his rich source of inspiration. In the opening poem 'An Tobar/The Well', Bríd, the speaker, advises the poet:

> Aimsigh do thobar féin, a chroí,
> óir tá am an anáis romhainn amach:
> Caithfear pilleadh arís ar na foinsí.

> *Find your own well, my lad,*
> *for the arid times to come.*
> *They dry up who steer clear of sources.*

(OO pp. 18–21)

He realises that in order to harvest his poetry he must:

> Umhlaigh do chrédhúil d'athartha,
> oibrigh go dúthrachtach
> ithir seo d'oidhreachta.
> Foilseoidh an fómhar do shaothar go hiomlán.
> Beidh gach gort ina dhán.

> *Bend like your fathers' fathers to land-worship*
> *and work like you were born to this heirloom.*
> *The harvest will be yours: every field a poem.*

('Umhlaigh'/'Submit', OO p. 56)

Ó Searcaigh is humbled by the dignity and richness in the life of an elderly local farmer in 'Cré na Cuimhne/Cast In Clay':

> Féach anois mé ag sléachtadh anseo roimh leathanach
> atá chomh bán leis an línéadach a leagadh sé amach

> Do theacht an tsagairt agus ar an altóir bhocht thuatach seo
> ceiliúraim le glóir an bhriathair a bheatha gan gleo [...]

> *See me now, humbled before a sheet*
> *as pale as the linen he'd lay out for the priest.*

> *Here, on this improvised altar,*
> *I celebrate through the ministry of the word*

> *his unspectacular life [...]*

(OO p. 34)

Bernard O'Donoghue celebrates the lives of similar neighbours in West Cork in his recent collection *Here Nor There*: 'this dark-dressed, nearly extinct escaper/From the nineteen-fifties Saturday night' in 'The Owls At Willie Mac's', and a sister and brother in 'Ter Conatus'.[4] O'Donoghue writes as an exile who left his native County Cork almost forty years ago. Perhaps being an academic, influenced by mainly anonymous medieval and earlier poets, the impetus for his poetry is less emotional than linguistic. In an interview after he was awarded the Whitbread Poetry Prize for his collection *Gunpowder*,[5] O'Donoghue said:

> I don't particularly want to write only about the same locale but it just happens. The place seems to be as resonant to me now as when I was young.

He believes that it is hindsight that provides the counterpoint that brings each poem into existence:

> you think yourself back into what you thought then from what you know now and these two perspectives provide the two poles that the poem operates between.[6]

Another contemporary poet who writes of place and its people is Kerry Hardie, whose first collection is entitled *A Furious Place*.[7] The 'furious place' of the title is the heart, according to the poem 'She Goes with her Brother to the Place of their Forebears':

> And I think what a furious place
> is the heart: so raw, so pure and so shameless.

Place here encompasses sea as much as it does land, both of which are often at odds with each other and, at times, at odds with the weather, as in 'Where were we, Who were we, What was the journey?':

> The ferry heaves, nudges the land back,
> pushes to sea. We turn to each other,
> butting our way into storm.

Hardie begins her collection with 'We Change The Map':

These Days I want to trace
the shape of every townland in this valley;
name families; count trees, walls, cattle, gable-ends,
smoke-soft and tender in the near blue distance.

It is a task which she undertakes purposefully. Ó Searcaigh's
response to his surroundings, however, is more immediate,
and emotional — he drinks from nature's font in order to
celebrate these surroundings and the lives of neighbours who
would otherwise be forgotten; in his case, there is no sense of
distance, no feeling of setting about a task.

In *Writing Poems*, Peter Sansom states that

> writing poetry is important to us, and personal, in a
> way that writing fiction, even the shortest of short
> stories, isn't. Perhaps the key word here is 'fiction'.
> We tend to feel that poems are true.[8]

This is an interesting statement. Is poetry true? What is truth?
Is a poem any less true because the poet changes the time,
location, character in an event, fictionalises that event,
embroiders it when crafting a poem?

Commissioned by the Letterkenny library, 'Gort na
gCnámh'/Field of Bones' (*OO* pp. 66–76) is a long poem of
seven thirteen line sections written in the first person. It tells
the harrowing tale of how a thirteen-year-old girl is raped by
her father, gives birth, smothers her child, and buries it in the
earth. More than likely, the character in question is an
archetype drawn from victims of abuse. It is a theme rarely
dealt with thoroughly until now in this country, although
many poets penned individual tributes in the wake of the
death of Ann Lovett. With typical skill, driven by an emotional
empathy few poets are capable of, Ó Searcaigh relates a similar
tragedy. The following lines show what a bleak, unrelenting,
demanding place the land can be:

> Is iomaí lá de mo chuid allais ag an áit ainniseach seo, á leasú
>    is á saibhriú;
> is iomaí deoir ghoirt atá caointe anseo agam ach cha dtig
>    a thart a shásamh.

*Many's a day*
*I sweated for this wretched place to fertilise it*
*and make it rich. Many's a tear I cried here*
*until the drought in me could not be slaked.*

(*OO*, pp 66–76)

The land has taken everything, even hope:

Anseo a chaill mé mo bhláth; anseo i nGort na
gCnámh a
    cuireadh mo dhóchas
i dtalamh [...]

*Here I was deflowered. Here in the Field of Bones*
*my hope was buried in the ground.*

(*OO*, pp 66–76)

This poem is not true in that the events portrayed were not, obviously, visited upon the poet. But perhaps he was violated in other ways — ostracised, forced to give birth to something beautiful, though terrible, something which he has had to suppress and inter. Something which has haunted him ever since:

Agus d'fhán mé anseo mar nach raibh mé ábalta
m'aghaidh
    a thabhairt orm féin
chan amháin ar an tsaol.

    *I waited unable to face myself,*
*never mind the world.*

(*OO* p. 70)

The blurb for the poetry collection *Unshed Tears/Deora Nár Caoineadh* by Áine Ní Ghlinn states that 'no other contemporary Irish poet has dealt so openly with child abuse'.[9] Certainly she and Ó Searcaigh are among the few contemporary poets who have done so in any depth. About two thirds of Ní Ghlinn's volume comprises poems on the theme of abuse. In one review, however, Victoria White complains that:

Ní Ghlinn resorts too often to the journalistic to
achieve her effect, rather than exploring the

possibilities of poetry. She does not exploit metaphor, sound or structure.

Rather than portraying an archetype, she records the experience of many different characters in poems, most of which are short, and some no less powerful on this account. The characters differ but it is the same story. White writes in the same review that:

> it is perhaps a shame that Ní Ghlinn does not give these characters a fictional life in prose, rather than giving us snapshots in poems.

In 'Gort na gCnámh/Field of Bones', Ó Searcaigh does give his character a fictional life in poetry, with metaphor, structure and sound that create snapshots of a truly miserable existence.

The advertising or 'PR' on Ní Ghlinn's book is an indication as to how publishers increasingly market their writers as though they were commodities on a supermarket shelf whose components, place of origin, and sell-by date must be listed. Do we need to know, for example, that the author is the son of a guard, the sister of a singer, or the victim of a debilitating illness? Surely the work itself should reveal as much of the author's persona and circumstances as is necessary for the reader? Surely it is up to the reader to glean what they wish from the work itself?

Part three of *Out in the Open* deals openly with the theme of homo-erotic love. Lillis Ó Laoire writes that 'homosexual love has until very recently been taboo in Ireland, although decriminalisation has created more openness in this area'.[10] Ó Searcaigh is gay, and poems in this section, which are autobiographical in tone, firmly bring him out into the open as regards his sexuality. There is, however, the danger that once a label has been applied to a writer, that writer will be pigeon-holed into one category or another, and regarded as a gay writer or a feminist writer or a writer with some other agenda, rather than regarded first and foremost as a writer.

Ó Laoire also writes that in many love poems:

> Ó Searcaigh draws upon the song poetry of the eighteenth and nineteenth centuries, which has come to be regarded as one of the great accomplishments of Irish literature.

Many songs concerned love that was unrequited or that could not be discussed openly. Male and female identity, for example, were often confused: women sang the songs of men, and vice versa. Messages were conveyed through song, veiled communication and secret contact made. According to Ó Laoire,

> Cathal Ó Searcaigh is the conscious heir of this tradition and is acutely aware of its possibilities for his poetry. That the songs may often not be gender-bound or even gender-specific has allowed him to exploit the ambiguity within the tradition and to create his own reality from it.

This would appear to be true of the poem 'Rúnsearc/Secret Love':

> Agus fiú mura dtig liom trácht ar an té atá le mo mhian,
> mura dtig liom a chuid gruaige, a shúile, a bheola a lua i gcomhrá [...]
> beidh siad anois agus i dtólamh
> ag tabhairt blais agus bolaidh do mo bhriathra.
>
> *And even if it's forbidden to refer to the one I'm after,*
> *to casually mention his eyes, his lips, his hair, [...]*
> *they will always scent and flavour my words, whatever thought*
> *I lay bare, whatever poem I concoct.*

> (*OO* pp. 92–93)

This same reason may go a long way to explaining why I am not affronted by these love poems — whether or not I am a 'feminist'.

Gabriel Fitzmaurice asks does Ó Searcaigh 'compromise women with all his talk of sex and his own pleasure'?, and answers that ultimately he thinks not. The days when sex was seen as a means to procreation only are long gone. What strikes me about these poems is not the fact that they deal unabashedly with same-sex love; it is their candour and deep emotion. Everyone wants to love and be loved, and if their journey through life involves the enjoyment of sex, so much the better. Few Irish writers, in any genre, write well about sex, regardless of their personal experience.

In 'An Ghualainn Ghortaithe/The Injured Shoulder', Ó Searcaigh describes how he lovingly dressed the wound of a young man. It is a poem in which the poet dramatically recalls — with total disregard for the danger inherent in his action — the few tender moments he spent with the object of his desire:

> Nuair a d'imigh sé, d'aimsigh mé os cionn na cathaoireach
> cuid den tseanchóiriú, bratóg bheag fhuilteach;
> ba chóir a chaitheamh sa tinidh láithreach:
> ach d'fháisc mé le mo bheola é le dúil agus le grá
> 's choinnigh ansin é ar feadh i bhfad; fuil an té a b'ansa
> liom thar chách
>
> fuil the a chroí ag deargadh mo bheola ...

> *When he left, I found in front of the chair*
> *some of the old dressing, a small bloodied rag.*
> *It should have been thrown on the fire immediately*
> *but I pressed it to my lips with love and longing*
> *and kept it there for ages; the warm blood of the one*
>
> *I love above all others darkening my lips ...*

(*OO* pp. 94–95)

But what is even more exciting about this section of poems is that not only does it draw on the traditional Irish love song for inspiration, it also draws on the love poems of the Greek poet C. P. Cavafy, in particular poems such as 'Afternoon Sun', 'Their Beginning' and 'In Despair'. In his introduction to *The Complete Poems of C. P. Cavafy*, W. H. Auden neatly summarises the Greek poet's method as follows:

> he neither bowdlerizes nor glamorizes nor giggles. The erotic world he depicts is one of casual pickups and short-lived affairs. Love, there, is rarely more than physical passion, and when tenderer emotions do exist, they are almost always one-sided. At the same time, he refuses to pretend that his memories of

moments of sensual pleasure are unhappy or spoiled by feelings of guilt. One can feel guilty about one's relation to other persons but nobody, whatever his moral convictions, can honestly regret a moment of physical pleasure.[11]

Another interesting aspect to these poems is that they form part of a journey. On first reading, some poems may appear to contradict each other: in 'Buachaill Bán' (*OO* p. 82), the poet writes that he would like to find the words in which to voice what it is like being in love with a man; in 'Spliontair/Splinters' (*OO* p. 120), he states that he and his lover weren't afraid to show to the world love that others hid; in 'Ccann Dubh Dílis/Dear Dark-Haired Love' (*OO* p. 112), he reassures his lover that he won't tell anyone about their love which is deemed to be 'on the wrong side of the gospel'. But these poems were obviously written at different times. Adrienne Rich has dated her poems from the moment she became politically aware. Most poets would, I'm sure, balk at such organisation. Whether or not Ó Searcaigh keeps such a record should prove interesting as regards future studies of his work.

In 'D'ainm/Your Name' (*OO* p. 100), the poet describes how he tried to bury the name of his lover, but that this name shot up through the dark like a seed. Perhaps it is the poet's love for other men that he was forced to suppress, and inter, like the child in 'Gort na gCnámh/Field of Bones'.

As Ó Searcaigh's poetry is tied to the land, so too is his homosexuality tied to his poetry. In 'Geasa/The Bond', the poet realises that he will never be sexually attracted to a woman. He implies that he must write about how he feels, and that his life, therefore, cannot be private, even if he wants it to be:

> is ba mhór an crá croí domh
> na geasa dubha draíochta
> a leagadh orm go síoraí
> as féith seo na filíochta.

147

*O, and it hurt so deep,*
*this black magic bond*
*placed on me forever*
*by Poetry.*

(*OO* pp. 78–81)

The decriminalisation of homosexuality may well be what sparked off poems in this section. It chronicles many brief encounters, some of which have the flavour of a holiday romance. 'Ag Na Pioctúirí Ar Na Croisbhealaí/At the Pictures on the Crossroads' (*OO* p. 104) recalls an erotic encounter that occurred twenty three years earlier; the trysts in 'Gorm/Blue' (*OO* p. 102) and 'Oíche/Night' (*OO* p. 90) happened twenty six years and eighteen years previously. 'Samhain, 1976'/November, 1976, 'Samhain', 1984'/November 1984, 'Samhain, 1994'/November, 1994 (*OO* pp. 106–111) recall the pain of relationships from these times. Perhaps these poems also recall memories buried until now. Why the poet has chosen to write about these now may well be connected to recent legislation. It may be also the onset of middle age, or any number of other factors, but most likely it is due to the poet's growing confidence in himself and courage (inherited from Cavafy and other writers) to speak or come out in the current social climate.

Many of the poems in Part Four have an urban setting; while poems in Part Five are set in America and Nepal. Were I to travel to Kathmandu, I would write about enforced polyandry, or about how girls as young as seven are consigned to a life of prostitution — not because I am a feminist but because I write about what moves me. Ó Searcaigh's brief acquaintance with sherpa Narayan Shrestha is what moved him. The resulting love poem, 'Do/For Narayan Shrestha', is about a man who, not unlike those elderly neighbours in Donegal, would have otherwise died unpraised:

Fágadh tú fuar fann folamh
ar laftán sneachta—
bláth bán an bháis ag liathadh
lí is dealramh d'áilleachta [...]

*You were left cold and emptied*
*on a bank of snow,*
*the white flower of death*
*peeling the colour from your complexion.*

(*OO* pp. 188–193)

Another poem in this section, 'Kathmandu', is a celebration of place:

le do chuid sráideacha de Saris lasánta ag luascadh mar lilíocha
    i mbog-ghaoth na tráchtála;
le do chuid sráideacha ar ar shiúil Bhúpi Sherchan [...]

*with your streets of bright Sari's swaying like lilies*
    *in a breeze of business*
*with your streets where Búpi Sherchen walked [...]*

(*OO* pp. 194–199)

The influence of Kerouac and the Beat poets is apparent in this section also. Here the poet has taken their rhythms and applied them to the rhythms of Irish.

In Part 6, the poem 'Cor na gCarachtairí/A Chorus of Characters' (*OO* p. 212) evokes the intrusive characters of Pirandello; while 'An Duibheagán/The Deep' (*OO* p. 228) is written thanks to the inspiration of Deidier. Influences and inspirations such as these provide an interesting injection into Irish language poetry. And it is this injection, and its concomitant eclecticism, that makes contemporary Irish language poets, Ó Searcaigh among them, so exciting. Ó Searcaigh's development can be observed in his individual collections, and the breadth of that development enjoyed in both of his dual-language selected works.

I do not know Ó Searcaigh as well on a personal level as critics such as Gréagóir Ó Dúill, or Lillis Ó Laoire, who have written incisively about his work. However, what I've written in this essay is my personal response to the work of one of the greatest poets working in the Irish language today. Ó Searcaigh is not ensconced in an ivory tower; nor is he removed geographically from his community, although his sexuality and his profession set him apart. He knows that the

Tollund and other men and women have lain in the soil for millions of years. But he is not preoccupied with unearthing the past and, although some poems involve the earth and what it yields, the poet consistently moves on in search of other pastures, both here and abroad. Whether the impulse be more emotional than linguistic, or at times more linguistic than emotional, whether the inspiration continues to gush forth from sean-Bhríd's/old Bríd's well, or from the peaks of Nepal, I know that his work will continue to grow. Now that his love poems are 'out in the open', it remains to be seen how his work on this theme will develop. I wait with baited breath.

## Notes

1      Seán Ó Tuama, Repossessions: Selected Essays on the Irish Literary Heritage (Cork University Press, 1995), p. 249.

2      See OO p. 48, p. 58, p. 60, respectively.

3      Gréagóir Ó Dúill, 'Cathal Ó Searcaigh: A Negotiation with Place, Community and Tradition', Poetry Ireland Review, 48 (Winter 1995), pp. 14–18 (p. 15).

4      Bernard O'Donoghue, Here Nor There (London: Chatto & Windus, 1999), p. 2 and p. 52, respectively.

5      Bernard O'Donoghue, Gunpowder (London: Chatto & Windus, 1995).

6      Bernard O'Donoghue interviewed by Penelope Dening, The Irish Times, 23. 01. 1996, p. 10.

7      Kerry Hardie, A Furious Place (Loughcrew: The Gallery Press, 1996).

8      Peter Sansom, Writing Poems (Newcastle-Upon-Tyne: Bloodaxe Books, 1994), p. 10.

9      Áine Ní Ghlinn, Unshed Tears/Deora Nár Caoineadh (Dublin: The Dedalus Press, 1996).

10    Lillis Ó Laoire, 'Dearg Dobhogtha Cháin/The Indelible Mark of Cain: Sexual Dissidence in the Poetry of Cathal Ó Searcaigh', in Sex, Nation and Dissent in Irish Writing, ed. Éibhear Walshe (Cork University Press, 1997), pp. 221–234 (p. 221).

11    The Complete Poems of C. P. Cavafy, translated by Rae Dalven with an introduction by W. H. Auden (London: The Hogarth Press, 1961), p. ix.

## (as) Is Glas na Cnoic

Anois piocaim suas Mín 'a Leá agus Mayfair
ar an mhinicíocht
mhire mhíorúilteacht amháin i m'aigne
sa *bhuzz* seo a mhothaím i mBerkley Square;
agus mé ag teacht orm féin le dearfacht
nár mhothaigh mé go dtí seo
mo *vibe* féin, mo rithim féin,
rithim bheo na beatha ag borradh agus ag *buzzáil*
i bhféitheacha mo bhriathra.

(*ABB* 206)

## (from) Faraway Hills

Now I pick up up Mín 'a Leá and Mayfair
On the same mad miraculous
Frequency in my mind
In this buzz I feel in Berkeley Square;
While I discover myself with a positiveness
I haven't already felt
My own vibe, my own rhythm
The exciting rhythm of life increasing and buzzing
In the arteries that are my words.

(trans. Lillis Ó Laoire)

Cathal with Jimmy Burke, hill farmer and shepherd in the Blue Stack Mountains, Donegal, 1985 (photo: Rachel Giese Brown)

Nobuaki Tochigi

## CATHAL Ó SEARCAIGH AND TRANSFIGURING REPRESENTATIONS OF THE NATIVE

'An Tobar'/'The Well' is the opening poem of the two editions of Cathal O'Searcaigh's selected poems with English translations, *An Bealach 'na Bhaile/Homecoming* and *Out in the Open*, both of which have expanded his audience to the English-speaking world, and increased public recognition of his poetry. The poem 'An Tobar/The Well' contrasts spring-water from a local well that gives you vital energy, and piped water from far-off hills that snakes its way to every kitchen. In the end, a wise old woman character advises the poet:

> Aimsigh do thobar féin, a chroí,
> óir tá am an anáis romhainn amach:
> Caithfear pilleadh arís ar na foinsí.

> *Find your own well, my lad,*
> *for the arid times to come.*
> *They dry up who steer clear of sources.*

> (*ABB* p. 20)

The precept is that the poet needs to seek out her/his own personal helicon which is neglected and 'hidden in bulrushes and grass' in the neighbourhood. Ó Searcaigh, commenting on the background of the poem,[1] pointed out that there was a great industrial boom in Britain in the late 1960s which affected life in Donegal; in particular, people came home from seasonal labour with a lot of money and they became wealthy enough to build new bungalows and have water pipes laid. In consequence, they began to neglect local wells. The irony is that the piped water came to the Gaeltacht from without. For Ó Searcaigh, the well is like the Irish-speaking people's indigenous culture whereas piped water signifies trans-Atlantic influences. He observes that it is of vital importance for 'a peripheral culture to raise a banner of self-identity' and, for this reason, believes that it is sad to find fast food restaurants with names like 'Smoky Joe's' or 'Sergeant Pepper's' in an area where his people have lived.

Ó Searcaigh, however, never wishes for his people's culture and language to be changeless and isolated. On the contrary, he himself has drawn from various sources to give his language fresh dimensions. It seems that his personal 'helicon' is not necessarily bound to his native place; he tries to avoid being trapped by what the reader traditionally expects from Irish poetry, while maintaining an alliance to his original well water. From the beginning, his psyche was omnivorous and bilingual, because oral Irish culture was not his only source: he educated himself in reading and writing English so that he could help his mother read letters from her husband who was a migratory worker. In addition, it was through reading English literature that he became aware of his own personal difficulties: 'there was nothing in Irish which was speaking directly to me [...] I read Whitman and Ginsberg, which began to explain my predicament as a young gay adolescent'.[2]

The young Ó Searcaigh saw a sense of liberation in English-language books: 'it was apparent from the beginning that I wasn't going to be a migrant labourer, once I discovered the second-hand bookshops on Charing Cross Road'.[3] The boy was fifteen-and-a-half years of age when he went to London for the first time, an encounter later dramatized in the poem 'Déagóir ag Driftáil/Drifting' set in 'Londain 1973':

> Caithim seal i siopaí leabhar Charing Cross Road
> ag *browse*áil i measc na m*Beats*;
> Iadsan a bhfuil *voodoo* i *vibe*anna a gcuid véarsaí,
> a chuireann mise craiceáilte
> sa chruth go bhfuil *buzz* ó gach beo agus go mbraithim
> i dtiúin leis an tsíoraíocht.

> *I hang out in the bookshops down Charing Cross Road*
> *browsing among the Beats,*
> *getting good vibes from the voodoo in their verses*
> *which crack me up and open*
> *until everything's a buzz and I feel in tune*
> *with eternity.*                    (*OO* p. 157)

Mín a Leá where Cathal lives (photo: Neil Martin)

The Beats came like a gift out of the blue to the young man who was alone and stuck in the metropolis: at the end of the poem, 'Ginsberg, Corso, and Ferlinghetti' are 'chirping in [his] pocket' like nightingales when he decides to sleep in the open in Berkeley Square. It was imperative for a man who has just come 'from hill and bog,/from small parishes of hypocrisy, from gossipy towns [...] sick-to-death of roots,/of digging in the past tense' (*OO* p. 155) to assimilate himself to the vagabond gay hipsters because, in this way, he could rid himself of obsessive bondage to his native place and prescribed sexuality.

Ó Searcaigh began as a poet in 'exile' in a big city and his first collection, *Miontraigéide Cathrach*/'a trivial city tragedy' which appeared in 1978, positioned him as a rightful successor to Máirtín Ó Direáin. The young poet followed the example of Ó Direáin, who wrote for those who had been displaced and had struggled desperately 'sa chathair fhallsa/in the deceitful city'.[4] The lines quoted below give an image of the young exile's traumatic experience in London:

Damnú orthu. ní dhéanfadsa bábántacht níos mó
ar theoiricí míofara as broinn tí chuntais. Go hifreann
le gach clic -- cleaic -- ac as clóscríobhán Miss Devereaux;
le gach *jolly good delineation, pop it up to Dodo or Boremann*;
le gach luas staighre, le gach clagairt chloig, le gach *ditto*;
leo siúd go léir a d'angaigh mo mhéinse le bliain. Amárach
pillfidh mé ar Ghleann an Átha, áit a nglanfar sileadh an
anró
as m'aigne, áit a gcuirfear in iúl domh go carthanach

go gcneasaíonn goin ach nach bhfásann fionnadh ar an
cholm.

*Damn them. I'll no longer tug my forelock*
*to loathsome theories from the womb of a counting house. To hell*
*with every click — clack — ack of Miss Devereaux's typewriter;*
*with every 'jolly good delineation, pop it up to Dodo or Boreman';*
*with every moving stair, every clattering bell, every ditto;*
*with all that festered in my spirit for a year. Tomorrow*
*I'll return to Gleann an Átha where this ooze of despair will be*
*drained*
*from my mind, where I'll be told, with kindness*

*that the wound heals but that no hair grows on the scar.*

(*ABB* p. 78)

These lines represent the dislocated Irish-speaking Donegal
man's psyche in an English-speaking milieu; the narrator's
experience is constructed in Irish, his mother tongue, while the
details are bound to be expressed in fragmented English
phrases. Business people's unceremonious, snobbish
utterances aggravate the narrator's psychological stress, and
the whole passage literally imitates the narrator's anxious
situation or position of being surrounded by tacitly menacing
language. As a result, the interferential use of English, which
breaks the linguistic purity, does open up, however, a new
possibility for the Irish language poem. By doing so, Ó
Searcaigh finds a way to express the 'native' speaker's mind
faithfully. And also, he learns how to redress the stereotype (of
the Gael), as he does in 'Cainteoir Dúchais/Native Speaker'
(*OO* p. 134) whose narrator, an Irish-speaker living in a flat in
London, coins verbs like 'a *hoover*eáil' and 'a *jeyes-fluide*áil'

from English brand names, and goes out 'a *chruise*áil'/cruising, which indicates that the speaker is also gay.

Thus, Ó Searcaigh's dislocated 'native' narrators may dissatisfy those who have only a stereotypical image of Irish people, mostly found in the world of picture postcards. Not appearing 'authentic' enough or, rather, conforming to the common stereotype, the narrators of certain Ó Searcaigh poems may even cause some readers discomfort. Such reactions can be compared to what Rey Chow, a Chinese Academic, calls 'the familiarly ironic scenarios of anthropology' which sometimes arise, for example, when Western anthropologists encounter what they perceive as the anomaly of 'inauthentic' natives who appear to them to 'have gone "civilized" or who, like the anthropologists themselves, have taken up the active task of shaping their own culture'.[5] Chow further underscores the predicament which an 'inauthentic' native can cause to anthropologists:

> Margaret Mead, for instance, found the interest of certain Arapesh Indians (from Highland New Guinea) in cultural influences other than their own 'annoying' since, as James Clifford puts it, 'their culture collecting complied hers'. Similarly, Claude Lévi-Strauss, doing his 'fieldwork' in New York on American ethnology, was affected by the sight, in the New York Public Library reading room where he was doing research for his *Elementary Structure of Kinship*, of a feathered Indian with a Parker pen.[6]

In this context, Ó Searcaigh's Donegal narrators in London, doing office work and speaking their native language interlarded with acquired English words, can be seen as 'inauthentic' natives. In other words, Ó Searcaigh's natives are no longer merely objects to be watched; they themselves are the ones who watch — from an urban as well as a rural perspective. Their cultural/linguistic background can be seen in two mirrors, that of the country and of the metropolis, the one held up to the other. Or rather, it is as if what emerges from these poems is a doubly exposed picture or pattern of images in which you can see Donegal through a London cityscape and vice versa.

This dual perspective can be seen, for example, in the following lines from 'Cór na Síog' / 'The Fairy Reel':

Tuirlingím den Tube i dTottenham Court Road
agus caithim seal ag spásáil thart i Soho
ón Chearnóg go Carnaby Street. Tá'n áit seo Uasal;
i bhfad Éireann níos uaisle ná mar atá Coillidh Phrochlais.
Anseo tá na síoga ag *cruise*áil sa chlapsholas.
Tá siad tagtha amach as liosanna na heagla, as rathanna an uaignis.

*I get off the Tube at Tottenham Court Road*
*where I wander around Soho from the Square*
*to Carnaby Street. This place is enchanting,*
*so much more than the hunting of Prochlas Wood.*
*Here, the fairies come out from fear's ring-forts*
*and the raths of loneliness to cruise the waves of twilight.*

(*OO* p. 162)

*Daoine maithe*/good people can transcend borders: the fairies 'cruising' in London's city centre are just as dusky and energetic as those in Prochlas Wood in remote Donegal. Ó Searcaigh, who has said half-jocularly that 'my mother made the fairies so real that they were no different from the neighbours to me: maybe that's why I became a fairy',[7] has his creatures frolic through London streets; along the way, he makes the best use of the double meaning of 'síog'/fairy. 'Cór na Síog' is the title of a traditional Irish tune commonly played for a dance (of the same name) which is very popular amongst little girls in green dresses and ringletted hair.[8] The tune is so common at céilí dances that it has almost become as much of a stereotype as the fairy-like image of those little dancers. Ó Searcaigh juxtaposes this stereotype with another stereotype, the image of the gay. With these two-fold images, he rejuvenates fairy-lore into a vehicle which accommodates homosexuality.

Unlike his hero Ó Direáin, whom he calls 'an fuascailteoir/the emancipator' in his poem by that name (*ABB* p. 186), Ó Searcaigh went back to his native townland in Donegal to settle down and, in doing so, rejected or abandoned the approved formula of literary 'exile'. Both poets are excellent portraitists in words, but their styles are very different.

158

Whereas Ó Direáin's Inishmore and its people are elevated to an enchanted and unreachable realm —

> Maireann a gcuimhne fós i m'aigne:
> Báiníní bána is léinte geala [...]
>
> *Their memory lives in my mind:*
> *White bawneen coats and gleaming shirts [...]*[9]

— those country people who inhabit Ó Searcaigh's poems are more like flesh and blood. They are wise, talk like ordinary people, and even keep an eye on the welfare administration. One such portrait by Ó Searcaigh is the notable poem 'Fiacha An tSolais/The ESB Bill' (*ABB* p. 121) in which a man from the Electricity Supply Board comes to a slated cabin to disconnect the electricity supply. The resident of this cabin had been found dead after a life of alcoholism. The poem conveys the *absence* of a man and, in the end, the reader is informed through the ESB man's sobering comment that, even in the Arcadia of remote Ireland, 'tá'n bás [...] dálta gearradh cumhachta/death is like being cut off by the ESB'.

Having migrated back to the place of his 'roots', Ó Searcaigh set himself a task of cultivating 'every field into a poem/gach gort ina dhán' (*OO* p. 56). It was in February 1983 that he wrote 'Cor Úr/A Fresh Dimension', which opens the collection *Súile Shuibhne*. This poem marks a renewed relationship between the poet and his beloved landscape. Lillis Ó Laoire remarks that 'the landscape for Ó Searcaigh is at once his long lost lover welcoming him home after years of absence and a sanctuary which gives meaning to his existence and his poetry'.[10] Calling the topography by its vernacular placenames, the poet summons up the *genius loci*. The poem closes with a scene of union:

> Ó ná ceadaigh domh imeacht arís ar fán:
> clutharaigh anseo mé idir chabhsaí geala do chos,
> deonaigh cor úr a chur i mo dhán.
> *Oh! don't let me stray again:*
> *Shelter me here between the bright causeway of your legs,*
> *add a fresh dimension to my poem.*

> (*ABB* p. 86)

The poem provides a superb example of how sensual 'dinnseanchas' or topography can be, but that is not all. Ó Searcaigh is also sensitive to what is lost in the English translation. The poet himself has helped me read the last line, remarking that besides 'dimension', 'cor' can mean 'a twist' and 'mo dhán' can mean 'my destiny' as well as 'my poem'. So, the poet went on, the line can mean 'permit me to put a new twist in my poem/destiny'. With this comment, we realize that the original line asserts that writing poetry is at one with the poet's life. Ó Searcaigh is happy to read the field as the poetry book or 'duanaire' of his people, and he takes it upon himself to be the mouthpiece of the place and its people because, he writes, 'anseo braithim go bhfuil éifeacht i bhfilíocht/here I feel the worth of poetry' (*ABB* p. 96).

However, Ó Searcaigh has to confront a problem: the fact that the language and culture to which he belongs are in a critical situation. 'Caoineadh/Lament' follows a convention associated, for example, with 'Caoineadh Airt Uí Laoghaire/The Lament for Art Ó Laoghaire', a convention in which the poet expresses both private mourning and public lamentation simultaneously. Remembering childhood grief concerning a pet ewe which was trapped on a ledge and tortured to death by predator crows,[11] the poet reflects on the present situation of the Irish language:

> Inniu tá mo Theangaidh ag saothrú an bháis.
> Ansacht na bhfilí -- teangaigh ár n-aithreacha
> Gafa i gcreagacha crochta na Faillí
> Is gan ionainn í a tharrtháil le dásacht.

> *To-day it's my language that's in its throes,*
> *The poets' passion, my mothers' fathers'*
> *Mothers' language, abandoned and trapped*
> *On a fatal ledge that we won't attempt.*

(*ABB* p. 208)

This is unmistakably a lament for a dying language, but it is not that Ó Searcaigh is observing the last glow of Irish. Paradoxically enough, the poet is witnessing the survival of the Irish language by being present at its death. To put it differently, Ó Searcaigh gives the dying language a new energy to survive by means of using it in his lament.

As we have seen, Ó Searcaigh has tried to rectify stereotypical images of the Irish language and its native speakers. His job as a 'rooted' poet based in his native townland is to be a witness of what is happening to his language, people, and place. To cite Rey Chow's view of the native again, the poet in the passage quoted above can be seen not as a 'native-as-subject' but a 'native' who has 'the ability to look'. Chow maintains that the native 'needs to be rethought as that which bears witness to its own demolition — in a form which is at once image and gaze, but a gaze that exceeds the moment of colonization'.[12] Actually, the native poets have long borne witness to the decline of the Irish language. The traditional Gaelic community and its language were already threatened when, in the late 18th century, Eibhlín Dhubh Ní Chonaill lamented for her husband Art Ó Laoghaire, who had been murdered by a colonizer. Ironically enough, the language is revitalized all the more as the widow's grief reaches its highest, and ultimate, point:

> is ar do chroí atá mo chumha
> ná leigheasfadh Cúige Mumhan
> ná Gaibhne Oileán na bhFionn.

> *Your grief upon my heart*
> *all Munster couldn't cure,*
> *nor the smiths of Oileán na bhFionn.*[13]

So, Ó Searcaigh, like his predecessors, witnesses the transformation, rather than the death in the literal sense, of the Irish language.

Some statistical figures show that the Irish language as a day-to-day language is slowly dying; on the other hand, the same language has proved that it can go beyond the boundaries of Irish-speaking areas, as is shown in the restored popularity of Irish in education, traditional music, and mass media since the late 1980s. Poets such as Nuala Ní Dhomhnaill and Cathal Ó Searcaigh, leading agents of this cultural ferment, seem to be in step with the liberal climate of Irish society in the 1990s — a decade in which there has been heated public debate of issues such as abortion, divorce, and the decriminalization of homosexual practice. Within this context, the two poets are considered not only of importance as fine word-smiths but also as influential advocates for women and gay people who are not necessarily fluent Irish-speakers. In addition, their bilingual collections of poems have been enthusiastically received in the English-speaking world; furthermore, Ní Dhomhnaill's selected poems was published in Japan with Japanse translations and Ó Searcaigh's selected poems is available in French as well. The community of the 'dying' language has paradoxically expanded to create a new and unexpected audience.

Cathal with Irish language poets Gabriel Rosenstock and Michael Davitt at Clondalkin, Dublin, 1983 (Photo: Michael Davitt)

In the case of Ó Searcaigh, his resilient stance toward the language has helped him gain this new audience. His imagination is flexible in that it can modify existing forms or themes — indigenous or not — for his poems. As we have seen, he is as much at home with the Beat poets as he is with fairy-lore. He is open and forward-thinking in 'translating', imitating or adapting whatever will draw out a previously unknown facet of his poetry. For instance, he employs long lines in poems such as 'Déagóir Ag *Drift*áil/Drifting' (*OO* p. 152) and 'Do Jack Kerouac/For Jack Kerouac' (*ABB* p. 188), whose style reminds the reader of Whitman or Ginsberg. Indeed Declan Kiberd notes a powerful American impact on Irish-language poets, stating, for example, that 'Davitt and Rosenstock share with Ginsberg and Corso a love of the list',[14] but, unlike Ó Searcaigh, Davitt and Rosenstock did not go as far as using Whitmanian long lines. As for Ó Searcaigh's long lines, there is no evidence as to whether they were actually inspired by Whitman and the Beat poets. The long lines could be, just like those of Ciaran Carson, inspired by the musical unit of a reel or by 'sean nós'/traditional Irish (literally, 'old style') singing. However, what we do know is that Whitman and the Beat poets are among Ó Searcaigh's favourites, and the fact that they are poetically congenial, and useful to him as models, is unmistakable. For example, he uses an applied version of the long-line form in a recent poem, 'Kathmandu', where the setting is based on his visit to Nepal, and the breath of his poetic voice seems freer:

> Ó a Khathmandu, a strainséir dhuibh, a Sadhu fhiáin an tsléibhe,
> bhuail mé leat aréir i mbeár buile na hoíche
> anois siúlann tú isteach i mo dhán
> suíonn tú síos ag béile bocht seo an bhriathar
> le do chlapsholas cnocach
> a thiteann mar chleite [...]

> *O Kathmandu dark stranger wild Sadhu of the mountain*
> *I met you last night in a rowdy night-club*
> *now you stroll into my poem*
> *you sit down at this poor altar of the word*
> *with your mountain dusk*
> *that falls like a feather [...]*

(*OO* p. 194)

The lines hereafter continue to celebrate the Kathmandu before the poet's mind's eye, making use of a Ginsbergian list with 'le do/with your ...'.

Ó Searcaigh is indeed a child of a post-Beat culture, but his poetics follows the learning process of oral culture: you are given a version in the first place, then practice it, and finally you present your own. This is how Ó Searcaigh digests the works of Kerouac and Ginsberg, exploiting positively the poetic forms provided, in order to localize them. Besides absorbing the poetic heritage of the Beat Generation, Ó Searcaigh (with apparent ease) composes haikus, and sings along with the blues in vernacular, using bilingual rhymes. It would be appropriate to say that he makes his own versions, learning from various forms that are open to everybody; Blues and Haiku, together with the literary styles associated with the Beats, are 'free-to-use' forms in the public domain of contemporary popular culture. Ó Searcaigh updates the forms and reinforces the whole frame of values by making modifications. There is no authoritative centre nor suppression caused by the expansion of the universal in this model of Ó Searcaigh's poetics. Instead, there are different versions and modified forms which echo one another, and which make up a web of inter-relationships. This model will grant us an alternative view of the 'inauthentic native', because we can find in Ó Searcaigh an 'inauthentic' native poet who is free to make his own versions of different kinds of songs and poems — Irish, American, and even Japanese.[15] By doing so, Ó Searcaigh remains 'authentic' to oral culture, and makes the best use of his people's indigenous ways.

Notes

1    From an interview I conducted with Ó Searcaigh in December 1996. Unless otherwise indicated, references hereafter to the poet's comments and explications stem from this occasion. I am grateful to Mr. Ó Searcaigh for his time and help.
2    Victoria White, 'Gay love as Gaeilge', *The Irish Times*, 1 March 1996, p. 11.

3   Djinn Gallagher, 'Irish, Gifted and Gay', *The Tribune Magazine*, 15 September 1996, p. 12.

4   See Máirtín Ó Direáin, 'Ár Ré Dhearóil/Our Wretched Era', in *Selected Poems/Tacar Dánta*, trans. Tomás Mac Síomóin and Douglas Sealy (Newbridge, Co. Kildare: The Goldsmith Press, 1984), p. 74.

5   Rey Chow, *Writing Diaspora: Tactics of Intervention in Contemporary Cultural Studies*, (Indianapolis: Indiana U. P., 1993), p. 28.

6   Chow, *Writing Diaspora*, p. 28.

7   Victoria White, 'Gay love as Gaeilge', *The Irish Times*, 1 March 1996, p. 11.

8   I owe Tom Sherlock for information about the tune 'Cór na Síog' and its popularity.

9   Ó Direáin, 'Cuimhní Cinn/Memories', in *Selected Poems/Tacar Dánta*, p. 6.

10  Lillis Ó Laoire, 'Introduction: A Yellow Spot on the Snow', *Homecoming/An Bealach 'na Bhaile*, pp. 13 40 (p. 34).

11  Formerly, in the Irish tradition, 'an préachán mór'/the big crow was a euphemism for England. Editor's note.

12  Chow, *Writing Diaspora*, p. 51.

13  Eibhlín Dhubh Ní Chonaill, 'Caoineadh Art Uí Laoghaire/The Lament for Art Ó Laoghaire', in *An Duanaire 1600–1900/Poems of the Dispossessed*, ed. by Séan Ó Tuama, with translations by Thomas Kinsella (Dublin: The Dolmen Press, 1981), pp. 198–219 (218–219).

14  Declan Kiberd, Introduction, *An Crann Faoi Bhláth/The Flowering Tree*, ed. by Kiberd, D. and G. Fitzmaurice (Dublin: Wolfhound Press, 1991), pp. xi–xlii (p. xl).

15  What he does can be compared with the technique of 'sampling' in modern music or with the production of variant 'cover versions' — to reapply a phrase which Frank Sewell has used in the context of translation (*OO* p. 15).

## (as) AN LILÍ BHÁNDEARG

An brú atá ormsa le mé féin a chur in iúl faoi scáth na bhfocal;
    níl aon ghá ag an lilí
lena leithéidí. Ní theastaíonn ealaín na bhfocal uaithi le í féin
    a nochtadh, a chur in aithne.
Is leor léithe a bheith mar atá sí, socair, suaimhneach, seasta,
    ansiúd sa tsoitheach chré.
Í fein a deir sí agus deir sí sin go foirfe, lena crot, lena cineáltas
    lena cumhracht, lena ciúnas.
Má shiúlaim róchóngarach dithe cuirim ar crith í, ar tinneall.
    Mothú ar fad atá inti
agus í ag breathnú agus ag braistint, ag ceiliúradh na beatha
    le niamh dhearg a hanama.
An é go bhfuil mé gafa i gciorcal draíochta an bhlátha seo, go bhfuil
    ciapóga ag teacht orm?
Ní hé go dteastaíonn uaim a bheith i mo lilí, cé go mbeinn sásta
    leis an chinniúint sin
in cé bith ioncholnú eile atá i ndán domh sna saoltaí romham amach.
    Níl uaim i láthair na huaire
ach a bheith chomh mór i dtiúin le mo nádúr daonna is atá
    an lilí seo lena dúchas lilíoch.
Níl uaim ach a bheith chomh mór i mo dhuine agus atá an lilí
    ina lilí - an lilí bhándearg.

(OO 238)

## (from) THE PINK LILY

What force I feel to drive my green self
through a fuse of words, the lily has long
mastered. She needs no more art than nature
to declare her genius. Enough for her to stay
put and placid in her clay vase, her own
fervent prayer in shape and sort; scent
and silence. If I step too near, she tenses.
Trembles. All feeling. Watching. Waiting.
Singing life with the tongues of her lustre-red soul.
Has this flower overpowered me? No.
Even though I'd be happy with that incarnation
in some future life, all I want now
is to be as human as the lily is *lilium*,
as much myself as that lily, in the pink.

(trans. Frank Sewell)

Brian Ó Conchubhair

## CATHAL Ó SEARCAIGH: TEIP AGUS TÉAGAR NA TEANGA / FALLING DOWN AND FALLING BACK ON LANGUAGE

Ireland's post-Revival discourse allotted the indigenous language and its literary traditions a highly privileged site in the emerging socio-political narrative. This position allowed the new cultural and political elite to emphasise positions and attitudes which served contemporary political and cultural requirements. In the process, this elite, both within and outside the language movement, inscribed a rigid and dogmatic image of the Irish language on the new state's cultural consciousness. The French philosopher Paul Ricoeur describes how a socio-political imaginary discourse 'serves to uncritically vindicate established political powers. In such instances, the symbols of a community become fixed and fetishized; they serve as lies'.[1] Only in recent decades has the fabrication of this cultural construct undergone a thorough interrogation. The *Innti* group and, in particular, Cathal Ó Searcaigh's creative engagement with the language and its traditions reveal the distortion and dissimulation which Irish suffered in the post-Revival discourse. In his poetry, Ó Searcaigh engages with the illusions, distortions and ideological falsehoods which Richard Kearney sees as deriving from narrative emplotment emanating from a desire for a homogeneous experience, order and unity.[2] This article examines how Cathal Ó Searcaigh challenges and subverts the homogeneous aspect of language and tradition as ordained in the post-Revival narrative in order to create space for alternatives and diversity. Perversely, therefore, it is a homosexual, Irish-language poet, Ó Searcaigh, who ruptures the nation State's homogeneous cultural paradigm by introducing a heterogeneous cultural narrative.

As a result of the Easter Rebellion of 1916 and the War of Independence in 1921, the Irish Free State came into existence on 6 December 1922. It followed the sporting, cultural, literary and linguistic revivals of the late nineteenth and early twentieth century. The new government, legitimized by the Anglo-Irish Treaty, perpetuated the legal and political structures inherited from English rule prior to independence. Same-gender relationships had been considered a crime within this inherited legal system since 1540, when it was legislated against as part of King Henry VIII's efforts to exert his control over Tudor Ireland.[3] The homosexual and bisexual scandals in 1880s England, the most famous being the trial of the Irish author Oscar Wilde, led to the 1885 Labouchere Amendment, which furthered this early measure.[4] The Irish Free State's main social dilemma concerned the expression of a distinctive culture which was Catholic, Irish and Gaelic. These characteristics epitomised a nation frantically attempting to establish its authenticity by opposing everything espoused by its former colonial master. For many in Ireland, English homosexual scandal signified a wider moral corruption. The new State imagined the ideal Irish citizen as a poor Irish-speaking peasant who worked the land on the west coast of Ireland, content with her/his life and finding comfort in the Catholic faith, in Irish culture and in the new political independence. The result: a state which defined itself in dogmatic Catholic terms in an attempt to be the opposite of low, 'immoral' English culture. Church and State solidarity on the homosexual issue ensured the prohibition of homosexuality in all spheres of society. This decolonising movement cemented the suppression of homosexuality:

Post-colonial countries like Ireland have particular difficulty with the real presence of the homoerotic. Colonialism itself generates a gendered power relationship and, inevitably, casts the colonising power as masculine and dominant and the colonised as feminine and passive. One of the consequences of this resistance to the imperial was an increased unease with the shifting and 'unstable' nature of sexual difference, and so a narrowing of gender hierarchies ensues. In Irish cultural discourse silencing sexual difference became imperative because of a supposed link between homosexuality and enfeebled, 'feminised' masculinity. The post-colonial struggle to escape the influence of the colonising power became a struggle to escape the gendered relationship of male coloniser to female colonised. Therefore the post-colonial culture could not permit any public, ideological acknowledgement of the actuality of the sexually 'other'... For a nation 'coming of age,' the lesbian and gay sensibility must be edited out, shut up.[5]

The new Ireland was supposedly populated with multiple local organic communities living in Catholic bliss. It was an Ireland barely tolerant of overt romance. Marriages, particularly in rural areas, were arranged on the basis of social class and often viewed as financial transactions. No space for homosexuality existed. Extreme censorship in Ireland in the 'twenties and 'thirties smothered all sexual reference regardless of orientation. De Valera, as the Irish President, drafted *Bunreacht na hÉireann*, the 1937 constitution, and it received Catholic hierarchy approval before its presentation to *An tOireachtas* (the upper and lower houses of the Irish assembly). Catholic Church support was vital to ensure Fianna Fáil's respectability as a political party recently emerged from the anti-treaty faction which had lost the Civil War. National newspapers adhered to Church teaching and guidelines in all aspects of journalism.[6] Ireland's social and intellectual isolation from mainland Europe continued up to and during World War II, in which the State remained officially neutral. This combination of strict censorship, the interdependence of Church and State and the absence of a challenging external European influence led to an Ireland in the 'forties and 'fifties which was largely insular, negative, defeatist and suspicious of outside influence. However, the structures of Church and State which for so long preserved a hermetic seal repressing sexuality and intellectual debate fractured once challenged. The international cultural revolution of the 60's hit Ireland in the early 'seventies and, to a large extent, the cultural boom of the late 'eighties and 'nineties is its offspring. The 'sixties, with its stress on the local, the organic and the natural, brought new life and respect to the Irish language and its culture.

All political parties in the new State extolled the revival and cultivation of the Irish language. The concept that a distinct, indigenous, pure and implicitly unBritish essence could be accessed through the language drove this agenda.

Paradoxically, the compulsory teaching of Irish in schools, its requirement for employment, a hypocritical political attitude and the absence of an effective methodology resulted in frustration and resentment towards the language in large sections of the public. In addition, emigration ravaged the pool of native speakers and exposed the culture of hypocrisy.[7] Within the cultural and literary world of the Irish language the most obvious effects of the rebel decade was the emergence of the *Innti* group, comprising a number of undergraduate students at University College Cork studying Irish under Professor Seán Ó Tuama. The group's interest and explorations in poetry resulted in the publication [of *Innti*], the title of which now identifies the literary movement. Today the journal *Innti* ranks among the top Irish literary journals in either language.[8]

Characterising this group and divorcing them from the previous generation of poets is their liberal attitude to a number of sacred cows: sex, language, politics and love. For this group of young, rebellious hippies, poetry is not all introspection, depression, alienation, existentialism and seriousness, as it had been for Ó Ríordáin, Ó Direáin, Mac an tSaoi and Ó Tuairisc.[9] The *Innti* writers envision poetry as a public art form that is funny, shocking and relevant. Their poetry is open to a diversity of influences ranging from the Beat poets, Rock and Roll, Zen Buddhism, Hinduism, Japanese haiku as well as the native Irish traditions. The original members were Michael Davitt, Gabriel Rosenstock, Nuala Ní Dhomhnaill and Liam Ó Muirthile.[10] Poetry workshops in the College were also attended by Cathal Ó Searcaigh, a student of French, Russian and Irish at the National Institute of Higher Education (now the University of Limerick) on the outskirts of Limerick city.

Language

For Cathal Ó Searcaigh, the failure of the Irish language (which is his first and native language) to verbalise his sexual orientation, and the absence of a homosexual strand within his tradition, provide the dynamic for much of his poetry. In the following discussion issues of language and tradition are interrogated in order to comprehend how Ó Searcaigh creatively engages with these issues, and what strategies he adopts to combat the obstacles they pose to him. Ó Searcaigh's language is the Donegal dialect of the Irish language.[11] Within the sociolinguistic world of Irish, the Ulster or Donegal dialect is perceived, unjustly, as difficult and 'inferior' to either the Munster or Connaught dialects. The Munster dialect dominated as the literary language in the early decades of the twentieth century, while the Connaught dialect became assertive as a literary mode from the middle of the century onwards. The Ulster dialect, despite fine individual writers (the Mac Grianna brothers, Tarlach Ó hUid, Breandán Ó Doibhlinn and Pádraig Ó Siadhail), has never assumed a dominant literary position. Lillis Ó Laoire, in his invaluable introduction to the selected poems of Cathal Ó Searcaigh, sums up the situation as follows:

Cathal's family home and dog Hiúdaí (photo: Rachel Giese Brown)

The variety of Irish spoken in Donegal forms part of a linguistic continuum which stretches from Lewis (in Scotland) in the north to Cape Clear in the south (of Ireland). Donegal Irish has many similarities to Gáidhlig (the native language of Scotland). These were formerly attributed to the movements which have just been referred to, but now some scholars take the view that they are indigenous and not due to any overt Scottish influence. Whatever their origin, these affinities render Donegal Irish different in many respects from the Irish spoken further south. This, together with Donegal's marginal location, causes many southern speakers to say that they cannot understand the dialect.[12]

But if Donegal suffers from a marginal location, Ó Searcaigh was to experience linguistic and social alienation when he emigrated to England. London's gay scene of 1973 provides the backdrop for a number of poems which deal with the experiences of the poet as a young man, and his efforts to come to terms with various components of his personality: failure to communicate, cultural identity, sexuality and heritage. The dynamic of these London poems derives from his difficulties in coping with loneliness, sexual orientation and the hypocrisy of the business world, among other things. But Ó Searcaigh's predicament is more perplexing than that typically facing a member of a fragmented, uncaring society. Not alone does he face the problem of expressing himself in the manner of a deracinated twentieth-century alien, but, in addition, his language is a rural language of unlettered peasants and fishermen. It is a language of *bóithríní*/country laneways, and not the cosmopolitan information superhighway. In addition to discovering his cultural identity in the city, he also explores his sexual orientation. These two concerns are variously interlinked. To express homosexuality involved a process of naming and of giving voice in a language which the Post-revival discourse had sanctified, and the heterogeneity of which had been silenced. The process of empowering this central aspect of his personality entails language, but the language of his people fails him at multiple levels. The Irish language is (officially) alien to both the modern city and the homosexual experience. Therefore, Ó Searcaigh's alienation in the modern urban environment is compounded by a series of factors: the confusion and complication of preparing 'to come out' as a gay man, the inability of his native language to verbalise and address issues of homosexuality, and the absence of a homosexual strand within his literary and cultural tradition. In 'Mise Charlie an Scibhí'/'I am Charlie the Scivvy', he refers to the inadequacy of his language by comparing the language to himself; both are raw and inexperienced, both from rural origins, both lost and inept at dealing with the modern urban experience, and both fumble and stagger awkwardly in their futile efforts to merge with an alien environment. Both Ó Searcaigh and his language are under attack from external forces. For example, the perilous state of the Irish language is addressed in 'Caoineadh'/'Lament'. Here Ó Searcaigh compares the fate of a pet sheep trapped on a cliff ledge and petrified into motionless terror to his language:

> Chaoin mé na cuileatacha ar ucht mo mháthara
> An lá a bhásaigh Mollie - peata de sheanchaora
> Istigh i gcreagacha crochta na Beithí.
> Á cuartú a bhí muid lá marbhánta samhraidh
> Is brú anála orainn beirt ag dreasú na gcaorach
> Siar ó na hailltreacha nuair a tímid an marfach
> Sna beanna dodhreaptha. Préacháin dhubha ina scaotha
> Á hithe ina beatha gur imigh an dé deiridh aisti
> De chnead choscrach amháin is gan ionainn iarraidh
> Tharrthála a thabhairt uirthi thíos sna scealpacha.
> Ní thiocfaí mé a shásamh is an tocht ag teacht tríom;
> D'fháisc lena hucht mé is í ag cásamh mo chaill liom
> Go dtí gur chuireas an racht adaí ó íochtar mo chroí.
> D'iompair abhaile mé ansin ar a guailneacha
> Ag gealladh go ndéanfadh sí ceapairí arán préataí.
>
> Inniu tá mo Theangaidh ag saothrú an bháis.
> Ansacht na bhfilí - teangaidh ár n-aithreacha
> Gafa i gcreagacha crochta na Faillí
> Is gan ionainn í a tharrtháil le dásacht.
> Cluinim na smeachannaí deireanacha
> Is na héanacha creiche ag teacht go tapaidh,
> A ngoba craosacha réidh chun feille.
> Ó dá ligfeadh sí liú amháin gaile - liú catha
> A chuirfeadh na creachadóirí chun reatha,
> Ach seo í ag creathnú, seo í ag géilleadh;
> Níl mo mháthair anseo le mé a shuaimhniú a thuilleadh
> Is ní dhéanfaidh gealladh an phian a mhaolú.

*I cried on my mother's breast, cried sore*
*The day Mollie died, our old pet ewe*
*Trapped on a rockface up at Béithí.*
*It was sultry heat, we'd been looking for her,*
*Sweating and panting, driving sheep back*
*From the cliff-edge when we saw her attacked*
*On a ledge far down. Crows and more crows*
*Were eating at her. We heard the cries*
*But couldn't get near. She was ripped to death*
*As we suffered her terrible, wild, last breath*
*And my child's heart broke. I couldn't be calmed*
*No matter how much she tightened her arms*
*And gathered me close. I just cried on*
*Till she hushed me at last with a piggyback*
*And the promise of treats of potato-cake.*

*To-day it's my language that's in its throes,*
*The poets' passion, my mothers' fathers'*
*Mothers' language, abandoned and trapped*
*On a fatal ledge that we won't attempt.*
*She's in agony, I can hear her heave*
*And gasp and struggle as they arrive,*
*The beaked and ravenous scavengers*
*Who are never far. Oh if only anger*
*Came howling wild out of her grief,*
*If only she'd bare the teeth of her love*
*And rout the pack. But she's giving in,*
*She's quivering badly, my mother's gone.*
*And promises now won't ease the pain.*

(ABB pp. 208–09)

'Caoineadh'/'Lament' juxtaposes the Irish language and the speaker's mother. The pet sheep, Mollie, perishes on the cliffs from starvation and the attack of the scavenging crows.[13] The language, similarly, is perishing because of lack of activity, lack of usage and attack.[14] The coupling of the sheep, harmless, loyal and docile as an animal, with the Irish language is not without design. It is the sheep, symbolically mirroring the language, which thrives in the poor, rocky, underdeveloped west coast of Ireland. As a farm animal, she serves as an important commodity in the local economy as she provides wool, meat, and of course, a valuable source of income in the form of European Union subsidies for disadvantaged areas. In this poem, her value increases because she has become a family pet. The crow, on the other hand, is perceived as a useless scavenger. Within the older Irish literary tradition the crow is associated with the death of the Ulster hero, Cú Chulainn. Weak from continuous single combat, he strapped himself to a boulder and continued to accept the challenge of Queen Medb's magical warriors. They feared to challenge him in contest until a crow rested upon the shoulder of the hero and pecked at his dry blood, thus indicating that he was indeed dead. The crow, therefore, is not alone associated with death and scavenging, but also with the demise of a hero and a time of great cultural loss.

In Ó Searcaigh's poem the speaker's emotional distress is tempered by his mother's care and affection. The paradox is that while the sheep starves and is ripped to death by the marauding crows, the child's distress is alleviated by food and his mother's care. With the death of his mother and the decline of his language, what now will comfort the poet in his hour of need? Neither is his mother there to console him, nor is his language available to him as a medium in which, and through which, to express and release the inner turmoil that befalls him. At the poem's conclusion, it is clear that a promise, similar to that at the end of the first stanza, will fail to soften the pain of losing what is familiar and what is comforting. The loss recalls the mother, who fulfilled a traditional role, as the teacher of language and prime carer. Thus, it is the mother who bestows on him the gift of expression, the medium of language. This 'gealladh' (promise, pledge, undertaking) refers, on the one hand, to the potato cakes of the first stanza; on the other hand it carries undertones of token government promises and glib manifestos at election time promoting the language and heralding civil rights for Irish speakers.[15] Ironically, it is in Ó Searcaigh's poetry that Irish does give the required 'liú amháin gaile — liú catha' ('one cry of warlike valour, a war cry'). The image of the poet left alone, without his mother or his language, is a despairing image, as is the representation of the language as a dying sheep isolated on the cliff. The concept that the poet needs to shout and find a language in which to express himself parallels the idea of articulating his sexuality. Without the solace of a caring figure (who can sustain, support and espouse), the poet must find an agent by which to articulate his personality and engage the world through a premise which he comprehends.

As the child seeks a parent figure who will nurture him, the narrator seeks a competent language through which to express his dilemma, the quandary of a young homosexual. Therefore, although not central to this poem, issues of gayness, and the need to be authentic and honest to oneself and one's culture reside at a subtextual level in 'Caoineadh'/'Lament'. The affinity between asserting and affirming, between survival and fidelity both to oneself and one's culture is heard more specifically in 'An Tobar'/'The Well':

> 'Cuirfidh sé brí ionat agus beatha,'
> arsa sean-Bhríd, faghairt ina súile
> ag tabhairt babhla fíoruisce chugam
> as an tobar is glaine i nGleann an Átha.
> Tobar a coinníodh go slachtmhar
> Ó ghlúin go glúin, oidhreacht
> luachmhar an teaghlaigh
> cuachta istigh i gclúid foscaidh,
> claí cosanta ina thimpeall
> leac chumhdaigh ar a bhéal [...]

> 'Is doiligh tobar a aimsiú faoi láthair,'
> arsa Bríd, ag líonadh an bhabhla athuair.
> 'Tá siad folaithe i bhfeagacha agus i bhféar,
> tachtaithe ag caileannógach agus cuiscreach,
> ach in ainneoin na neamhairde go léir
> níor chaill siad a dhath den tseanmhianach.
> Aimsigh do thobar féin, a chroí,
> Óir tá am an anáis romhainn amach:
> Caithfear pilleadh arís ar na foinsí.'

> *'Twill put a stir in you, and life,'*
> *says old Bridget, spark in her eyes*
> *proffering a bowl of spring-water*
> *from the purest well in Gleann an Átha,*
> *a well that was tended tastily*
> *from generation to generation, the precious*
> *heritage of the household*
> *snugly sheltered in a nook,*
> *a ditch around it for protection.*
> *a flag stone on its mouth [...]*

*'Tis hard to find a well nowadays,'*
*says Bridget filling the bowl again.*
*'They're hidden in rushes and grass,*
*choked by green scum and ferns,*
*but, despite the neglect,*
*they've lost none of their true mettle.*
*Seek out your own well, my dear,*
*for the age of want is near:*
*There will have to be a going back to sources.'*

(*ABB* pp. 42–45)

While this poem may be read as addressing sociolinguistic concerns and cultural issues, its pertinence to social outcasts, and in particular to a gay audience and community, cannot and should not be underestimated. It may be viewed as an exhortation to return to sources and reappropriate entities and attitudes obscured by the dominant cultural and political elites. Nor should this quest for a return to the original sources be detained by opposition or rhetoric. The retrieval of what is true and original will energise the individual and the wider social setting: a reference to both language and society.

One note resonates throughout all the London poems: hope, no matter how faint, is always present. Hope persists even when surrounded by hobos, down-and-outs and the dregs of society. In fact, hope is discovered precisely when the narrator identifies and empathises with the vagrant street people in London, and later, the social outcasts in Donegal: the poet expresses the belief in 'Mise Charlie an Scibhí'[16] that he will overcome the confusion and awkwardness of this time and that he will master the turmoil by naming it. He is convinced that both he and his language will grow, mature and assimilate the new cultural and linguistic experience and benefit from it:

Teangaidh bhocht an tsléibhe!
I gculaith ghlas caorach
an tseantsaoil, tá sí chomh saonta
liom féin, i *slickness* na cathrach;
chomh hamscaí faoi na soilse seo
le damhsóir brógaí tairní
i *mballet* Rúiseach. Ach lá inteacht
tiocfaidh muid beirt, b'fhéidir,

Ar phéirspicíocht dár gcuid féin
a bhéarfas muinín dúinn
ár n-aghaidh a thabhairt go meanmnach
ar ár ndán; tráth a mbeidh
ár mbriathra ag teacht go hiomlán
lenár mbearta, is cuma cé chomh fada
agus a bheas muid ar fán
ónár ndomhan dúchais.

*The poor mountain Tongue!*
*Clad in old world homespun*
*She is as gullible as myself*
*In the city slickness;*
*As ungainly under these lights*
*As a hobnailed stepdancer*
*In a Russian ballet. But some day*
*perhaps we will discover*

*A perspective of our own*
*Which will give us confidence*
*To face our destiny with courage;*
*When our words will completely*
*Match our deeds, no matter*
*How far we stray*
*From our native world.*

(*ABB* pp. 204–05)

The poet's choice of words in the original emphasises his ineptitude and that of the Irish language itself to express the conflict. The poet's conflict concerns his inability to express his homosexuality. The language's dilemma concerns the incorporation of the modern urban experience. The words 'slickness' and 'ballet' appear in the original (Irish) text in English, the poet deliberately not employing the official Irish dictionary terms (*clisteacht/ábaltacht* and *bailé*). The reference to Russian ballet acts as a representation of the poet's experience. The hobnailed boots of the dancer are a familiar feature in rural farming life. Ballet is an art form which the Irish language never assimilated into its culture. It barely exists on the fringes of mainstream Irish cultural life in the English language, even in Dublin, a city which prides itself on its European multicultural heritage. The poet, however, also expresses the belief that he will overcome the confusion and awkwardness of this time and that he will master the turmoil by naming it, that the *dán* (fate/poem) of the language, and of the poet himself, will be resolved satisfactorily. He is convinced that both he, as a gay man, and his language will grow, mature and assimilate this new urban experience and benefit from it. What is of importance here is that Ó Searcaigh accepts that both he and his language will emerge with a new 'perspective'. The word for perspective in the original poem is not an English loan word as occurred in the case of 'slickness' and 'ballet', but an adaptation of an international cognate into an Irish spelling and pronunciation. This may be an indication that the future of both the language and the gay community lies in a productive assimilation and alliance with larger and non-native entities.

'Déagóir ag *Drift*áil'[17] and 'Cor na Síog'[18] are two long poems which deal with the London gay scene in the 1970s and the poet's interaction with that world. The intertwining of language and gay issues is made explicit in the latter where the narrator finds himself alone in a strange city in which neither he nor his language is at home. 'Cor na Síog' ('the Fairy Reel') is the title of a complicated traditional Irish group-dance which is common at *feiseanna* (dancing competitions).[19] 'Fairy' also serves as a derogatory term for a homosexual. This poem describes how the poet undertakes a physical and a psychological journey. Geographically, Ó Searcaigh travels across London through Willesden, Walm Lane, Finchley Park, Tottenham Court Road, Soho, and St. John's Wood. On the abstract level the poem recounts a sexual encounter of the poet's, and explores the inspiration and hope which he derives from a diversity of literary, musical and artistic sources: the beat poets, Hinduism and jazz. It deals with Ó Searcaigh's rejection of heterosexual love, and his descent into the hidden world of office workers on the Tube underground transport system.[20] The poet encounters a friend from his own district in Ireland who is 'subbing' (working on the building sites in London), and their conversation sparks the poet's imagination and recalls memories of home. In the domain of the tube, speaker and fellow countryman are united by the presumed homogeneity of the Irish national narrative. Both are emigrants, exploited 'Paddies' on the streets of London, longing for the homes of Donegal. This shared identification is exposed as a lie. Like the national narrative itself, the fellow countryman presumes that the narrator is heterosexual; and in the submerged world of the underground, the narrator chooses to pass as one of the inhabitants of the city. In the dark, the narrator can pass as one of the crowd who inhabit the city — citizens, heterosexuals, inhabitants all. This identification with his fellow compatriot is false since it relies on a lie: his compatriot's assumption that he is heterosexual. He emerges from the underground into the daylight, — honesty and authenticity — at Tottenham Court Road. Here he mingles openly with gays whom he describes in terms of the Irish fairies (from the folklore tradition) emerged from their fairy forts of love. They were banished to the fairy mounds and can only emerge at night to sing, play and roam the countryside. The poet encounters a young man on Greek Street — again the location is significant — and accompanies him home:

> Anois tá *mantra* a anála ag oibriú ionam, á mo thabhairt thar na harda,
> amach san Aoibhneas, áit a bhfuil na réaltóga ag déanamh cor na síog
> do Jazzman na Gealaí.
> Fágaim slán aige ar an Abbey Road ach féachaim ina dhiaidh go tochtach
> agus é ag imeacht uaim, ag gabháil as aithne cheana féin
> i *Samsara* na sráide, i measc Ciaróga agus Cuileoga na hoíche ...
> In Aois seo an *Kali yuga* siúlaim 'na bhaile sa tsolas
> lán dorchadas ...
>
> *His breath's mantra feels warm on me, and the odour*
> *carries me up into the sky to see the stars*
> *dance the fairy reel for the Jazzman in the moon.*
> *We say goodbye on Abbey Road, and I sadly watch him go,*
> *disappearing into the night's shadows with the Beetles and Moths*
> *...*
> *In the* Kali yuga, *I walk home in the light full of darkness.*
>
> (*OO* pp. 164–65)

This brief encounter, however, is more than a one-night stand. The casual lover is well versed in Hinduism and jazz, and he expounds his philosophy to the poet who learns eagerly. The poem concludes with the narrator walking home alone, 'In Aois seo an *Kali yuga* siúlaim 'na bhaile sa tsolas lán dorchadais .../in the Kali yuga, I walk home in the light full of darkness'. 'Cor na Síog', therefore, is a poem describing a rite of passage, a coming of age, a new sense of being and awareness. Kali is a Hindu goddess who consumes her adherents with a darkness before imbuing them with a clearer level of knowledge and understanding. She is associated with violent forces and sexuality. In popular Hinduism, she is the Mother goddess who kills demons and impersonations of evil. From an Irish-language perspective, it is interesting to note that Kali is the originator of Sanskrit. Each of the human skulls she wears on a necklace represents a letter of the Sanskrit alphabet. The reference may be read as Ó Searcaigh's arrival at a deeper understanding of himself and his sexuality through this encounter. The goddess not only imbues him with new light and understanding by dominating his body, but she bestows on him the language through which to express himself and his sexuality.[21]

'Déagóir ag *Drift*áil' is also set in London's 'seventies gay scene. The poem opposes heterosexuality and homosexuality by contrasting the narrator with a mother and child in a city park. A young soldier is an object of desire for both, but the woman's love has born fruit while the poet never can. The poet in his appeal for a window is echoing, perhaps, C. P. Cavafy. Written in 1903, 'Windows' too was written by a poet attempting to express his homosexuality.[22] Ó Searcaigh echoes Cavafy's sense of futility and entrapment resulting from involvement in failed romances and barren chastity:

> Tá an tsráid anásta seo as anáil i marbhtheas an mheán lae
> > agus í ag ardú na malacha
> I nDollis Hill lena hualach de chúraimí an tsaoil;
> > línte níocháin a clainne
> ag sileadh allais i gclúideanna salacha a colainne;
> > gearbóga gránna an bhuildéala
> ag déanamh angaidh ina haghaidh liathbhán chráite;
> > smug bhréan an bhruscair
> ag sileadh ó ghaosáin gharbhdhéanta a cuid cosán.
> > Siúlaim thairisti go tapaidh

agus léimim ar bhus atá ag gabháil go Cricklewood Broadway.

*This struggling street wheezes in the midday heat*
  *as she lumbers up the slope*
*of Dollis Hill with the worries of the world on her shoulders,*
  *her family washing-lines*
*streaming in the dirty corners of her body, ugly scabs of building sites*
  *festering in her worn anguished face,*
*filthy snotty rubbish streaming from the coarse nostrils*
  *of her alleys. I run from her sight*
*and hop on a bus to Cricklewood Broadway.*

(*OO* pp. 154–5)

The poet experiences a sense of camaraderie with his fellow immigrants from the West of Ireland, but perceives the futility of an existence which centres on pub life, abusive drinking, and life-sapping work. Ó Searcaigh's London ghettos are where wave upon wave of Irish emigrants settled over time so that they are now readily identified in the Irish imagination. Seasonal migration workers from the west of Ireland remain an isolated minority suffering from negative stereotypes in these ghettos:

[...] fir fhiáine mo chine
a bhfuil talann na dtreabh iontu go fóill
ach a chaitheann an lá ag cur troda ar thaibhsí tormasacha a n-aigne;
  ná deamhain óil a chuir deireadh lena nDóchas.
Níl mé ag iarraidh go ndéanfaí faobhar m'óige a mhaolú is a scríos
  le meirg an díomhaointis i seomra beag tais
an uaignis, i g*Kilburn* nó i d*Tufnell Park*, i *Walthamstow* nó i *Holloway*;
  i g*Cricklewood*, i g*Camden Town* nó in *Archway*.
Ní mian liom mo shaol a chaitheamh anseo leis an Uasal Uaigneas
  gan éinne ag tabhairt cuairt ar mo chroí,
Ina lámh deis tá duairceas agus díomá, ina lámh chlé tá scian fola agus Bás.
  Teastaíonn uaim tábla na féile a leagan don Áthas!
Teastaíonn uaim laethannta na seachtaine a ghléasú in éide an Aoibhnis.

*the wild men of my race who still have the tribal spirit*
  *but who spend the day fighting*
*the griping ghosts of their mind, the demon drinks*
  *that have poisoned their hope.*
*I don't want my youth blunted and ground down with rust,*
  *put to no good use in a damp lonely bedsit,*
*in Kilburn or Tufnell Park, in Walthamstow or Holloway,*
  *in Cricklewood, Camden Town or Archway.*
*I don't want to spend my life here with no-one*
  *warming to my heart but Mr Loneliness,*
*in his right hand - darkness and despair; in his left -*
  *a razor and death. I want to roll out the carpet*
*for happiness! I want to wrap my days up in joy!*

(OO pp. 156–7)

America's Beat poets — Ginsberg, Corso and Ferlinghetti — offer Ó Searcaigh, in contrast to his companions, examples of ways by which to escape from the city's hazards. These poets and eccentrics defy convention. They inspire and invigorate the narrator, both spiritually and poetically. The Beats' poetry and their philosophy transforms Ó Searcaigh's London into a lively bustling city in which he revels.

In 'Déagóir ag *Drift*áil' (literally, 'Teenager Drifting'), a cottaging episode in a Picadilly cubicle temporarily fulfils the narrator's physical needs, but it is no more than an ephemeral encounter. The influence and presence of the Beat poets is what endures, however. Inspired by their example the narrator discerns that regardless of exigency, necessity or inconvenience the Beat poetry convinces him that he can persevere, endure and possibly triumph:

  ach tá mo thriúr féin liomsa
ag ceiliúr i mo phóca, ag tógáil cian domh san oíche -
  Ginsberg, Corso agus Ferlinghetti.
Agus má sháraíonn orm leabaidh na hoíche a aimsiú
  dhéanfaidh siadsan mo shamhlaíocht
a shiopriú i bpluid ghleoite na spéire, mo bhrionglóidí
  a shuaimhniú ar adhairt chinn na gealaí ...

> *Still I've got three of my own*
> *chirping in my pocket, lighting up my nights -*
> *Ginsberg, Corso and Ferlinghetti;*
> > *and if I don't find a bed tonight,*
> *they will wrap my imagination*
> *in a star-spangled blanket of sky, tranquillise*
> > *my dreams on a pillow-moon ...*

(OO pp. 158–9)

Ó Searcaigh's best known poem, 'Do Jack Kerouac',[23] also pertains to the Beat poets, and represents Ó Seacaigh's victory mantra. It is a tribute to his inspiration and muse, Jack Kerouac, but it is also a victory song of survival and of return or 'homecoming'. It signifies the return of the prodigal son and his acceptance of the local with its beauty and its warts. It indicates both Ó Searcaigh's Kerouac-ising *and* Kavanagh-ising of his Donegal hinterland. No longer the stony gray soil and source of repression and depression, it is now exoticised into a Donegal version of the Beats' domain.[24]

One source of this enthusiastic hope for rejuvenation, in the poem 'Londain', is the belief that the insidious nature of the office world will be neutralised by a return to Donegal, the poet's homeplace. Ó Searcaigh does not refer to Donegal by name, but instead by a specific, local place-name, Gleann an Átha. In the original this means 'the glen/valley of the crossing point/ford', usually a point where a river is forded. Such vantage points were important as they functioned as sites of development and habitation. Rivers functioned as markers of territorial distinction, and a ford was the point at which one moved from one political domain to another, from one social and cultural grouping to another. The poet crosses more than a river, he is bridging a divide between modes of living and articulation. Again Ó Laoire's insight is helpful:

Cathal Ó Searcaigh is a poet of this place [Donegal] and this landscape. His voice gives vivid expression to his feeling of intimacy with his Gleann Átha [sic], the Valley of the Ford. This is not only a geographical location but a country of the imagination which the poet recreates in each poem. As Dante Della Terza has stated in the introduction to the work of Rocco Scotellaro, an Italian poet from Luciana with whom Ó

Searcaigh strongly identifies: 'His poetry gives us not a realistic topography, but the internal measure of space: an *espace du dedans* which is farther reaching and more telling than any geographical remoteness'. The landscape for Ó Searcaigh is at once his long lost lover welcoming him home after years of absence and a sanctuary which gives meaning to his existence and his poetry. Nevertheless the claustrophobia which is part of all small communities emerges from his verse in no uncertain terms and perhaps this serves to temper his celebratory lyricism.[25]

Ó Searcaigh does not present an idyllic romanticisation of homecoming. Fortified by the sagacity accrued in London he is aware 'go gcneasaíonn goin ach nach bhfásann fionnadh ar an cholm'[26] ('that wounds will heal, even though hair will not grow on the scar'). This concerns a gay man's ability to adapt and survive in a community which resists his vision and his culture. The hostility he encounters can be ignored and an accommodation can be reached with the community despite the fact that they do not share his values and vision; hence the wounds will heal, but regardless of this progress, the aberrant individual will always exist as queer, thus removed from the core community. This distinction is conveyed by the absence of hair on the scar; although similar to other parts of the communal body, the narrator as eccentric will stand out due to the lack of hair on the healed wound. This is an experience which can be dealt with and ignored, but never fully forgotten.[27]

The poet returns to this aspect in 'An Díbeartach'.[28] Here, he compares himself to the Biblical character Cain. Both are social outcasts and will never be fully accepted into the tribe of humanity or the local community. They are part of a tribe and as such they have a feeling of belonging and sense of place which is in stark contrast to the apathy and craving experienced by the poet in London:

> (i)
> Ní thuigeann siad an buachaill seanchríonna
> a bhíonn ag cumadh ar feadh na hoíche

thuas i gcnoic Bharr an Ghleanna.
Tá a bhfuil ar siúl aige amaideach
a deir siad thíos i dtigh an leanna --
macasamhail an mhadaidh bháin
a bhíonn ag cnaí chnámh na gealaí
i bpolláin uisce ar an bhealach.

Ach fós beidh a chuid amhrán
ina n-oileáin dúchais agus dídine
i bhfarraigí a ndorchadais.

(ii)
Ní duitse faraor
dea-fhód a dhéanamh den domasach
ná an Domhnach a chomóradh mar chách
ná grá na gcomharsan lá na cinniúna
ná muirniú mná faoi scáth an phósta
ná dea-chuideachta an tí ósta.

Duitse faraor
dearg dobhogtha Cháin
a bheith smeartha ar chlár d'éadain.

(i)
*They don't get it. The boy,*
*older than his years, versing*
*all night, away up in the glen.*
*What he's up to is daft,*
*they say down the pub,*
*like the white dog*
*baying for the bone he sees*
*in a puddle on the road - the moon.*

*And yet his songs will be*
*islands of hope and protection*
*in their mind-dark seas.*

*(ii) Not for you, it seems,*
*making the best of the badland,*
*suiting Sunday like everyone,*
*a Samaritan when you're in need,*
*loving under licence,*
*the good cheer of the pub.*

(*OO* pp. 48–49)

The home Ó Searcaigh makes for himself in Donegal, 'or the smithy of human existence in which he forges a conscience', is an environment where he connects with the land and its people. Later poems such as 'Cuisle an Chaoráin'[29] and 'Súile Shuibhne'[30] display the ease and naturalness which the poet feels in this locality. Suibhne in the Irish tradition is the madman, an outcast to all, exiled to live in the trees as a result of a dispute with a cleric. There is a sense of home and belonging in these poems which is alien to the London poems. 'An Díbeartach' makes clear that Ó Searcaigh will never be an inner member of the community, but to exist on the fringes of a community is to have a community to which one belongs, even if the relationship is of a marginal and ostracising nature. In response, Ó Searcaigh writes celebratory poems of other *éin chorr* (eccentrics) from the locality; poems such as 'Bean an tSléibhe'[31] and 'Cré na Cuimhne'[32] These poems serve to populate the poetic and imaginary landscape with individual people to whom, and of whom, Ó Searcaigh can relate. Mirroring the hobos and down-and-outs on park benches in London, the rural eccentrics of Dún na nGall/Donegal represent for Ó Searcaigh fountains of humanity in a desert otherwise parched of human concern. These individuals, despite their adherence to community values, fail to provide heirs for the land which they spent their lives cultivating, heirs who in turn would work the land and bequeath it to the next generation. Similar to the homosexual, these people are 'disgraced' in the eyes of the rural tradition which places premium value on land and inheritance. It is these marginalised members of society that Ó Searcaigh befriends and with whom he empathises. He sees value and humanity in them and, above all else, they act as examples of survival in a society often hostile to those on the fringes, those who fail a rural society's requirements.

It may be beneficial here to consider another reference to an *áth* as a crossing point into Ulster. In *Táin Bó Cúalnge*, Conall Cearnach guards the portage into Ulster for the following reason:

> 'Maith lim, a maccáin, prímsligeda in chóicid d'iarfaigid. Cia airet imthéit?' 'Téit co Áth na Foraire i Sléib Fhúait,' ar Ibar. 'Cid 'ma n-apar Áth na Foraire fris in fetar-su?' 'Rafhetar-sa omm,' bar Ibar. 'Dagláech de Ultaib bís ic foraire ocus ic forcomét and arná tíset óic *nó* echtranna i nUltu do fhúacra comraic forru, corop é in láech [sin], conairr comrac dar cend in chóicid uli. Dá ndig dano áes dána fo dímaig a Ultaib/ocus assin chóiciud, corop é conairr séta ocus maíne, dar cend aenig in chóicid dóib. Dá tí dano áes dána 'sin crích, corop é in fer [sin] bas chommairge dóib co rrosset colbo Conchobuir, corop siat a dúana-sain ocus a dréchta gabtair ar tús i nEmain ar ríchtain'.[33]

> 'Wherefore is it called "the Ford of Watching," Knowest thou?' 'Yea, I know it well,' Ibar made answer. 'A stout warrior of Ulster is on watch and on guard there every day, so that there come no strange youths into Ulster to challenge them to battle, and he is a champion to give battle in behalf of the whole province. Likewise if men of song leave the Ulstermen and the province in dudgeon, he is there to soothe them by proffering treasures and valuables, and so to save the honour of the province. Again, if the men of song enter the land, he is the man that is their surety that they win the favour of Conchobhar, so that songs and lays made for him will be the first to be sung after their arrival in Emain'.[34]

The *áth*, therefore, is more than a mere physical location: it is a crossing point of culture and integrity and allows one to move from one socio-cultural milieu to another. The crossing point, therefore, represents the completion of the journey which began with a departure from Tír Conaill (Dún na nGall/Donegal) and whose homeward leg began after an epiphany on Greek Street in London. The 'bealach 'na bhaile' (the way into home) returns Ó Searcaigh to his *áit dhúchais*, his home place, the home of his language and dialect, but with an enriched understanding and facility for that medium.

## Tradition

The preceding section looks at the manner in which the Irish language to some extent fails Ó Searcaigh and 'falls down' on him; this section considers how Ó Searcaigh approaches literary tradition as a gay man seeking to express himself. The issue of language and linguistic empowerment is central to the poetry of Ó Searcaigh. Tradition, including the application of that tradition, is also fundamental to any reading of his work. The native Irish tradition, which extends over two thousand years, was a self-contained, robust, relatively independent culture until the late eighteenth century. The late nineteenth and early twentieth century witnessed a revival and re-energizing of this tradition which suffered greatly in the intervening decades. The revival, however, constructed this tradition as exclusively heterosexual. All scholarship concerning Irish language literature and culture was conducted within a heterosexual discourse, with a few dissenting voices emerging in recent years. Some arguments suggest a homosexual relationship between the Irish chieftains and their bards/*baird* and *filí*[35] within the classical Irish tradition which existed from the tenth to the sixteenth century. Máire Mhac an tSaoi addresses this issue and her opinion is that:

> We know from Aristotle that the Celts esteemed homosexuality; so also, it would appear, did the Gaels – at least for ritual purposes. The Irish chief was wed to the sovereignty, to the Goddess under one of her many names – Éire, Banba, Fodhla; perhaps Bridget or Íte; almost certainly Macha, Emer, Medb and Gormfhlaith ... She (the Goddess) experiences this not only allegorically, but in the actual person of her priest, almost certainly a man. For the Irish poet never abandoned his supernatural role. When his verse legitimised the ruler his was a ceremonial marriage with the Goddess in her incarnation as the totem of the tribe, as, for example, a white mare. In the bardic poetry this practice is refined to a convention of romantic attachment between the ruler and the poet, in which the poet plays the role of the woman. To this convention we owe one of the most splendid dramatic apologues to be found in any language, that where

189

Eochaidh Ó hEoghusa, the late 16th century author of,
among other works, 'O'Hussey's Ode to Maguire',
speaks to his patron in the character of a wife torn
between loyalty to an absent husband and the
passionate demands of a present lover. What he
actually means is that if his present patron does not
reward him adequately he will find another who will.
In spite of this ulterior motive, or because of it, the
poem is a superb and exquisitely expressed insight
into the female mind and emotions. There are two
tempting speculations to account for O'Hussey's
explicitness in handling this convention – and it is
found not only here, but throughout his work – one,
that he was in fact an actual homosexual and two –
which I think is more probable – that he was a
genuine poet and a modern, a man of his time,
exploiting a once sacred device for kicks. Perhaps
indeed both. It may be interesting to consider
Shakespeare's homosexual sonnets in this context.[36]

When one considers this argument from a distance, it seems
quite reasonable that the love songs of the seventeenth,
eighteenth and nineteenth centuries be interpreted as texts
accessible to both homosexual and heterosexual artists. These
folk compositions came to prominence when the nobles
emigrated en masse between 1607 and 1609 to continental
Europe to maintain their social status.[37] Given that no
authenticity can be established regarding the songs' authors, as
Máire Ní hAnnracháin suggests, there is no logical reason for
positioning all of these compositions solely and dogmatically
within a heterosexual discourse.

Is é an caoineadh an genre is mó is dual do mhná agus
an t-aon chorp mór fileata a d'fhágadar againn (ach
amháin na hamhráin ghrá a gcuirtear an oiread sin
acu ina leith, cé nach féidir a bheith cinnte gur mná a
chum iad).[38]

A song such as 'Ceann Dubh Dílis',[39] while conforming to all
the requirements of a *Chanson de Jeune Fille*, reads as a same-
gender love poem as easily as a heterosexual love song. Lillis
Ó Laoire suggests in the introduction to *Bealach 'na
Bhaile/Homecoming* that:

The lyric song poetry of the eighteenth and nineteenth centuries, with its intricate vowel rhyming and sinuous grace, provide him [Ó Searcaigh] with possibilities for experimenting with theme and form. The passionate, intense simplicity of the love songs continue to inspire and delight him [...] The bare translation gives an idea of the original, even without its word music and its melody, which in the hands of a skilled traditional singer becomes a poignant statement of lost love, speaking directly from the heart. This song is a well known standard in the living repertoire of Donegal singers. The precedents set by these songs are an important resource for Ó Searcaigh, enabling him to explore this area of his emotional life in a truly personal fashion. 'Ceann Dubh Dílis'/'My Blackhaired Love' is perhaps the most obvious example of such exploration. From a lyric of the same name, Cathal adapts the song to his own experience, dealing with homosexual love, a theme which has until now seldom appeared in Irish language literature.[40]

In fact, Ó Searcaigh adopts this tradition and especially the forms, motifs and style of *na hamhráin ghrá* (the love songs) to write gay love poems, such as 'Ceann Dubh Dílis'.[41] Therefore, while conforming to all the requirements of the *Chanson de Jeune Fille*, it may be read as a same-gender love poem as easily as a heterosexual love song, as Ó Laoire suggests. Thus 'Ceann Dubh Dílis' exemplifies Ó Searcaigh's adoption of the literary, and in particular the oral, tradition to express gay issues, namely same-gender love. The poem/song adapts old motifs of *na hAmhráin Ghrá*: illicit love, vows of silence, fears of retribution, Church opposition and steadfast loyalty. This is an appropriation of older material to address contemporary, if not perennial, concerns. How, then, does tradition assist him and function in a positive manner in Ó Searcaigh's poetry? In the poem 'Laoi Chumainn',[42] Ó Searcaigh again parodies the dogmatic heterosexual interpretation of the Irish tradition by writing a love poem which centers on extended imagery of gallant feats and language associated with the heroic tales of Ireland. It is this manipulation of heroic language and phrases affiliated with romance tales that elevates this poem from a simple love lyric to a poem which is a conscious orchestration of the poet's heritage. Similarly, it is this same strategy which distinguishes 'Laoi Chumainn' from 'Ceann Dubh Dílis'. 'Ceann Dubh Dílis' represents a reclaiming of a genre. 'Laoi Chumainn' is a whole new edifice utilising the tools and resources (cultural and linguistic) of the language. It is a poem which disputes the exclusive heterosexual interpretation of the Irish tradition and through that tradition gives this poem a distinctive Irish literary flavour.

The first stanza contains the phrase 'mo laoch, an curadh caol cruaidh', which possesses a distinctive literary echo, obviously from a heroic tale. 'Cú na gCleas' refers to a heroic figure, specifically to Cú Chulainn. In the second stanza 'luan laoich' puns with 'gríos gréine', and refers to 'gleam/halo of a warrior', emphasizing the military and heroic element. The final line in the third stanza, 'a bhearnú chugam fríd plúid agus piliúr', is another echo from the tales where the hero cuts a gap (bearna) through his opponents. There is also a sexual double meaning here with which Ó Searcaigh mischievously plays. Other examples abound in the remaining stanzas, where obvious echoes and lexicon from the heroic tales are present (in Ó Searcaigh's Irish-language original, at least). In the fourth stanza, 'macaomh' and 'macghníomhartha' are archaic words from the hero tales. In the fifth stanza, the words 'tearmann' (sanctuary), 'dún daingean' (strong fortress) and 'treabha' (tribes) all sustain the heroic warlike image. The phrases 'ceithre creasa na cruinne' (the four zones/belts of the world) and 'a thiocfá i dteann is i dtreise is go mbeadh gach ball do mo bhallaibh' are clearly calcified phrases from the folk tales of ancient Ireland which survived on the western seaboard in oral form until the middle part of this century. These allusions and the reference particularly to 'Cú na gCleas' mark this text as having a close affinity to the ancient sagas. The final stanza again echoes the myths and legends with the description of the two lovers safe inside the magic circle, but aware that they will have to pay the traditional penalty of 'fiach na fola' (the penalty or debt of love). An additional archaism is the use of the word 'cluain' in the final verse.[43]

This poem is noteworthy, not alone for the occurrence of archaic locution and vocabulary but also for the literary references which enrich the text. The final lines of the first stanza and the opening lines of the second stanza bear a marked resemblance to Eibhlín Dhubh Ní Chonaill's eighteenth-century lament for her dead husband, 'Caoineadh Airt Uí Laoire'. The reference to 'do bhealach féin' comes from Mac Grianna's novel *Mo Bhealach Féin*, and is a phrase which Ó Searcaigh uses frequently in interviews and essays to describe his efforts to forge his own identity.[44] The fifth stanza contains the line, 'leis na beo agus leis na mairbh' and refers to the title of a famous short story by Máirtín Ó Cadhain. Ironic as it may seem, there appear to be allusions to the 'Lord's Prayer' and the 'Apostles' Creed' in this poem. The sense in the fourth stanza that this is the fulfilment of a prophecy is typical of the ancient Fenian and heroic tales of Middle Irish, especially the 'macghníomhartha macnais'. Ó Searcaigh's early poetry earned recognition from critics and, in particular, English-language critics because of his use of placenames and his refusal to translate placenames from their original Irish to English. The use of the human body as a physical location and the adaptation of placenames to describe limbs and bodily features is nothing new in the poetry of Ó Searcaigh but it is particularly evident in this poem.

Rather than being a repetition of an earlier poetic device, this represents an advanced and more accomplished use of the same technique. The narrator assumes a passive role and the dominance of verbal adjectives and autonomous verbs give this text a lazy exuberance. There is a sense that the narrator is in control of the situation and is almost a goddesslike figure welcoming the warrior prophesied to rescue her, which carries overtones of the *aisling* poems. The poem abounds with phrases and half-lines from *na hAmhráin Ghrá* of the seventeenth, eighteenth and nineteenth centuries.[45] A typical feature of Ó Searcaigh's poetry is the interwoven vowel sounds and consonants.[46]

It would be a mistake and an artistic injustice to Cathal Ó Searcaigh to presume that this use of a specialized lexicon and a crafted selection from an ancient word-hoard is a matter of chance or the natural talent of a native speaker. It is the product of a poetic imagination allied to a sharp and sophisticated mind. He uses ancient mythology, a rich learned lexicon, cultural motifs and modern literature to craft a love poem which happens to be homosexual. The subtext is distinctively and undeniably Irish. This tradition is, rather, the oldest, and most enduring of all the traditions on the island. In 'An Lilí Bhándearg',[47] dedicated to another wordsmith, Seán Ó Ríordáin, Ó Searcaigh captures a writer's creative tension and also the reality for many students of Irish (and other languages) who strive to live their lives through the medium of a language other than their mother tongue:

> Scuabaim an t-urlár, ním na soithí, tugaim spléachadh go tapaidh
> fríd fhoclóir an Duinnínigh;
> Caithim seanleathanaigh leathscríofa isteach i dtinidh na cisteanadh
> agus mé an t-am ar fad
> Ag cuartú na cuimhne, ag ransú na haigne, ag tóraíocht sa tsamhlaíocht,
> ag lorg briathra béal-líofa,
> Focla a bheadh beacht, braitheach, beannaithe, briathra bithbheo
> a bhéarfadh brí agus beatha
> do mo dhán, a dhéanfadh a shoiléiriú agus a thabhairt chun solais [...]

> *I brush the floor. Do the dishes. Flick through my Dinneen.*
> *Throw old half-written pages into the fire, and search*
> *the whole time through memory, mind and imagination*
> *for words flowing fast with feeling. Holy and precise words*
> *to fuse my poem with eternal worth. Words to bring it into the*
> *light.*

(*OO* pp. 236–7)

Ó Searcaigh's latest poems focus more on the wonder of everyday life and the miracle of life rather than the oppression and alienation which dominated so much of his early work. Several are located in the Himalayas where the poet undertook a climbing expedition. Extracts from his diary appeared recently in *Comhar*.[48]

In 'Cainteoir Dúchais',[49] Ó Searcaigh subverts both language and literary tradition in a humorous poem which has serious undercurrents. The Irish language poets of the pre-World War II generation (Liam S. Gógan and Piaras Béaslaí) were primarily language enthusiasts who dabbled in poetry as a cultural hobby. Much of their composition reflects this. Poems acclaiming the language, the nation's glorious past, and exhorting others to speak the language festoon periodicals of the era. Ó Searcaigh and his generation are poets first and foremost, whose literary medium happens to be Irish, a minority language. Ó Searcaigh, however, does not regard himself as a custodian of the language, even less a guardian of its purity. His poem 'Cainteoir Dúchais' would appal any old style Nationalist *Gaeilgeoir*[50] on two counts. Its extensive use of *Béarlachas* (the assimilation of English words directly into Irish and/or the use of English syntax and word order) would represent a total corruption for a traditionalist, and the whole concept of a gay native speaker of Irish lies beyond the realm of possibility, as we have seen in the Irish discourse since the Revival. The puns and loan-words, typical of the early *Innti* group, lose all context in an English-language translation just as something (usually poetry!) is lost in all translation, but even their visual contraposition in the Irish text conveys a sense of the speaker's language contamination:

> Bhí sé flat-out, a dúirt sé
> i gcaitheamh na maidine.
> Rinne sé an t-árasán a *hoover*eáil,
> na boscaí bruscair a *jeyes-fluid*eáil,
> an *loo* a *harpick*áil, an *bath* a *vim*eáil.
> Ansin rinne see an t-urlár a *flash*áil
> na fuinneoga a *windolene*áil
> agus na leapacha a *eau-de-cologne*áil.
>
> Bhí se shagáilte, a dúirt sé
> ach ina dhiaidh sin agus uile
> rachadh sé amach a *chruise*áil;
> b'fhéidir, a dúirt sé, go mbuailfeadh sé
> le boc inteacht
> a mbeadh Gaeilge aige.
>
> *He was flat-out, he said,*
> *after the morning.*
> *He had the place all hoovered,*
> *the bins jeyes-fluided,*

*the loo harpicked, the bath vimmed.*
*Then he flashed the mop over*
*the floor, windowlened the windows*
*and eau-de-cologned the beds.*

*He was shagged-out, he said,*
*but even so, he was all set*
*to go out cruising;*
*you never know, he said,*
*he might run into someone*
*with a* cúpla focal.[51]

(*OO* pp. 134–35)

The whole concept of a gay speaker of Irish, native or otherwise, is beyond the Pale of possibility in the Irish discourse since the revival — that is, prior to the arrival of Micheál Mac Liammóir, Pearse Hutchinson, Cathal Ó Searcaigh and Mícheál Ó Conghaile, who challenge this discourse and oblige it to acknowledge and engage with their writings.[52] The ability to laugh at, as well as to laugh with, are signs of Ó Searcaigh's belief in the current strength of the language. This short, witty poem challenges the exclusive heterosexual image of the native speaker, who since the revival was envisioned as an inhabitant of the western seaboard surviving by the dint of his struggle with the elements and the land. Here this stereotype is subverted by depicting the narrator, *an cainteoir dúchais*/the native speaker, in a non-traditional non-heroic role, that of an urban dweller, domestic servant, friend, homosexual. This is an open assault on the falsehood and homogeneity enshrined in the tradition during the Revival.[53]

Conclusion

One of the highpoints of *Na Buachaillí Bána* is the long poem 'Gort na gCnámh',[54] commissioned by Leitir Ceannain Public Library.[55] Its theme is a father's abusive and incestuous relationship with his daughter. Since gay issues dominate this collection, a poem focusing on incest and gender issue appears strange. When *An tOireachtas* legalised homosexuality in 1994 it was reasonable to presume that gay writers and activists after achieving constitutional and legal rights would concentrate on combating homophobic fears, resentment and uncertainty. Therefore, it may seem surprising that this poem deals with incest, another sexual taboo. What appears to be happening in the recent work of Ó Searcaigh and in the highly acclaimed short-story collection *An Fear a Phléasc*, by Mícheál Ó Conghaile, is that gay writers working in the Irish language are attempting to incorporate the gay experience within mainstream opinion by stressing the otherness of and abhorrence for sexual acts which all social groups oppose. In short, gay writers are joining the settlers inside the encircled wagons, and now are leading the attack on the wild 'savages' who attack the wagon train. To restate this in Irish terms, the writers are joining the colonists within Dublin Castle and the Pale and are advising the King's court on how best to subdue the wild Irish in the provinces.[56] It is also feasible, however, to argue that Ó Searcaigh and Ó Conghaile link homosexuals with other marginalised and victimised groups in society.

Cathal at Gortahork Technical School (photo: Cathal Ó Searcaigh)

The lonely deprived life which this teenager in 'Gort na gCnámh' endures echoes sentiments from Ó Searcaigh's entire corpus to date. A notion which appears repeatedly throughout the poetry of Ó Searcaigh is that, compared with the barbarity of certain acts within the heterosexual domain and the loneliness and frustration of chastity, gay love is a wonderful alternative. The image of gay love in his poetry, although idealised, is more appealing and genuine than the image of chaste lonely farmers and abused young women. This representation is open to many criticisms, but it may serve to counteract centuries of negatively portrayed homosexuality.[57]

Ó Searcaigh is a fine poet, amongst the finest in Ireland. He writes poetry which is rooted in the urban cosmos of the late twentieth century. This poetry is informed by a long tradition, but this tradition is a force which the poet can call upon at will; it never threatens to engulf him and obscure the unique voice which sounds in these poems. His poetry is a wonderful synthesis of a liberal, compassionate voice informed by personal experience, Irish culture and a wide array of world cultures and international writers. His language is fresh and modern. He moves from turf sod to tube station with graceful ease. Rather than the language enriching him, he enriches the language by bringing new realms of experience within its compass. Here one sees Ó Searcaigh engaging, subverting and extending the oldest vernacular tradition in Northern Europe: a tradition and language which, through the translations of Dubhghlas de hÍde and his *Amhráin Ghrá Chúige Chonnachta/Love Songs of Connacht*, inspired George Moore, Lady Augusta Gregory, W.B. Yeats and James Joyce at the turn of the century. In Ó Searcaigh one finds that same tradition furnishing inspiration and innovation to a poetic talent once again a century later. But rather than inspire creativity in English as occurred one hundred years ago, the tradition renews itself in the work of Ó Searcaigh. The circle turns and may it may well be that Ó Searcaigh's work will in turn contribute to a flowering in the English tradition of a future century. Admittedly, Eoghan Ó Tuairisc, Liam S. Gógan, Máire Mhac an tSaoi and Máirtín Ó Direáin have mined the tradition and its older language for literary purposes, but few with the success and contemporary vision of Ó Searcaigh. When one reads or, more to the point, when one listens to Ó Searcaigh read his poetry in the original, statistics, figures, demographics disappear and become meaningless. One is mesmerized by the fluidity of language, the cacophony of vowel sounds, the richness of alliteration and assonance, the vitality of metaphor and image. One is in the presence of a master poet who is comfortable in his medium, aware of his culture and literary heritage, one who is far more than a *cainteoir dúchais*, a native speaker. He is, in essence, an active tradition bearer, a tradition interrogator, an enricher and enhancer of that tradition. In the work of Ó Searcaigh, the tradition lives and thrives. The modern city experience, the street schools of Soho and Clapham Common College hone his perspective. Through his accomplishment, the language gives the cry of defiance which he appeals for in 'Caoineadh,' for he marries the Irish language community's concerns with those of the aerach/gay community. His poems, while remaining highly personalised, appeal to and express the reality for gays and *gaeilgeoirí*, for dykes and *díograiseoirí*, for fanatics and faggots, for queers and *caomhnóirí* alike.[58]

To conclude, Ó Searcaigh succeeds in forging poems from the smithy of personal experience and a wide literary tradition. Rather than resort to silence, cunning and exile, which would be an understandable reaction for a speaker of a minority language and a member of a marginalised group, he chooses to speak to a diverse audience at a multiplicity of levels. Ó Searcaigh's poetry is a locale of respite in which social outcasts, marginalised people, deracinated individuals, closet gays, green environmentalists, language learners, schizophrenic native speakers, molested and abused victims can find solace and temporary shelter, safe in the knowledge that somebody else understands, empathises and, above all else, grants hope.

## Notes

My thanks to the following individuals who shared their knowledge and advice with me: Alex Chasin, Kaarina Hollo, Mathew Lambertti, Philip O'Leary, Richard Murphy, Joe Nugent, and James M. Smith. Different versions of this paper were presented at the Graduate Irish Studies

Conference, University of Connecticut 1998, and The Lavender Language and Linguistics Conference, American University, Washington D.C. 1998. This paper was written with the assistance of a Government of Ireland Scholarship from The Interim Council for Humanities and Social Sciences.

1	Paul Ricoeur, 'The Creativity of Language', in Richard Kearney (ed.), *States of Mind: Dialogues with Contemporary Thinkers on the European Mind*, Manchester Univ. Press, Manchester, 1995, pp. 29–30.

2	Richard Kearney, 'Between Tradition and Utopia: The Hermeneutical Problem of Myth', in David Wood (ed.), *On Paul Ricoeur: Narrative and Interpretation*, Routledge, London, 1991, p. 65.

3	See Éibhear Walshe, 'Introduction: Sex, Nation and Dissent', in *Sex, Nation and Dissent in Irish Writing* (ed. Walshe), Cork UP, Cork, 1997.

4	In 1916 the accusation of homosexuality ensured that public sympathy would not be mobilised to seek a royal pardon preventing the execution of Sir Roger Casement, one of the leaders of the 1916 Irish Rebellion.

5	É. Walshe, op.cit., p. 5.

6	Exceptions to this would include journals such as *The Bell* and *An t-Éireannach*. The *Irish Times* was dismissed as a Protestant and Ascendancy publication.

7	Conor Cruise O'Brien describes Irish political discourse in a controversial article as follows: 'There is another aspect, not so bearable: the establishment of an atmosphere of intellectual dishonesty, solemn lipservice to dead men whose aims have long since been abandoned in practice, but who themselves remain the object of a vague cult on the part of the State. Intellectual dishonesty of this kind pervades parliament and the media, befuddles the public mind and provides the killers who operate in a culture with the kind of justification that legitimizes their deeds, or half legitimizes their deed, or half legitimizes them. Everything is done by halves in the half-dark. In some moods — the mood of 3 o'clock in the morning, for example — I am scared stiff, and not laughing at all, at the clammy green cloud that permeates, clogs and corrodes our Irish discourse and thought processes whenever the phantom shapes of our national aims heave dimly into view. The official national aims, I need hardly remind you, are the restoration of the Irish language and the unification of the national territory. Most people in the Republic don't give a tinker's curse about either of these aims: if anything they are opposed to both of them. But they do like to elect people who proclaim their dedication to these aims. They elect them on the tacit understanding shared by both electors and elected that the proclaimed dedication reflects no practical purpose at all. It is a kind of bleep, a signal of a shared ethnicity, and of a comfortable if bleary righteousness in terms of the ethnicity'. See 'Revolution and the Shaping of Modern Ireland', *The Celtic Consciousness*, Braziller, New York, 1982, p. 429.

8	*Innti*: the Group's name is derived from a slang expression in West County Kerry. It refers to visiting Dingle town, the capital of the region: literally 'into her'. It is also a sexual reference.

9   These are the major Irish language poets of the 'fifties and 'sixties —
    Seán Ó Ríordáin, Máirtín Ó Direáin, Máire Mhac an tSaoi and Eoghan
    Ó Tuairisc. They are accredited with laying the foundations of
    modern Irish language poetry. Seán Ó Ríordáin was writer in
    residence in University College Cork when the *Innti* generation were
    undergraduate students there.

10  In a manner similar to the beat poets in the United States there is
    some confusion regarding the original members of this group. With
    the passage of time more and more poets are included under the
    umbrella term, but it is generally accepted that the four original
    members are those named above.

11  *Bunreacht na hÉireann* (The Irish Constitution) describes Irish as the
    first language of the country and English as the second language. In
    practice English is the first language with only a minority of citizens
    using Irish as their first language. Cynics (disposed towards the Irish
    language) would comment that Irish is indeed the first language of
    the country — the first to be ignored, ridiculed, abused and deprived!

12  Lillis Ó Laoire, 'Introduction: A Yellow Spot on the Snow'/'Réamhrá:
    Ball Buí ar an tSneachta' (*ABB* pp. 14–15).

13  'Caoineadh' echoes Seán Ó Ríordáin's poem to his mother on the
    occasion of her funeral entitled 'Adhlacadh mo Mháthar'. Seamus
    Heaney translates Ó Searcaigh's 'Caoineadh' as 'Lament' (*ABB* pp.
    208–9). Lillis Ó Laoire also translates it as 'Lament' (*ABB* p. 32).

14  For the most recent and alarming analysis of the decline of the Irish
    language, see Donncha Ó hEallaithe, 'Uair na Cinniúna don
    Ghaeltacht', in *Cuisle*, Eagrán 5, 1999.

15  There may be a sense here, that critics and translators are scavengers
    who feed off the dying language, while not attempting to make any
    effort to extricate the language from its plight.

16  'Mise Charlie an Scivvy': Frank Sewell translates this as 'I'm Charlie
    the Scivvy' (*OO* pp. 144–47); Lillis Ó Laoire translates it as 'I am
    Charlie the Scivvy' (*ABB* pp. 202–5) . Ó Searcaigh is clearly satirising
    the famous poem, 'Mise Raifteraí an File'.

17  'Déagóir ag *Drift*áil': Sewell translates it as 'Drifting' (*OO* pp. 152–9).

18  'Cor na Síog': Robert Wavle and Anna Ní Dhomhnaill translate it as
    'The Fairy Reel'(*OO* pp. 160–65).

19  In particular for young girls in Ireland. It is rarely found at adult
    social gatherings.

20  The tube, like the national narrative, can only service the major
    centres and cannot meander to service all sections of the community.
    In the midst of the many the narrator can mix with the dominant
    group and pass unnoticed.

21  My thanks to Lisabeth Buchelt for discussing this point with me.

22  Ó Searcaigh's most recent Irish language collection, *Na Buachaillí
    Bána*, contains translations and adaptations of the Greek poet's work.
    Ó Searcaigh admits, in the preface, his debt to Cavafy as a source of
    inspiration.

23  F. Sewell translates this as 'Let's Hit the Road, Jack' (*OO* pp. 180–83);
    Sara Berkeley translates it as 'To Jack Kerouac' (*ABB* pp. 188–91)

24  See L. Ó Laoire, 'Réamhrá/Introduction', (*ABB* pp. 38–40).

25    Ó Laoire, Ibid., p. 34.

26    'Londain': Aodán Mac Póilín translates this as 'London' (*ABB* pp. 78–9). F. Sewell translates it as 'Capital' (*OO* pp. 148–49).

27    This may be a reference to Eavan Boland's essay, *A Kind of Scar: the Woman Poet in a national tradition*, Attic Press, Dublin, 1989. It echoes the lines from her poem, 'Mise Éire': 'who neither/knows nor cares that/a new language/is a kind of scar/and heals after a while/into a passable imitation/of what went before'.

28    'An Díbeartach': F. Sewell translates this as 'Outcast' (*OO* pp. 48–9).

29    'Cuisle an Chaoráin': F. Sewell translates this as 'Mountain Pulse' (*OO* pp. 40–3).

30    'Súile Shuibhne'. F. Sewell translates this as 'Sweeney's Eyes' (*OO* pp. 50–1); and Sara Berkeley translates it as 'Sweeney's Eyes' (*ABB* pp. 180–81).

31    'Bean an tSléibhe'. F. Sewell translates this as 'Mountain Woman' (*OO* pp. 22–5); and L. Ó Laoire translates it as 'Mountain Woman' (*ABB* pp. 116–19).

32    'Cré na Cuimhne'. Literally, clay or faith of memory; F. Sewell translates it as 'Cast in Clay' (*OO* pp. 26–35).

33    *Táin Bó Cúalnge* from the Book of Leinster (ed. Cecile O'Rahilly), Dublin Institute for Advanced Studies, Dublin, 1970, lines 992–1003.

34    *The Ancient Irish Epic Tale: Táin Bó Cúalnge* (trans. Joseph Dunn), David Nutt, London, 1914, pp. 64–65. Dunn's translation and register emphasise the problems and dilemmas inherent in the translations of a literary text.

35    Literally 'poets', but much more than a composer of verse is implied. A *file* was a seer, a creator of verse, a historian, a custodian of tradition and a chronicler amongst other things. See Katherine Simms, 'The Poet as Chieftain's Widow', in *Sages, Saints and Storytellers: Celtic Studies in Honour of Professor James Carney* (ed. Donncha Ó Corráin et al.), An Sagart, Maynooth, 1989.

36    Máire Mhac an tSaoi, 'The Celtic Continuum', in *The Celtic Consciousness*, pp. 250–251. Later, in the same article, she suggests a homosexual relationship between the fourteenth-century poet, Gearóid Iarla, and Dermot McCarthy. Cathal Ó Searcaigh suggests other homosexual bardic relationships in an interview with Marion Kelly in 'Ón Taobh Istigh, Agallamh le Cathal Ó Searcaigh', *Macalla 1996–97*, Cumann Éigse agus Seanchais, Gaillimh, 1997, pp. 35–49.

37    See Seán Ó Tuama, 'Love in Irish Folksong', *Repossessions: Selected Essays on the Irish Literary Heritage*, Cork UP, Cork, 1995, pp. 134–158.

38    'The Keen is the genre which is most usual to Irish women poets and it is the only large corpus of poetry that they have bequeathed us (except the love songs so many of which are attributed to them but of which we cannot be certain that women were the composers)'. Máire Ní hAnnracháin, 'Ait liom bean a bheith ina file', in *Léachtaí Cholm Cille* XII, An Sagart, Maigh Nuad, 1982, p. 155. My translation.

39    'Ceann Dubh Dílis': Gabriel Fitzmaurice translates this as 'My Blackhaired Love' (*ABB* pp. 140–41). F. Sewell translates it as 'Dear Dark-Haired Love' (*OO* pp. 112–23).

40    L. Ó Laoire, 'Introduction/Réamhrá' (*ABB* pp. 27–28).

41      See L. Ó Laoire, 'Dearg Dobhogtha Cháin/The Indelible Mark of Cain: Sexual Dissidence in the Poetry of Cathal Ó Searcaigh', in *Sex, Nation and Dissent in Irish Writing*, pp. 229–230.

42      'Laoi Cumainn': G. Rosenstock translates this as 'Hound of Ulster' (*ABB* pp. 166–69); F. Sewell translates it as 'Serenade' (*OO* pp. 86–9).

43      This word for 'deceit' is cited in Dinneen's dictionary as existing in the title of a Monaghan folk tale, *An Fear a chuir cluain ar an mBás*. Patrick S. Dinneen, *Foclóir Gaedhilge agus Béarla*, Educational Company of Ireland, Dublin and Cork, 1927, p. 209.

44      See Séamus Deane, '*Mo Bhealach Féin* by Seosamh Mac Grianna', *The Pleasures of Gaelic Literature* (ed. John Jordan), The Mercier Press, Dublin, 1977, pp. 52–61. See also L. Ó Laoire, 'Réamhrá/Introduction', pp. 26–27.

45      L. Ó Laoire, 'Dearg Dobhogtha Cháin/The Indelible Mark of Cain', pp. 228–231. See also Ó Laoire, 'Réamhrá/Introduction', pp. 27–30.

46      The second stanza contains a conscious repetition of an *ae* vowel combination and the fourth stanza contains six slender *l*s.

47      'An Lilí Bhándearg': F. Sewell translates this as 'The Pink Lily' (*OO* pp. 236–39).

48      C. Ó Searcaigh, 'Cín Lae ó Bharr na Cruinne', *Comhar*, Nollaig, 1998, pp. 17–21.

49      Translated as 'Native Speaker'. A *cainteoir dúchais* is a not alone a speaker whose first language is Irish, but one who speaks out of a tradition, an active tradition bearer.

50      *Gaeilgeoir* — A language enthusiast, often but not necessarily identified by *An Fháinne*, a plain circular broach/pin which indicates one of two levels of proficiency in the language. *Gaeilgeoirí* (plural) are often derided by native speakers for their naiveté and accused by anti-Irish factions of being fanatical. Traditionally the stereotypical *Gaeilgeoir* possessed the missionary zeal of the convert in all matters relating to Irish which made him/her more of a liability than an asset.

51      A glossary of some key terms seems appropriate given the cultural specificity of some items utilised: 'flat-out' (had not-stopped, i.e. was extremely busy and now exhausted); 'hoovered' (vacuumed; 'hoover' is also a brand-name); 'jeyes-fluided' (a brand-name for a disinfectant); 'loo' (a bathroom or toilet-bowl); 'harpic[k]' (a bathroom disinfectant brand-name); 'vim' (a scouring agent brand-name); 'flash' (brand-name for floor polish, cleaning agent); 'windowlene' (brand-name for a polishing agent for glass/windows); 'shagged' (exhausted, also has sexual connotation); 'cruising' (seeking to pick up a partner for sex); '*cúpla focal*' (literally 'a few words'), used to describe the fluency of a speaker. In practice it may imply anything from a few words to near fluency. It is often used sarcastically or in reference to a token use of the language at official functions.

52      David Norris' comment applies to both languages: 'There remained in the minds of many people a doubt to whether the term "Irish" and "Homosexual" were not mutually exclusive'. See 'Homosexual People and the Christian Churches in Ireland', *The Crane Bag*, 2, 1981, p. 3. Neither Mac Liammóir nor Hutchinson are 'native' speakers: both men acquired Irish as a second language. Hutchinson discusses

homosexuality and Irish in ' "Rus in Urbe": Comhrá le Pearse Hutchinson', *Innti* xi, 1998, pp. 55–68.

53    The right wing, staunch Catholic anti-liberal group dominated the Irish language movement during the revival and rejected the views of the liberal European-influenced group comprised of Pádraic Ó Conaire, Liam P. Ó Riain and Pádraic Mac Piarais on occasions.

54    F. Sewell translates this as 'Field of Bones' (*OO* pp. 66–76).

55    A final word needs to be said regarding the controversy which arose over the front covers for Ó Searcaigh's *Na Buachaillí Bána* and *Out in the Open* — both of which feature nudes. For example, on the dust-jacket of *Out in the Open*, also published by Cló Iar-Chonnachta, there appears a reproduction of Henry Scott Tuke's 'The Bathers' which hangs in the Leeds City Art Gallery. The bathers are a group of nude boys, in their early teens, lying on a boat deck preparing to dive into the water. The boys' age provoked negative comment in several quarters. They were considered too young, and even those who defended Ó Searcaigh conceded that, in the present climate of fear in Ireland regarding child abuse, it was an unfortunate selection. It would be a travesty if this were to adversely affect Ó Searcaigh's standing as a poet either in Ireland or elsewhere, or if this dust jacket were to become a stick with which homophobic interest groups may attack Ó Searcaigh. Regarding the Irish-language collection's title, *Na Buachaillí Bána*, the following note by Micheál Mac Craith on the schism in Irish nationalism between the Clergy and secret political societies may explain the title's origin: 'Thug na Buachaillí Bána aghaidh a gcraois ar an gcléir freisin agus is spéisiúil an ní é gur le linn na seacht déag seascaidí a briseadh den chéad uair an aontacht idir an chléir Chaitliceach agus aon léinn na Gaeilge maidir leis na Stíobhartaigh, aontacht arbh ann di ó thús an tseachtú haois déag' [from 'Foinsí an radacachais in Éirinn' in *Éirí Amach 1798 in Éirinn*, ed. Gearóid Ó Tuathaigh, Cló Iar-Chonnachta, Indreabhán, 1998, 11–28. My translation is as follows: 'The White Boys turned their fury on the clergy also and it is interesting that it was during the 1760s for the first time that the alliance between the Catholic clergy and the intellectuals of Irish literature regarding the Stewarts, a unity which had existed from the beginning of the seventeenth century, was severed'.] Ó Searcaigh may be drawing a parallel between Ireland's gay community and the eighteenth-century White Boys: a clandestine organisation supported by the masses but condemned by the Church, and performing illicit and illegal nocturnal acts while awaiting the arrival from afar of a male redeeming figure.

56    Pádraic Standún's novel *Cion Mná*, which contrasts marital abuse and lesbianism, may be interpreted in a similar fashion.

57    The most obvious criticism concerns 'Gort na gCnámh'. How well can a male writer interpret and represent a young woman's experience?

58    Editor's note: a neutral translation of *gaeilgeoirí* would be 'Irish speakers' who are also likely to be described as *díograiseoirí* and *caomhnóirí*; *díograiseoirí* could be translated as 'enthusiasts'; and *caomhnóirí* could be interpreted as (small 'c') conservatives or preservationists.

## (as) CUISLE AN CHAORÁIN

Chrom sé agus phóg sé
plobar úscach an tsléibhe -
cíocha silteacha Bhríde, bandia na gcríoch, Bé:
deoch a bhí lena mhian;
lán de mhilseacht aduain,
a mheiscigh is a mhearaigh é gur mhothaigh sé
an croí beag ina chliabh,

ag craobhú agus ag síneadh,
ag leathnú amach
go meanmnach míorúilteach; ag lonnú sa tsliabh
agus a thaobhú mar chliabh.
Anois nuair a labhrann sé amach
i bhfilíocht, labhrann, mar nár labhair ariamh,
go macnasach, mórchroíoch ...

as croí an tsléibhe...

(OO 40)

## (from) MOUNTAIN PULSE

He bent and kissed
the wet neck of the mountain,
the weeping breasts of Brid, mountain-goddess, Muse;
a drink to his taste,
filled with a strange sweetness
that turned him on and cn until he felt
the little heart in his breast

rippling and reaching,
spreading out
boldly and miraculously, clinging
to the mountain, flesh to flesh.
Now when he speaks out
in poetry, he speaks, as never before,
wildly, whole-heartedly ...

from the heart of the mountain...

(trans. Frank Sewell)

# Niall McGrath and Cathal Ó Searcaigh

## 'CHALLENGING OUR CONFORMITIES':
### CATHAL Ó SEARCAIGH IN CONVERSATION WITH NIALL McGRATH

NMcG:
Is 'home' a sanctuary for you? What does 'home' mean to you as a person and as a writer?

COS:
I became acutely aware of home when I went to London in the early seventies. I remember galooting around Piccadilly and Trafalgar Square, taking a walk on the wild side. It was the first time I began to look into that terrible dark pool of the Self, the *Duibheagán* as I call it in Irish. At times like that you realise you're an abyss, a pitch black pit. There's only a deep darkness. You get dizzy looking down into the gulf, the chasm of Yourself. You realise there's a terrible deadening, deafening Silence ... that there are no answers. A poem became for me an act of defiance thrown in the face of that Silence.

Cathal at National School, Casheal na gCorr (photo: Cathal Ó Searcaigh)

I wrote in English, poems of adolescent angst, mostly. A poetry of pimples. I wrote bad poems because I didn't have the humility to read really great poems. Until one evening in the Autumn of 1975 a man who worked in the storeroom of Oxford University Press walked into the pub where I worked — the 'Ox & Gate', halfway between Cricklewood and Neasden — and handed me a copy of Derek Mahon's latest collection, *The Snow Party*. That book had a profound effect on me, especially the first poem called 'Afterlives', dedicated to James Simmons,[1] whom I work with now since he moved the Poets' House from Portmuck to Muckish. Little did I know at the time that James' fate and my fate would become so closely intertwined further down the road of years.

Anyway, Derek Mahon had gone to London at the beginning of the troubles and I think he felt it on his conscience that he hadn't accounted for those terrible times in his poetry. So 'Afterlives' is a homecoming poem, in that Mahon comes back to Belfast. The last verse was a real shock of recognition:

> But the hills are still the same
> Grey-blue above Belfast.
> Perhaps if I'd stayed behind
> And lived it bomb by bomb
> I might have grown up at last
> And learnt what is meant by home.

Home! The word just winged its way off the page. I felt the word as an intense desire to be reunited with something from which I felt I was cut off. The word was a smell from another world; the lost domain of my Dúchas. Dúchas is a difficult word to explain in English, but briefly it means a sense of connection; a feeling of attachment to a place, a tongue and a tradition; a belief that one belongs to a sustaining cultural and communal energy; that one has a place and a name. Suddenly I realised that I was an exile in an alien city where I neither had a face nor a name or a place. I had to return 'home' to reclaim my heritage, my Dúchas. I also realised that Irish was my emotional language and not English. Intuitively I knew more about the texture and the tone, the aura of words in Irish. In Irish we refer to the language as 'she'. Everything in Irish is either masculine or feminine; everything is alive and throbbing, so to say, we don't neuter things with a detached, callous 'it'. Anyway, I became aware that I was a native of 'her' psyche, or that she inhabited my consciousness, perhaps in a way that English didn't. From then on I would write poetry in Irish. 'She' would connect me with the vital creative energies of my Dúchas. She would bring me back home.

Cathal with poet Derek Mahon and Patricia King, Wake Forest, North Carolina, 1984 (photo: Rachel Giese Brown)

NMcG:
So how does nature and the landscape of rural Donegal affect you and your poetry? You write of being 'in tune with my fate and environment...'.

COS:
Well, I'm in love with the green spirit of mountain and moor. That, I think, accounts for the impulse of many of my poems. Creativity, according to Gary Snyder, is an expression of gratitude and a celebration of place. In that sense my work is devotional; a homage to tongue, place and tradition. I use place names a lot in my poems. The sense of place, the

sacredness of place is a common motif in Irish poetry. Dinnseanchas — the lore of placename — was an important part of the poets' education. For me there's an urgency to name things. This comes from a sense of crisis. The placenames are being forgotten. This happens more in my area as the Irish language shrinks and the English language spreads. It's so sad, this communal amnesia. This detailed naming of the land that my people did was their way to transform the wilderness into a place where they could feel at home. For a lot of people, nowadays, the landscape is silent. They no longer have the name to invoke the spirit of the place. You can't converse properly with a hill, a field, a hollow or a rock without addressing it by its name.

Poetry for me is a means of making memorable what is being forgotten. I love these names. My persistent recitation of them in my poems is a way of bringing the past into the present; hoping that there will be a future for that past. Other than that, I can only say that this area around the foot of Mount Errigal is my physical and spiritual home. Here I feel in harmony with myself, 'in tune with my fate and environment' as I say in the poem that you have just quoted, 'Here at Caiseal na gCorr Station'. Next stop Nirvana!

NMcG
What early influences had you? How did you first develop an interest in poetry and literature?

COS:
The first poems that actually engaged my attention were the poems of Robbie Burns. I remember my father reading these poems to me when I was four or five. On winter nights after he returned home after seasonal work in Scotland, he would read these poems out loud to myself and my mother, while we were sitting around the fire. I was enthralled by these sonorous fireside readings. My father chanted these poems in the same way that the priest intoned the Latin Mass in church. I didn't have any English at the time but I knew that the sounds my

Mickey Ó Searcaigh, father, April 1982 (Rachel Giese Brown)

Cathal and his mother, Agnes, 1981 (Rachel Giese Brown)

father made were the strange and secret spells of a magician. He read them out of this big, fat forbidding-looking book that he handled with great care and always kept well out of my reach when he wasn't using it. I knew that if I could match these sounds, mimic them even, I would have power over the adults that inhabited and controlled my world. That was my first realisation, I suppose, of the hypnotic, oracular powers of language. Once I began to read, my father brought books back from Glasgow. He always arrived with a sackful of books. He picked them up at random, I think, in the Barrows — Glasgow's famous flea-market. He certainly wasn't censorious in his selections. In 1968, for example, he brought back Gore Vidal's *The City and the Pillar*. That was the first time I encountered gay characters in a book and although their relationship was merely an unspoken grope — tortured, frightened and doomed to failure — it was an acknowledgement of the public reality of homosexuality. For me, a young adolescent in the wilds of Donegal, coming to terms with my sexual difference, that book was a testament of hope and promise. It was an admission and an affirmation that I wasn't on my own. Out there, somewhere, were others of a similar 'bent'. For many the constrained isolation of the closet leaves them timid, vulnerable, fearful. It leaves them with an aching cramp in the heart.

Anyway, I was lucky. At an early age literature lured me out of the 'lios'. The Lios is where the fairies dwell. It's my gaylic for closet. I also became familiar in my early teens with the American 'Beats' — Kerouac, Ginsberg, Corso, Snyder. Kerouac's *On the Road* became my travelogue; a travelogue for my interior regions; the America of my Imagination. It made me want to travel, to cross borders, to experience the thrill of new frontiers. 'If you can't go on a journey,' the Persian poet Rumi said, 'go on a sightseeing tour of the Self,' or words to that effect. For me these trips provide the stories that I tell in my poems.

NMcG:
How has religion affected you?

COS:

I was brought up a Catholic but I copped out a long time ago. You could, I suppose, call me a 'Copp-tic' Catholic. I was reared in a household that straddled two worlds: this world and the Otherworld. My mother, who was illiterate, believed fervently in the fairies. She believed that another reality coexisted with ours; a hidden, supersensory domain inhabited by the Sí (the fairly people). According to her, we were in and out of this world unbeknown to ourselves. She was, anyway. She was always telling my father and myself to tread carefully in case we would bother our otherworldly neighbours. They were very touchy, you see. My mother would sit in front of the fire and tell long convoluted tales about her travels and ordeals in the Otherworld. Her journeys were often enforced ones. They took her forcibly to assist at a birth or to perform some menial chore. She also went there on her own steam to appease them over some transgression committed by myself or my father. Occasionally she told us that she travelled there by blue. And I, with the rational, no-nonsense approach the primary school tried to instil in me, would say, 'But, Mammy, you can't travel on a colour'. And she, without showing the slightest doubt or unease, would say, 'If you're stuck in the night, child, you'll take a lift from anything that is passing'. Years later when I read Gabriel Garcia Marquez's *One Hundred Years of Solitude*, I felt comfortable with his vision of things. My mother with her stories had prepared me for 'magic realism'. She herself was a living embodiment of it.

I know now that she suffered from deep depression. Perhaps these journeys were descents into her own dark self, into her own nether regions in order to come face to face with the demon of her illness.

All in all, I think that my mother's faith in the fairyworld had a stronger formative and shaping effect on me than Catholicism ever had. It instils in me a sense of awe at the Mystery; a green attitude to my surroundings. And finally I became a 'fairy' myself. My mother's attitude and approach to them made it acceptable. As a young child I was awe-struck by the solemnity, the grandeur, the ritual of certain Catholic ceremonies: the Midnight Mass on Christmas Night; the

Benediction; the funeral services. The colourful vestments left me gaping in astonishment; the smell of incense had me in a swoon. As a teenager I became appalled at the Dogma; the unyielding, harsh, Canonical tenets that seemed to me to be downright totalitarianism. I abandoned Orthodoxy for Mystery. Poetry became, I suppose, a means of salvation. Sometimes I wear a little badge which states: 'My Karma ran over my Dogma'.

NMcG:
And Buddhism?

COS:
Buddhism is like a length of cloth that you tailor into an outfit, a garment that suits your needs. It's an attitude of attentiveness. You must work out your own salvation; find the path through your own efforts and diligence. The Buddha himself said: 'Look within, you are the Buddha'. At the heart of Buddhism is the realisation that humanity's lot is 'suffering'. We suffer all sorts of psychic injuries on our path through life: the trauma of birth; the pain of sickness; the affliction of old age; the agony of death. We are possessive, greedy, egocentric beings and this also causes great suffering. The Four Noble Truths and the Eightfold Path of Buddhism provide the guidelines to free ourselves from delusions and to attain self-discovery. In a nutshell it's about mindfulness; the conquest of the Ego and the Oneness of all Life. I should say, however, that Buddhism differs from Judeo-Christian doctrines in that Buddhism offers kindly, compassionate advice rather than stern Dogma. It says: 'It would be better for you and for everyone else if you desisted from ...', rather than 'Thou shalt not ...'.

NMcG:
Buddhists believe in reincarnation. Do you share that view?

COS:
Yes, I believe in the Wheel of Life; what goes around, comes around. Day and night; the cycle of the seasons; the Earth circling the sun. It seems to me that Life occurs in the same cyclical dimension. It sometimes happens, of course, that we

Cathal, Prem and his wife Sunita, Kathmundu, Nepal, 2002 (photo: Cathal Ó Searcaigh)

have an innate knowledge of things, of subjects we have not acquired or learned in our present lives. There are, I believe, deposits or repositories from a past life. And most of us, I think, have intimations, dim flickerings of other lives. We have faint memories, we hear whispers from a shadowy past. Like the Buddhists I believe in a cyclical rather than a linear reality. The Tibetan Buddhists have worked out and systematised what I can only call a science of dying. You will find it all in an amazing book called the *Tibetan Book of the Dead* — the *Bardo Thödol*. That book will help you acquaint yourself with Death while alive and prepare you for the post-Death state so that you are enabled to make a re-entry into the cycle of Life.

NMcG:
You've written about Nepal. How did visiting that country affect you and your writing?

COS:
Over the last two years I have been very fortunate that filming and writing projects brought me to Nepal. No one going to Nepal can be immune to the charms of its people. They welcomed me with open hearts and open doors. They who had nothing shared that nothing with me in abundance.

'It takes little talent to see clearly what lies under one's nose', according to Auden; 'a good deal of it to know in which direction to point that organ.' Yes, the nose of my pen has always been pointing East. It was inevitable that I myself would follow, eventually.

At present I'm trying to sort out and shape up a diary that I kept while travelling in Nepal. Other than plays, its my first attempt at an extended prose piece in Irish. In Nepal, I'm much more aware than I am here; much more alert to the Improbable and the Inexplicable. Perhaps at that altitude my senses became unblocked. Anyway, while I was in Nepal, I was having the most unexpected encounters; the strangest coincidences; the 'synchronicities' that Carl Jung talked about. This is one example: I have a close friend in Nepal called Pemba Thamang. He lives in a very remote part of Nepal quite close to the Tibetan border.

I got to know him on my first trip when I was there on a mountain-climbing expedition with Dermot Somers and Robbie Fenlon of the Irish Everest Squad. Pemba was one of our porters. And he shone out from the crowd. He had a tremendous sense of presence. Pemba became very attached to me and I to him. And so on my last trip to Nepal I decided to visit him in his mountain home. I went on a long journey by bus to the nearest village to Pemba. I wasn't sure exactly where Pemba lived. He had given me a scribbled address. He doesn't read or write and he speaks very little English and so we communicated by nods and smiles in a speechless, psychic way. So I arrived in this little village and then started to climb towards Gatland, where I knew he lived.

Now, Pemba Thamang, I discovered, is as common a name there as Johnny Gallagher is in Donegal and I wasn't sure where in this vast area Pemba lived. But on top of a mountain where myself and the two porters I had with me sat down to take a rest after ascending, there were quite a lot of other Thamang people sitting around, all dressed in the beautiful, traditional, red homespun cloth. There was one young man dressed in tattered Western clothes. And while I was sitting down I saw him staring at me; and I wasn't sure what was happening — whether he was 'cruising' me, which was unlikely, as that doesn't really exist in Nepal. After a while he came over and said to me, on top of this mountain among strangers, he said: 'Excuse me, are you Pemba Thamang's friend?' I had never seen this man before in my life and he certainly hadn't seen me, or so I thought. And then the whole story came to light. During the year I had sent Pemba a letter with some photographs but I wasn't very hopeful of it getting there. The postal service in Nepal is extremely unreliable. But it did arrive and Pemba, not being able to read or write, brought the letter to this man, who was the teacher in the local school. And so in exchange for reading him the letter, Pemba had given him a photograph of me. This was the only photograph that this man had, and so he was quite mesmerised to see the living image of that photograph right in front of his eyes. And I was equally amazed by this amazing coincidence. And, of course, he knew where Pemba lived. And that facilitated my journey into the mountains to find Pemba.

I usually spend December and January in Nepal. It's become a second home to me. In Kathmandu, on my second trip to Nepal, I met Prem Timalsina — a young man with incisive insights into the secular and spiritual traditions of his country. On that first meeting with Prem, it was extraordinary to find out that Dhungkorka, the mountain village which he came from, meant the same thing as my mountain townland of Mín a' Leá, namely 'the reclaimed flat land of flagstones in the mountain'. Since then, I have been to Dhungkorka many times, and Prem has been with me here in Mín a' Leá on extended visits. His real father is dead and I have become his surrogate father. I'm thrilled to have such a lovely son not by propagation but by providence. He is a being of Light.

Nepal is not Shangri La, despite what the holiday brochures say, but it is an extraordinary opportunity to step back in time and experience a less frenetic way of life, a simple, dignified, abstemious existence, completely at variance with the push and shove of our western lifestyles and the insatiable greed of our affluence. I'm not suggesting that Nepal is the last word in laid-back serenity. It's not. Nepal is one of the world's poorest nations and, of course, the twenty-first century is creeping up on them furtively. I fervently hope that they find the right balance between their past and our present. I feel enriched by their humble homes. They who have nothing give me abundantly. In their midst, I learned, I hope, to unburden myself of a lot of my ephemeral accretions.

NMcG:
And you write in Irish. What does this language mean to you?

COS:
I write in Irish because it's the language I know best; it's my emotional language. Poetry is language articulating itself at its most acute. To quicken language to that pitch of arousal you have to be in bed with the Muse of that Language. I write in Irish but my work only became well known when it was translated into English. I know that some Gaelic enthusiasts with a Golden Age complex are wary and opposed to innovation. The outside world of English cannot impinge or intrude. Translation into English is a blasphemy. Those smug,

self-appointed 'defenders of the flame' would say that I have squandered my integrity and honour as an Irish language writer by giving in to the lure and cheap thrill of English. As far as I'm concerned translation in English has given me a new lease of life; an opportunity to survive as a poet in the Irish language. To be known, to be recognised, it is imperative to receive the imprimatur of English. The Ireland Literature Exchange has, however, in recent times provided an opportunity to bypass English and find a home abroad in French, Breton, Italian, German, Catalan, Danish. As we speak, a Hindi version of my poems is in preparation. This means, of course, that the thrust of translations is no longer Anglo-centric. Gabriel Rosenstock, our greatest traveller across linguistic and cultural borders, said that translation was like a blood transfusion between friends. In this country, English and Irish have been colliding with each other for centuries, both physically and psychically. English poetry, I think, has benefited from and has been enriched by those encounters ... Clarke, Kavanagh, Heaney, Montague, Muldoon, Meehan. The ghost, the spectre of Irish is continually making an appearance in English language poetry in this country. It's like a poltergeist, upsetting the furniture of the poem; shuffling with the syntax; breathing through the metrics; uttering its own strange sounds. It's now time, I think, for Irish language verse to benefit from the scope and range of English. In my own case, I'm delighted with the way that Frank Sewell has managed to invoke my poems in English. He has found a voice and a register for them that seems to me to be acceptable in English. By deft and clever handling of tone and texture he has succeeded in making the poems speak in Poetry and not in Translationese. It just goes to prove, as someone said, that Poetry has many tongues but a single language.

NMcG:
The journey motif is important in your work. In recent years, you have travelled extensively ...

COS:
I love journeys; mystery tours; rambles. Every evening I take my mind out for a jaunt in the mountains and the moors. Even a long walk around the table can be awe-inspiring. It can be an

outing in the imagination. If you can't go on a journey, you can always take a sight-seeing tour of the Self. There are more things in the heaven and the earth of our minds than we know of ... To benefit from a journey, you have to cultivate a sense of awareness, a sense of openness; a readiness to experience whatever the journey brings forth. I remember my old friend, Maggie Neddie Dhonnchaidh, my next door neighbour; a woman who never left her home except once in her lifetime; a long epic journey to West Clare on a June day in 1963. And back home again on the self-same day. Her sister, Biddy, was married to a Clare man and they lived in London. That year, they decided to spend a holiday with his relations in Co. Clare and Maggie was invited to visit them. She did, but it was a flying visit. She hired a local driver, Charlie John Óig, one of the few locals to have a car at that time, to drive her there and back on the same day. From that day onwards, her favourite topic of conversation was 'the day I went to County Clare'. She would describe every detail of that trip; the people that she met and the places that she saw; every twist and turn, every snatch and scrap of conversation. She remembered everything: what she had seen, heard and felt. Years later, when my friends and I told her of our adventures while travelling in Europe or in America, her innocent face would light up and she'd say: 'well, isn't that strange? That's exactly what happened to me the day I went to Co. Clare'. And that was her off on her journey of wonder once more. As she got older, this one-day Odyssey became more magical and more epical. She kept reinventing it, renewing it. She made a spirited connection with her vital creative energies on that journey. The journey restored her enriched to the real world of her everyday life. Her only journey became all journeys. She found a space to move in with her whole body, her whole mind. She became attentive and attuned to the sights and sounds of eye and ear. She became a seer, a *file*. And what is a *file*? A poet ... but a child, according to Umberto Saba, a favourite Italian poet of mine, who marvels at what befalls him when he grows up. Maggie Neddie Dhonnchaidh is beneath the sods of Gort a' Choirce graveyard but I'm sure that her youthful spirit is hitchhiking in Eternity.

Listening to Maggie's wonder-voyage to Co. Clare and reading *On the Road*, Kerouac's rip-roaring tale of wanderlust, made me want to travel, to experience the euphoria of being on the road. The journey is, of course, a recurring motif in literature and in life; be it Kerouac's wild quest in search of himself in *On the Road* or the Hopi Indians' ritual journey into the wilderness, to gain some worthwhile spiritual knowledge. The Celts have always, I think, felt the need to journey. They voyaged in their literature into the unknown; to the isles of dreams; the isles of the ever young; the isles of fire. But they were always duty-bound to return, to share with their people the wonders they experienced, the spiritual wisdom they gained. Those things were of no consequence until they were channelled back into the community. Thus the importance of storytelling, of poetry recitation. The artist brings back in his art — be it a painting, poem, or piece of music — the golden fleece of his vision; the Holy Grail of his wisdom; the treasure-trove of his story. This type of artist prevents stagnation by risking new options, by shaping new strategies. We always need the inspiration, the vision, the stimulation of the creative artist in our society to open up new outlooks and outlets for the future, to provide insightful perceptions of the present, and to suggest a reliable reading of our past. The artist in our society is the challenger to our conformities; the punk angel in our midst.

NMcG:
How and in what ways do you believe being gay has contributed to your writing? Was such self-realisation difficult in rural Donegal?

COS:
I come from an area where people still believe in the Fairies, and for those with that Fairy-faith, I'm the living embodiment of their beliefs. Anyway, what is straight? A line can be straight — according to Tennessee Williams — or a street, but the human heart, oh no! It's curved like a road through mountains, and the Donegal mountain roads, as you know, are quite bent. You know the lines by Robert Frost, 'two roads diverged in a wood ... and I took the one less travelled by and that has made all the difference'? Well, that road has taken me

to Sodom. I read somewhere that the emperor Justinian (483–562) legislated against homosexuality because he was convinced that the act of sodomy was the cause of earthquakes. I never had a sexual experience that shook the bedrock of the world but I did have one or two that shook the bedposts ... Edmund White is a writer that I admire very much. In a marvellous collection of essays called *The Burning Library*, he says, 'no homosexual can take his homosexuality for granted. At a certain point, one undergoes a violent conversion into a new state, the unknown, which one then sets about knowing as one will'. Like many gay men, I had to figure things out for myself, from the bottom up, so to speak. We are all, as Edmund White remarked, forced to become reflective; to become 'gay philosophers' — although, that's changing now. I meet young people in gay clubs and bars who have never been *in*, they have always been *out*. Like myself, they have never been in the closet. I say that about myself because we never had anything as fashionably snazzy as a 'closet' in our poor household. Anyway, the sort of bizarre conditions under which I was brought up allowed me to be myself from a very early age. My gayness, something which I intimated intuitively when still a child, gave me a strong sense of being different. This, I think, pushed me inwards and opened up for me the magic realms of books. There is no ship like a book, according to Emily Dickinson, to take us lands away. In my adolescent years, I lived, to a large extent, in this rarefied world of books. It wasn't easy to obtain the books I wanted but somehow I did manage, on trips to Dublin and later to London, to pleasure myself with Oscar Wilde's *Portrait of Dorian Gray*; Christopher Isherwood's *Goodbye to Berlin*; André Gide's *The Immoralist*; Jean Genet's *The Thief's Journal*; James Baldwin's *Giovanni's Room*; and the poetry of Walt Whitman and Alan Ginsberg. By putting together this bookish Who's Who of Homos, I felt that I was being initiated into a gay fraternity of literature; a pinkish place where I had no fear of rejection.

Walt Whitman vowed that he would plant male friendships thick as trees along the riverbanks of America. I knew he was talking to me directly when he said:

I mind once how we lay such a transparent summer
morning
How you settled your head athwart my hips
And gently turned over upon me
And parted the shirt from my bosom bone
And plated your tongue to my bare stripped heart
And reached till you felt my beard
And reached till you held my feet …

After reading Whitman, especially the 'Calamus' section of
*Leaves of Grass*, I became a deft hand at the emissionary
position. As a teenager in the wilds of Donegal, it gave me a
tremendous shot of self-confidence and cockiness, of course, to
read authors who were confessing their gayness in their
writings. It was a mighty assuring 'Yes' to my condition. It
muffled and stifled all the denying, negative No's that the state
and society, church and community proclaimed. I also realised
that I was not some sort of fiend, cursed and ill-fated.
*Abumi*nable I may be, but not abominable. My falling in love
with boys rather than with girls was a biological predilection.
Unlike the swimming pool, the gene pool does not have a
lifeguard to straighten you out when you get into the turbulent
deep-end of the biochemical waters. Psychically, you either
sink or swim. Once I accepted what I was, I got as much
satisfaction out of my gay genes as I did out of my teenage
blue jeans.

NMcG:
The Greek poet Constantine Cavafy (1863–1933) is a strong
presence in your life and in your poems.

COS:
Wherever I go, I bring his poems along with me,
companionable presences to liven up my journeys. They are
extraordinary poems; lean and laconic; devoid, to a large
extent, of any metaphorical or metrical extravagance. They
impress by their 'unique tone of voice'. What Cavafy has that
surmounts the risks of translation, according to W. H. Auden,
is 'a tone of voice'. He shunned the full-throated rhetoric of
much of his contemporaries. His poems rarely raise their voice,
yet they insinuate themselves into our inner ear. We listen
enthralled to their quiet, ironic, self-deprecatory speech as they

talk with a total lack of sentimentality about the evanescence of life and love. Many of his poems are miniature dramas presented with a detached irony, set in a remote historical past somewhere between 200 BC and 600 AD — his favourite age being the Panhellenic world of the diasporic Greeks in Europe and Asia Minor after the collapse of the Alexandrian Empire. When I read him for the first time, in the mid-70s, I was intrigued by his resourceful use of an assemblage of characters from the ancient world — an imaginative masking device that allowed him to distance himself from his own contemporary angst and, at the same time, enabled his poems to become universal statements.

I also loved, of course, the frankly homosexual poems; his own autobiographical erotica, set in Alexandria. The direct way he had of evoking an erotic event or a sensual emotion with electrifying drama made a lasting impression on me. The no-linguistic-frills but plenty-of-erotic-thrills mode of poem that he wrote about his youthful pick-ups, excited me physically and imaginatively. I was having my own first fine careless raptures at the time, artistically speaking, and indeed, my first fine careless ruptures, anally speaking. These poems of Cavafy's intensified both experiences. Poems in which past pleasures, the intoxicating pleasures of the flesh, are remembered so fiercely, so keenly that they come alive again with a throbbing immediacy. By means of memory, the fleeting erotic encounters of his youth, the passionate short-lived affairs in the seedy neighbourhoods of Alexandria, are recreated so that they achieve a permanence through the transforming power of his poetry, the timelessness of his Art.

This Cavafian notion of memory — the redemptive power of memory to hold and to transform into Art the ephemeral passing life of the senses — appealed to me enormously. In Greek mythology, Mnemosyne is the spirit of Remembering. The Greeks hold her to be the foremost Muse. Memory is a brilliant faculty. It's the stuff of genius, really — having the capacity to explore our buried self, the shards and fragments, the buts of this and that ... joy, sorrow, grief, happiness, loneliness. These excavations of the psyche are akin to archaeology. We have many lost worlds buried deep in the earth of our psyche, a whole Atlantis of feelings. Nothing is ever forgotten by the body. Memory is the means to dig, to unearth, to discover the ages of our Being, the artefacts of our feelings.

Another thing about Cavafy that interests me is his sense of place. The city of Alexandria, for example, is evoked with a strong specificity in his poems, be it the mythical or the actual Alexandria. It became for him a city of the imagination, a city where the 'Greek way of life' found its most complete expression. For me, perhaps, Caiseal na gCorr has become a townland of the mind. Caiseal na gCorr could be construed as 'stone fort of the queer'. This etymologically bent reading of Caiseal na gCorr is, I suppose, the subtext when I use that placename in my poems. It's my attempt to Hellenize my surroundings. Close to Caiseal na gCorr, there's another townland called Baile an Gheata, meaning the townland of the gate but mysteriously rendered into English as 'Gaytown'. I think Cavafy would appreciate that creative corruption. Anyway, when I read him for the first time, I was enthralled by the exotic and erotic locations of his poems. And I marvelled at the way he brought those places alive for me; far-flung places, for me then, of romance and mystery, charm and colour; places like Alexandria, Antioch, Selefkia, Cappadocia, Ithaka, Tyana, Ionia, Nicomedia, Sidon, Syracuse — places that glow, of course, in the literary imagination of all of us who are devoted to Cavafy. Needless to say, I wanted, and still want, to give my Caiseal na gCorr and its environs a literary aura, a kind of Cavafian charm so that An Bhealtaine would become as erotically charged as Byzantium in the gay imagination.

NMcG:
You also have an affinity with the Japanese Arts, particularly the Haiku ...

COS:
The Japanese Hailku has, it seems to me, the ability to see into the innerness and the hiddenness of things; the mystery at the centre of the commonplace. I love their Oriental stillness. It's a type of poem that is balanced, pure, tranquil, so that it calms the mind, promotes harmony. The haiku thrives on the

nourishing traits of Silence. After all, the whole of the Cosmos is encapsulated within seventeen syllables. For the haiku poet, it's a question of seeing; seeing clearly and intently. He becomes — by virtue of seeing — a visionary of the real. A haiku by Buson[2] goes like this:

> Pissing through the doorway
> I make a clear hole
> in the snow.

I love the clarity and brevity of that. Its purity of attention. Being one with what he's doing. Suzuki, the great exponent of Zen Buddhism, remarked 'when you do something you should burn yourself completely like a good bonfire leaving no trace of yourself'.[3] Around the same time that I was reading my first haikus, I got to know the teachings of Krishnamurti.[4] In order to savour the full potential and promise of Being, it was necessary, according to Krishnamurti, to be attentive to the immediate: 'to have the capacity of meeting everything anew from moment to moment, without the conditioning reaction of the past'. This heed for a sense of openness appealed to me. Too often we become walled-in by fixed convictions, blinkered beliefs and arrogant assumptions. It's vital for our well-being to keep opening new doors onto Life. In the absence of any meditational technique, the haiku became for me a means to achieve some degree of attentiveness in my life. Haiku writing is, perhaps, a meditational exercise in that it concentrates the mind. It enables us to become more aware; more alert to our surroundings. It intensifies our perceptions. The Haiku, as Kuno Meyer, the great German Celtic scholar, pointed out, and rightly so, is akin to early Irish lyrics — those poems of insightful clarity from the sixth, seventh and eighth centuries, written by monks and hermits who achieved a oneness with themselves, their environment and their Creator, whoever he, she or it may be. Like the Haiku, these poems are usually brief. They are small luminous moments of insight. They taught me, I hope, a lesson in compactness; that it was possible to evoke by suggestion; to be emotive without being sentimental and gushy. I think it was Dorothy Parker who quipped about some over-eager artist, who didn't know to economise with his paints, that 'when he painted a snake, he couldn't refrain from adding feet'. Keats, if my memory serves me right, said something similar about Coleridge; something to the effect that he would write one beautiful, mysterious line and then write twenty more lines trying to explain it. So the lesson to be had from the Haiku and the early Irish lyric is that a wise man doesn't overblow his knows. Likewise with Japanese painting, it has a minimalist approach to subject matter. Less rather than more. A few brushstrokes and a whole scene is evoked by suggestion. And I am a fervent admirer of Hokusai's thirty-six views of Mount Fuji.[5] They are stunning impressions of the sacred mountain from a multiplicity of viewpoints. I have my own Fuji, of course. Mount Errigal seems to me to have the same contours, the same character as Fuji. It's equally as elusive as Fuji. It's a shape-shifter. Sometimes it's casually elegant in a cashmere of cloud or shimmeringly sexy in a negligée of snow. At other times, it's a Cailleach, ashen grey and hag-like in its ferocious scowl. But whatever its moods, it's my beloved Mount Errigal. It has cast its shadow across my life and my lines; my lifelines. I have never been able to entice it in its entirety into my poem. My approach has to be more alluring.

Cathal with Ted and Annie Deppe, American poets outside his house in Mín a' Leá, 1999 (photo: Cathal Ó Searcaigh)

Cathal with Prem and Billy Collins, Amerian poet at the Poet's House, Falcarragh, 1999 (photo: Cathal Ó Searcaigh)

Cathal with the late poet James Simmons at the Poet's House, Falcarragh, 1999

# Notes

In the course of his interview Cathal refers to many poets, writers and artists who are well known in 'the West', included below are some 'Eastern' influences. The editors gratefully acknowledge the assistance of Prof. Mitsuko Ohno and Prof. Nobuaki Tochigi in providing the notes for this chapter.

1   James Simmons (1933–2001). A poet, musician/singer-songwriter, teacher, and founder of *H.U./The Honest Ulsterman* magazine, 'Jimmy' Simmons has sadly passed away in the period since Cathal gave this interview.

2   Buson (1716–83), second only to Basho, is one of the best known haiku poets. He was born in Settsu, and flourished in Edo and then in Kyoto. He was a very fine painter, too. Often referred to simply by his pen-name 'Buson', if you add his family name, his full name is Yosa Buson.

3   Daisetsu Suzuki (1870–1966) is a Buddhist philosopher who has travelled in Europe and America extensively and taught at various universities including Columbia University. He wrote many books on Buddhism with an emphasis on Zen both in Japanese and in English. His English books are widely read in the English speaking world.

4   Jiddu Krishnamurti (1895–1986) is an Indian mystic and theosophist. He was associated with the Krishanmurti Foundation in California and the Order of the Star in the East.

5   Hokusai (1760–1849) is possibly the best known Japanese Ukiyo-e painter whose works provided a source for French impressionists. His full name is Katsushika Hokusai, and 'Hokusai' is actually one of his more than thirty pen names. Not unlike Picasso, he lived a long and energetic life, developing an original style (or, rather, styles — in the plural).

## TRASNÚ

Ó, tá muid ag fí ár dtodhchaí as ár ndúchas;
ag Magee-áil ár mbréidín brocach buí,
ag Levi-áil ár mbrístí de chorda an rí,
Ó, tá muid ag fí ár dtodhchaí as ár ndúchas.

Tá muid ar strae
áit inteacht
idir Cath Chionn tSáile
agus an *Chinese takeaway.*
Tá snáithe ár scéil
in aimhréidh
idir Tuirne Mháire agus Fruit of the Loom.
Tá ár gcuid Gaeilge ag lobhadh
le *plaque* an Bhéarla,
cé go sruthlaímid ár dteanga gach lá
i dtobar an dúchais.
Tá ár mbolg thiar ar ár dtóin
i ngorta an éadóchais
is gan de chothú le fáil
lenár dtarrtháil
ach na slisíní seanchais
agus na grabhrógaí grinn
a thit
idir an Greim Gasta agus an Golden Grill.

Tá muid ag fí ár dtodhchaí as ár ndúchas;
ag Magee-áil ár mbréidín brocach buí,
ag Levi-áil ár mbrístí de chorda an rí,
Ó, tá muid ag fí ár dtodhchaí as ár ndúchas.

Tá muid leath-réamhstairiúil
agus leath-*postmodern intertext*úil.
Gheofá muid inniu
go tiubh sa tsiúl
ag buachailleacht *dinosours*
le Fionn Mac Cumhaill;
agus amárach thiocfá orainn
ag súgradh go searcúil
le Cáit Ní Queer;

nó teannta go teolaí
i gcluiche *strip poker*
le Méabha Chonnachta.
Amanta eile
i marbhthráth na hoíche
tchífeá muid ag *joyride*áil
ar luas na gaoithe,
ag Subaru-áil i Leitir Ceanainn
i gceann de chuid *chariots*
Chú Chulainn.

Tá muid ag fí ár dtodhchaí as ár ndúchas;
ag Magee-áil ár mbréidín brocach buí
ag Levi-áil ár mbrístí de chorda an rí
Ó, tá muid ag fí ár dtodhchaí as ár ndúchas.

Tá muid teach ceanntuíach
Agus bungaló *mod con*ach;
Tá muid seanbhean bhochtach
Agus Marilyn Monroeach;
Tá muid scadán gortach
agus *takeaway microwave*ach;
Tá muid seanscéal báiníneach
agus *scoop*scéal Sky-ach;
Tá muid turas an tobaireach
agus *rock 'n roll walkman*ach;
Tá muid dún daingeanach
agus *mobile home*ach;
Tá muid carr capallach
agus Vauxhall Cavalier-each;
Tá muid béadán baileach
agus *porn internet*ach;
Tá muid bairín breacach
agus *pina colada cheesecake*ach;
Tá muid rince seiteach
agus hócaí pócaí cairiócaíach.

Tá muid ag fí ár dtodhchaí as ár ndúchas;
ag Magee-áil ár mbréidín brocach buí,
ag Levi-áil ár mbrístí de chorda an rí,
Ó, tá muid ag fí ár dtodhchaí as ár ndúchas.

(Cathal Ó Searcaigh, *ATLS*, pp. 277–79)

## SIC TRANSIT

*Somewhere or other*
*we've lost our way*
*between the Battle of Kinsale*
*and the Chinese takeaway.*

*The threads of our story*
*have broken loose*
*between Four Green Fields*
*and Fruit of the Loom.*

*Our Irish is rotting*
*with the plaque of English*
*though we dip our tongues*
*in* tobar an dúchais.

*Our stomachs stick out*
*over our arses,*
*with nothing to keep us*
*but shreds of* seanchas

*and crummy jokes*
*that tumble and fall*
*between the Bistro*
*and the Golden Grill.*

Oh, we're weaving our futures from our past,
McGee-ing our homespun wraps,
Levi-ing our kacks with King Billy's flax—
oh, we're weaving our futures from our past.

*We're half-prehistoric*
*and half-intertextual,*
*half-postmodern*
*and half-bisexual.*

*One day you find us,*
*a people on the prowl,*
*herding dinosaurs,*
*with Finn McCool;*

*next day we're feeling up*
*Katie McWeir*
*or beating the pants*
*off Queenie at poker.*

*Some nights, we joy-ride,*
*quick as a shot,*
*subarooing Letterkenny*
*in a hot-wired chariot*

*nicked under the nose*
*of the Hound of Ulster...*

Oh, we're weaving our futures from our past,
McGee-ing our homespun wraps,
Levi-ing our kacks with King Billy's flax—
oh, we're weaving our futures from our past.

*We're thatch-roofed*
*and bungalow mod-conned;*
*we're Marilyn Monroed*
*and Poor Old Womaned;*

*we're salmon-shortaged*
*and microwaifish;*
*we're Old Wives' Taled*
*and satellite-dished;*

*we're traditional welled,*
*and CD walkmaned;*
*we're cross-bordered*
*and station wagoned;*

*we're horsepowered*
*and Vauxhall Cavaliered;*
*we're local gossiped*
*and search engineered;*

*we're barmbracked*
*and pina colada'd,*
*we're cheesecaked,*
*and tossed salad;*

*we're set-danced*
*and hokey pokeyed;*

*we're* sean nós-*ed*
*and karaoke'd.*

Oh, we're weaving our futures from our past,
McGee-ing our homespun wraps,
Levi-ing our kacks with King Billy's flax—
oh, we're weaving our futures from our past.

(trans. Frank Sewell)

Cathal in Kathmandu, Nepal with Prem, Prem's mother and Cathal's Friend
Shantaram Sapkota (photo: Cathal Ó Searcaigh)

**Celia de Fréine** – poet, dramatist, and screenwriter. Many of her plays have been produced including most recently *Nára Turas é in Aistear* by Amharclann de hÍde in 2000. Her television work was shortlisted for the Celtic Film and Television Festival (1998). Her poetry has won many awards, including the Patrick Kavanagh Award (1994), Duais Chomórtas Filíochta Dhún Laoghaire (1996), the British Comparative Literature Association Translation Award (1999), and Duais Aitheantais Ghradam Litríochta Chló Iar-Chonnachta (1999). A collection *Faoi Chabáistí is Ríonacha* was published by Cló Iar-Chonnachta in 2001. She was awarded Arts Council Bursaries in 1997 and in 2000.

**James E. Doan** – received his Ph.D. in Folklore and Celtic Studies from Harvard University in 1981. He is Professor of Liberal Arts at Nova Southeastern University, where he teaches courses in Irish and comparative literature, the arts and humanities. He edits *Working Papers in Irish Studies* and the *ACIS* (American Conference for Irish Studies) *Newsletter* and has published numerous books and articles on Irish literature and history, including *The Romance of Cearbhall and Fearbhlaidh* (Portlaoise: Dolmen Press, 1985), *Cearbhall Ó Dálaigh: An Irish Poet in Romance and Oral Tradition* (New York: Garland Press, 1990), and *Scotch-Irish and Hiberno-English Language and Culture* (Fort Lauderdale: Nova Southeastern University, 1993). He is also Vice-Chair for North America of the International Association for the Study of Irish Literatures (IASIL) and President of the South Florida Irish Studies Consortium.

**Kieran Kennedy** – received his B.A. from the Dept. of English at University College Dublin, and his Ph.D. in English Literature at Columbia University, New York. He received a postgraduate fellowship at the Huntington Library. Currently at the University of California, Los Angeles, he is engaged in research on the work of Oscar Wilde. He has written several articles dealing with postcolonial and gender issues relating to 19th and 20th-century Irish literature.

**Eoin Mac Cárthaigh** – from Raheny in Dublin, he now lives in Dublin's Liberties with his wife, Mary Hassett, and their son, Caoimhín. He is a lecturer in the School of Irish, Trinity College, Dublin. His main research interest is *dán díreach*.

**Niall McGrath** – received his MPhil from the University of Ulster (Coleraine) in 2000 for a study entitled *Priest and Shaman Characters in Selected Drama by Brian Friel*. He is the founder and editor of the innovative journal *Black Mountain Review* ("BMR")

**Brian Ó Conchubhair** – is a Visiting Assistant Professor at the Keough Institute for Irish Studies at the University of Notre Dame. A graduate of NUI, Galway, he has taught at Boston College, the University of California, Berkeley and the Catholic University of Lublin, Poland. He has published articles in *Éire-Ireland*, *New Hibernian Review* and *Irisleabhar Mhá Nuad*.

**Mitsuko Ohno** – Professor of English Literature at Aichi Shukutoku University in Japan. She graduated with an MA from Nagoya University (1976) and a Ph.D. from Nara Women's University (2000). She is the author of *Yeats and the Tradition of Anglo-Irish Literature* (Kyoto, 1999) and *Women's Ireland* (Tokyo, 1998), both written in Japanese. Her most recent publication is *Pharaoh's Daughter: Selected Poems of Nuala Ní Dhomhnaill* (Tokyo: Shichosha, 2001), a bilingual edition of the original Irish poems plus Japanese translation with an accompanying CD; this publication is the result of a close collaboration between the poet and the translator. She has also lectured and taught (1997 and 2001) at the Yeats International Summer School in Sligo.

**Frank Sewell** – a writer, translator, musician and teacher, he currently works at the University of Ulster (Coleraine). His poems have previously been published in *Outside the Walls* by Frank Sewell and Francis O'Hare (Belfast: An Clochán, 1997), and also in many journals and newspapers. His English-language translations of poems in Irish by Cathal Ó Searcaigh, published in *Out in the Open* (Indreabhán: Cló Iar-Chonnachta, 1997), were nominated for the Aristeion European Translation Prize. He received the University of Ulster McCrea Literary Award for poetry in 1996 and a Literature Award from the Arts Council in 1999 and 2001. Most recently, he co-edited *Artwords: an Ulster anthology of contemporary visual art and poetry*. His literary criticism includes 'Where the Paradoxes Grow': the Poetry of Derek Mahon (Coleraine: Cranagh Press, 2000) and *Modern Irish Poetry: A New Alhambra* (Oxford: Oxford University Press, 2000).

**Mutsuo Takahashi** – a poet, first and foremost, but also a novelist, playwright, essayist. His poems have been written in diverse forms, ranging from modern free verse to traditional haiku and even more ancient Saibara; excelling in all of these forms, Takahashi is a widely recognised as a unique master of verse among contemporary Japanese poets. His over 60 books, including *Sleeping, Sinning, Falling* (English trans. by Hiroaki Sato, 1992) and, more recently, *Houkosho* (Poems Modelled after Ancient Rhymes), won him prestigious awards and acclaim both nationally and internationally. Takahashi's *Saku-no-Mukou* (Beyond the Hedge, currently being translated into English by Ohno and Sewell) is a collection of poems inspired by his trip to Ireland, and includes 'Uncovering a Well', a poem dedicated to Cathal Ó Searcaigh.

**Nobuaki Tochigi** – Professor of English at Waseda University in Tokyo. He is the author of *From the Irish Pub: Explorations in Irish Oral Culture* (1998) and *An Alternative Guide to Contemporary Irish Poets* (2001), both in Japanese. He is also co-editor of *The Tree of Strings: An Anthology of Contemporary Poetry in English* (1995), which comprises Seamus Heaney, Derek Walcott, Les Murray, and Tony Harrison, among others. Tochigi's recent articles include 'Cathal Ó Searcaigh and Aspects of Translation' (*Éire-Ireland*, XXXV: I&II, 2000) and 'Narrative Metamorphoses in Ciaran Carson's Fishing for Amber: A Long Story' (Journal of Irish Studies, XVI, 2001).

Cathal Ó Searcaigh
*Miontraigéide Cathrach* (Falcara: Cló Uí Chuirreáin, 1975)
*Súile Shuibhne* (Dublin: Coiscéim, 1983)
*Suibhne* (Dublin: Coiscéim, 1987)
*An Bealach 'na Bhaile/Homecoming* (Indreabhán: Cló Iar-Chonnachta, 1993)
*Na Buachaillí Bána* (Indreabhán: Cló Iar-Chonnachta, 1996)
*Out in the Open* (Indreabhán: Cló Iar-Chonnachta, 1997)
*Ag Tnúth leis an tSolas: 1975–2000* (Indreabhán: Cló Iar-Chonnachta, 2000)
*Caiseal na gCorr*, with Jan Voster (Indreabhán: Cló Iar-Chonnachta, 2002)
*Seal in Neípeal* (Indreabhán: Cló Iar-Chonnachta, 2003)


Secondary Sources featuring, or specifically concerning, Cathal Ó Searcaigh
Bolger, Dermot, and G. Fitzmaurice (eds.), *An Tonn Gheal/The Bright New Wave* (Dublin: Raven Arts Press, 1986)

Brown, John (ed), 'Interviewing Cathal O Searcaigh', *In the Chair: Interviews with Poets from the North of Ireland* (Cliffs of Moher, Co. Clare, Salmon Publishing, 2002)

Denvir, Gearóid, *Litríocht agus Pobal* (Indreabhán: Cló Iar-Chonnachta, 1997)

Dorgan, Theo, (ed.), *Irish Poetry Since Kavanagh* (Blackrock: Four Courts Press, 1996)

Duffy, Noel and T. Dorgan (eds.), *Watching the River Flow: A Century in Irish Poetry* (Dublin: Poetry Ireland, 1999)

Gallagher, Djinn, 'Irish, Gifted and Gay', in *The Tribune Magazine*, 15 Sept. 1996, 12

Hegarty, Ciarán, *File an Phobail/Poet of the People* (BBC Northern Ireland, 1994)

Hughes, A. J., 'Cathal Ó Searcaigh, file', in A. J. Hughes (ed.), *Le chemin du retour/Pilleadh an deoraí* (La Barbacane: Fumel, 1996)

Kelly, Marion, 'Ón Taobh Istigh: Agallamh le Cathal Ó Searcaigh', *Macalla 1996–97* (Gaillimh: Cumann Éigse agus Seanchais, 1997), pp. 35–49

Kiberd, Declan and G. Fitzmaurice (eds.), *An Crann Faoi Bhláth/The Flowering Tree* (Dublin: Wolfhound Press, 1991)

Longley, Michael, 'A going back to sources', *Poetry Ireland Review*, 39 (Autumn 1993), 92–96 [A review of Ó Searcaigh's *An Bealach 'na Bhaile*]

O'Carroll, Íde and E. Collins (eds.), *Lesbian and Gay Visions of Ireland: Towards the Twenty-first Century* (London: Cassell, 1995)

Ó Conghaile, Micheál, (ed.), *Sláinte: Deich mBliana de Chló Iar-Chonnachta* (Indreabhán: CIC, 1995)

Ó Dúill, Gréagóir, 'Mórfhile le teacht?' [review of *Miontraigéide Cathrach*], *Comhar* 35, No. 12, 1975, 17–18

—'An File is dual. Filíocht Chathail Uí Shearcaigh: I dtreo anailís théamúil', *Comhar* 52, No. 12, 1993, 35–41

—'Filíocht Chathail Uí Shearcaigh', *An tUltach*, Eanáir/January 1993

—'Cathal Ó Searcaigh: A Negotiation with Place, Community and Tradition', *Poetry Ireland Review*, Issue 48, Winter 1995, 14–18

Ó Laoire, Lillis, 'Introduction: A Yellow Spot on the Snow', in Cathal Ó Searcaigh, *Homecoming/An Bealach 'na Bhaile* (Indreabhán: Clo Iar-Chonnachta, 1993), pp. 13–40

—'Dearg Dobhogtha Cháin/The Indelible Mark of Cain: Sexual Dissidence in the Poetry of Cathal Ó Searcaigh', in Éibhear Walshe (ed.), *Sex, Nation and Dissent in Irish Writing* (Cork: Cork University Press, 1997), pp. 221–34

Ó Searcaigh, Cathal, 'Cín Lae ó Bharr na Cruinne', *Comhar*, Nollaig, 1998, 17–21

Rosenstock, Gabriel, 'Searcach na Seirce', interviewing Cathal Ó Searcaigh, *Feasta* (July 1996), 4–5

Sealy, D., [untitled review of *An Bealach 'na Bhaile/Homecoming*], *Comhar* 52, No. 6, 1993, 21–2

Sewell, Frank, *Modern Irish Poetry: A New Alhambra* (Oxford: Oxford University Press, 2000)

Walshe, Éibhear (ed.), *Sex, Nation and Dissent in Irish Writing* (Cork: Cork University Press, 1997)

Welch, Robert (ed.), *The Oxford Companion to Irish Literature* (Oxford: Clarendon Press, 1996)

White, Victoria, 'Gay love as Gaeilge', *The Irish Times*, 1 March 1996, 11

General

Andrews, Elmer (ed.), *Contemporary Irish Poetry: A Collection of Critical Essays* (Houndmills: MacMillan Press, 1992)

Auden, W. H., *Secondary Worlds* (London: Faber and Faber, 1968)
—*W. H. Auden: Collected Poems*, ed. by Edward Mendelson (London: Faber and Faber, 1976)

Ballard, Linda May, *Forgetting Frolic: Marriage Traditions in Ireland* (Belfast: The Institute of Irish Studies, University of Belfast, 1998)

Bergin, Osborn (ed.), *Irish Bardic Poetry* (Dublin: Dublin Institute for Advanced Studies, 1970)

Berman, Marshall, *All That Is Solid Melts Into Air: The Experience of Modernity* 2nd edn (London: Verso, 1983, repr. 1995)

Blake, William, *Blake: Complete Writings (with variant readings)*, ed. by Geoffrey Keynes (London: Oxford University Press, 1966)

Blasius, Mark, *Gay and Lesbian Politics: Sexuality and the Emergence of a New Ethics* (Philadelphia: Temple University Press, 1994)

Blasius, Mark and Shane Phelan (eds.), *We are Everywhere: a Historical Sourcebook of Gay and Lesbian Politics* (London, New York: Routledge, 1997)

Boland, Eavan, *A Kind of Scar: the Woman Poet in a national tradition* (Dublin: Attic Press, 1989)
—*Object Lessons: The Life of the Woman and the Poet in Our Time* (London: Vintage, 1996)

Bourke, Angela, 'Wild Men and Wailing Women', *Éigse: A Journal of Irish Studies*, 18 (1980), pp. 25–37

Brown, Terence, *Ireland: A Social and Cultural History 1922–1985* (London: Fontana Press, 1985)

Butler, Judith, *Bodies That Matter: on the Discursive Limits of 'Sex'* (New York: Routledge, 1993)

Carney, James, *The Irish Bardic Poet* (Dublin: Dolmen Press, 1967)

Cavafy, C. P., *The Complete Poems of C. P. Cavafy: translated by Rae Dalven with an introduction by W. H. Auden* (London: The Hogarth Press, 1961, repr. 1966)

Chow, Rey, *Writing Diaspora: Tactics of Intervention in Contemporary Cultural Studies* (Indianapolis: Indiana U. P., 1993)

Condren, Mary, *The Serpent and the Goddess: Women, Religion And Power in Celtic Ireland* (San Francisco: Harper and Row, 1989)

Cronin, Michael, *Translating Ireland: Tradition, Languages, Cultures* (Cork: Cork University Press, 1996)

Davitt, Michael, *Bligeard Sráide* (Dublin: Coiscéim, 1983)

de Blacam, Aodh, *Gaelic Literature Surveyed*, 2nd edn (Dublin: Talbot Press, 1929, 1973)

Deane, Seamus, 'Mo Bhealach Féin by Seosamh Mac Grianna', in John Jordan (ed.), *The Pleasures of Gaelic Literature* (Dublin: The Mercier Press, 1977), pp. 52–61
—(ed.), *Field Day Anthology of Irish Writing* (Derry: Field Day Publications, 1991)

de hÍde, Dubhglas (ed.), *Abhráin agus Dánta an Reachtabhraigh* (Dublin: Foilseacháin Rialtais, 1933)
—*Amhráin Ghrá Chúige Chonnachta/Love Songs of Connacht*

Dinneen, Patrick S., *Foclóir Gaedhilge agus Béarla* (Dublin and Cork: Educational Company of Ireland, 1927)

Doan, James E., Introduction to *The Romance of Cearbhall and Fearbhlaidh* (Mountrath: Dolmen Press, in association with Humanities Press, 1985), pp. 11–34

Foucault, Michel, *The History of Sexuality, Vol. 2 The Use of Pleasure*, trans. Robert Hurley (New York: Pantheon, 1985)

Frazier, Adrian, 'Queering the Irish Renaissance: The Masculinities of Moore, Martyn, and Yeats', in Bradley, A. and M.G. Valiulis (eds.), *Gender and Sexuality in Modern Ireland* (Amherst: University of Massachusetts Press, 1997)

Freeman, A. M., (ed.), *Annála Connacht: The Annals of Connacht* (Dublin: Dublin Institute for Advanced Studies, 1944)

Hardie, Kerry, *A Furious Place* (Loughcrew: The Gallery Press, 1996)

Heaney, Seamus, *Death of a Naturalist* (London: Faber and Faber, 1966)
—*Seeing Things* (London: Faber and Faber, 1991)
—*The Spirit Level* (London: Faber and Faber, 1996)

Hindley, Reg, *The Death of the Irish Language: A Qualified Obituary* (London: Routledge, 1990)

Hussey, Gemma, *Ireland Today: Anatomy of a Changing State* (Dublin: Townhouse, 1993)

Hutchinson, Pearse, ' "Rus in Urbe": Comhrá le Pearse Hutchinson', *Innti* xi, 1998, pp. 55–68

Johnston, Dillon, *Irish Poetry After Joyce*, 2nd edn (Syracuse, New York: Syracuse University Press, 1997)

Kearney, Richard, 'Between Tradition and Utopia: The Hermeneutical Problem of Myth', in David Wood (ed.), *On Paul Ricoeur: Narrative and Interpretation* (London: Routledge, 1991)

Kiberd, Declan, *Idir Dhá Chultúr* (Dublin: Coiscéim, 1994)
—*Inventing Ireland: The Literature of the Modern Nation* (London: Vintage, 1996)

Kinsella, Thomas, trans., *The Táin*, Dolmen Editions 9 (Dublin: Dolmen Press, 1969)

Luddy, Maria, *Women in Ireland, 1800–1918: A Documentary History* (Cork: Cork University Press, 1995)

Mac Cana, Proinsias, *Literature in Irish* (Dublin: Dept. of Foreign Affairs, 1980)

Mac Cionnaith, L. (ed.), *Dioghluim Dána* (Dublin: Oifig an tSoláthair, 1938)

Mac Craith, Micheál, 'Foinsí an radacachais in Éirinn', in Gearóid Ó Tuathaigh (ed.), *Éirí Amach 1798 in Éirinn* (Indreabhán: Cló Iar-Chonnachta, 1998), pp. 11–28

McGuinness, Frank, *Plays 1* (London: Faber and Faber, 1996)

MacNeice, Louis, *Collected Poems*, 2nd edn (London: Faber and Faber, 1979, repr. 1986)

Manalansan IV, Martin F., 'In the Shadows of Stonewall: Examining Gay Transnational Politics and the Diasporic Dilemma', in Lisa Lowe and David Lloyd (eds.), *The Politics of Culture in the Shadow of Capital* (Durham & London: Duke University Press, 1997), pp. 485–505

Meehan, Paula, *The Man Who Was Marked by Winter* (Loughcrew: Gallery Press, 1991)

Mhac an tSaoi, Máire, 'The Celtic Continuum', in *The Celtic Consciousness* (New York: Braziller, 1982), pp. 250–251

Miller, Kerby A., *Emigrants and Exiles: Ireland and the Irish Exodus to North America* (Oxford: Oxford University Press, 1985)

Morrison, Blake and Andrew Motion (eds.), *The Penguin Book of Contemporary British Poetry* (London: Penguin, 1982)

Ní hAnnracháin, Máire, 'Ait liom bean a bheith ina file', in *Léachtaí Cholm Cille* XII (Maigh Nuad: An Sagart, 1982)

Ní Dhomhnaill, Nuala, *Féar Suaithinseach* (Maynooth: An Sagart, 1984)
—*Selected Poems: Rogha Dánta*, trans. Michael Hartnett (Dublin: Raven Arts Press, 1986)
—*Pharaoh's Daughter* (Loughcrew: Gallery Press, 1990)
—*Feis* (Maynooth: An Sagart, 1991)
—*The Astrakhan Cloak*, trans. Paul Muldoon (Loughcrew: Gallery Press, 1992)
— 'Why I Choose to Write in Irish: the Corpse That Sits Up and Talks Back', in Susan Shaw Sailer (ed.), *Representing Ireland: Gender, Class, Nationality* (Gainesville: University of Florida Press, 1997), pp. 45–56
—*Cead Aighnis* (An Daingean: An Sagart, 1998)

Ní Ghlinn, Áine, *Unshed Tears/Deora Nár Caoineadh* (Dublin: The Dedalus Press, 1996)

Norris, David, 'Homosexual People and the Christian Churches in Ireland', *The Crane Bag*, 2, 1981
—'Criminal Law (Sexual Offences) Bill 1993: Second Stage Speech, Tuesday 29 June 1993', reprinted in Íde O'Carroll and Eoin Collins (ed.), *Lesbian And Gay Visions of Ireland: Towards the Twenty-first Century* (London and New York: Cassell, 1995)

O'Brien, Conor Cruise, 'Revolution and the Shaping of Modern Ireland', in *The Celtic Consciousness* (New York: Braziller, 1982)

O'Brien, F., *Duanaire Nuafhilíochta* (Dublin: An Clóchomhar, 1969)

O'Connor, A., 'Women in Irish Folklore: the Testimony Regarding Illegitimacy, Abortion and Infanticide', in *Women in Early Modern Ireland*, ed.

M. Mac Curtain and M. O'Dowd (Edinburgh: Edinburgh University Press, 1991)

Ó Direáin, Máirtín, *Cloch Choirnéil* (Dublin: An Clóchomhar, 1966)
—*Dánta 1939–1979* (Dublin: An Clóchomhar, 1980)
—*Craobhóg Dán* (Dublin: An Clóchomhar, 1986)
—*Selected Poems/Tacar Dánta*, trans. Tomás Mac Síomóin and Douglas Sealy (Newbridge: The Goldsmith Press, 1984)

O'Donoghue, Bernard, *Gunpowder* (London: Chatto & Windus, 1995)
— *Here Nor There* (London: Chatto & Windus, 1999)

O'Donoghue, Bernard interviewed by Penelope Dening, *The Irish Times*, 23 January 1996, 10

Ó hEallaithe, Donncha, 'Uair na Cinniúna don Ghaeltacht', in *Cuisle*, Eagrán 5, 1999

O'Rahilly, Cecile (ed.), *Táin Bó Cúalnge*, from the Book of Leinster (Dublin: Dublin Institute for Advanced Studies, 1970)

O'Rahilly, T. F., *Early Irish History and Mythology* (Dublin: Dublin Institute for Advanced Studies, 1946)

Ó Ríordáin, Seán, *Eireaball Spideoige*, 2nd edn (Dublin: Sáirséal – Ó Marcaigh, 1952, 1986)
—*Brosna* (Dublin: Sáirséal agus Dill, 1964, 1987)

Ó Tuama, Seán, *Repossessions: Selected Essays on the Irish Literary Heritage* (Cork: Cork University Press, 1995)

Ó Tuama, Seán (ed.) and T. Kinsella (trans.), *An Duanaire, 1600–1900: Poems of the Dispossessed* (Dublin: Dolmen Press, 1981)

Plummer, Ken (ed.), *Modern Homosexualities: Fragments of Lesbian and Gay Experience* (London: Routledge, 1992)

Ricoeur, Paul, 'The Creativity of Language', in Richard Kearney (ed.), *States of Mind: Dialogues with Contemporary Thinkers on the European Mind* (Manchester: Manchester Univ. Press, 1995), pp. 29–30

Rose, Kieran, *Diverse Communities: The Evolution of Lesbian and Gay Politics in Ireland* (Cork: Cork University Press, 1994)

Rylance, R. (ed.), *Debating Texts: A Reader in Twentieth Century Literary Theory and Method* (Milton Keynes: Open University Press, 1987, 1990)

Sansom, Peter, *Writing Poems* (Newcastle-Upon-Tyne: Bloodaxe Books, 1994)

Sedgwick, Eve Kosofsky, *Epistemology of the Closet* (Berkeley, Los Angeles: University of California Press, 1990)

Seoighe, Mairín, *An Bealach 'na Bhaile/The Road Home* (Scannáin Dobharchú, 1993)

Simms, Katherine, 'The Poet as Chieftain's Widow', in Donncha Ó Corráin et al. (eds.), *Sages, Saints and Storytellers: Celtic Studies in Honour of Professor James Carney* (Maynooth: An Sagart, 1989)

Simon, Sherry, *Gender in Translation: Cultural Identity and the Politics of Transmission* (London, New York: Routledge, 1996)

Stahlberger, Lawrence Leo, *The Symbolic System of Majakovskij* (The Hague: Mouton and Co., 1964)

Standún, Pádraic, *Cion Mná* (Indreabhán: Cló Iar-Chonnachta, 1993)

Thuente, Mary Helen, 'Liberty, Hibernia and Mary Le More: United Irish images of women', in *The Women of 1798*, ed. by Keogh, Dáire and N. Furlong (Dublin: Four Courts Press, 1998), pp. 9–25

Titley, Alan, *Chun Doirne: Rogha Aistí* (Belfast: Lagan Press, 1996)

Todd, Albert C. and Max Hayward with Daniel Weissbort (eds.), *Twentieth Century Russian Poetry: selected with an introduction by Yevgeny Yevtushenko* (London: Fourth Estate, 1993)

Tóibín, Colm, 'Roaming the Greenwood', Review of *A History of Gay Literature: the Male Tradition* by G. Woods (1998), in *London Review of Books*, Vol. 21, No. 2, 21 January 1999, 12–16

Valiulis, Maryann G. and Mary O'Dowd, *Women & Irish History* (Dublin: Wolfhound Press, 1997)

Yevtushenko, Yevgeny, *Selected Poems*, ed. by R. Milner-Gulland and P. Levi, S. J. (Middlesex: Penguin Books, 1962, repr. 1964)
—*A Precocious Autobiography*, translated by A. R. Mac Andrew (Harmondsworth: Penguin Books, 1965)
—*Sobranie sochinenii v treh tomah* (Moskva: Hudozhestvennaya Literatura, 1984)

Cathal in Nepal, 2000 (photo: Cathal Ó Searcaigh)